Managing Subcontracts:
Optimizing the
U.S. Government's Supply Chain

2011-2012 Edition

Gregory A. Garrett

WEST®

A Thomson Reuters business

For Customer Assistance Call 1-800-328-4880

Mat #41083879

Dedications

To My Wife,

I cannot imagine my life without you and our children. Thank you for your friendship, love, and support!

To My Father & Father-in-Law,

I appreciate and value your guidance, coaching, life-examples, and service to our country!

Acknowledgements

I would like to thank the following people for their support and contributions to this book!

Robert Burton, Esq.
Paul Debolt, Esq.
Terry Elling, Esq.
Steven M. Masiello, Esq.
Phillip R. Seckman, Esq.

I would like to extend a special thank you to the following people for their outstanding and professional administrative support services.

Barbara Hanson
Julie McKillip

About the Author

Gregory A. Garrett, is the Chief Operating Officer of AST LLC. He leads AST's consulting and support services for firms who perform aircraft maintenance, repair, overhaul, logistics, sustainment services, and provides a wide range of U.S. government contract, subcontract, and project management training. He is an internationally recognized expert in U.S. government contracting, cost estimating, project management, and supply-chain management. He is also a best-selling and award-winning author of 20 books and more than 100 published articles. He is an international educator, renowned business consultant, and dynamic professional speaker, who has taught, consulted, and motivated over 30,000 business professionals in 40+ countries. He is the recipient of numerous national and international business awards for his writing, teaching, consulting, and leadership.

For more information contact www.aircraft-llc.com.

Preface

This book provides an insightful, practical and compelling picture of the challenges which the U.S. Government faces to improve how it acquires products, services, systems, and integrated solutions. Realizing the record levels of U.S. federal government spending it is vital that the government agencies, prime contractors, and subcontractors work together to optimize the government and industry supply chains. Further, the author Gregory A. Garrett does an outstanding job of providing thoughtful and practical advice of what the U.S. government agencies, prime contractors, and subcontractors can do to improve performance results and save tax payers dollars.

In this newest edition, there is an excellent addition, Chapter 12— Terminating Subcontractors, which provides some valuable insights on the subcontract termination process and some proven best practices.

I highly recommend *Managing Subcontracts: Optimizing the U.S. Government's Supply Chain*. It is the most comprehensive, realistic, and process-oriented book ever written on this vital topic!

Robert Burton, Partner Venable LLP &
Former Deputy Administrator,
Office of Federal Procurement Policy

Introduction

The focus of this book is to provide a clear, comprehensive, and compelling discussion of what needs to be done to improve how the U.S. federal government agencies acquire products, services, systems, and solutions via prime contractors and subcontractors. This book begins with a review of how the U.S. Government's supply chains are structured, what challenges they encounter, and recommendations for improvement.

Next, the book discusses the challenges which government prime contractors and subcontractors face and best practices industry applies in managing their respective supply chains in support of U.S. government agencies and the public.

The remaining chapters of the book are focused on providing practical advice to improve managing subcontracts via providing a proven effective subcontract management process, composed of subcontractor sourcing, negotiation and subcontract formation, subcontract administration and closeout and other important related topics.

Table of Contents

CHAPTER 12. TERMINATING SUBCONTRACTORS: CHALLENGES & BEST PRACTICES

APPENDICES

Chapter 1

Optimizing the U.S. Federal Government's Supply Chains

> **KeyCite®:** Cases and other legal materials listed in KeyCite Scope can be researched through the KeyCite service on Westlaw®. Use KeyCite to check citations for form, parallel references, prior and later history, and comprehensive citator information, including citations to other decisions and secondary materials.

§ 1:1   Introduction

Like it or not, we live in a world of outsourcing. The practice of outsourcing work is growing worldwide in both the public and private sectors. For years, companies and government organizations have realized it is often more cost-effective and efficient to focus their critical resources (people, time, and money) on their respective core competencies, and outsource, or subcontract, their non-core functions to other companies. Clearly, some companies and government agencies have gone too far and outsourced key functions, which are indeed mission critical, and/or not realized the cost savings or efficiencies they had anticipated. However, in most cases the facts have proven that organizations have made reasonable business outsourcing decisions. Yet the decision to buy versus make a product, service, system, and/or solution is not sufficient; an organization must learn how to appropriately master their supply chain.

Optimizing the U.S. Government's supply chains is no easy task. However, the U.S. Government's supply chains are vital to U.S. taxpayers, and mission essential to ensure government agencies receive the quality products and services they require at a fair and reasonable price. The U.S. Government cannot meet the growing needs of its citizens without a strong, viable, and ethical supplier base. This chapter focuses on understanding (1) the world we live in and (2) the U.S. Government's current supply chains: what they consists of, how they are structured, and what are their challenges. Plus, this chapter offers several recommendations for optimizing the U.S. Government's supply chains for the benefit of U.S. taxpayers, government agencies, and industry.

§ 1:2   Understanding the world we live in

The world we live in is changing at an ever-increasing rate. Likewise, business paradigms are shifting significantly for organizations and for individuals. Downsizing, outsourcing, horizontal supply chain relationships, globalization, and increased pressures to achieve high-performance results are affecting nearly everyone—especially business leaders. Within the buying and selling communities, organizations are struggling to advance from classic stovepipe structures to talent-based integrated project teams. With the power of tremendous communication technologies, individuals are now challenged to overcome the overwhelming daily e-mails, voice mails, and instant messages, to establish focused priorities and to ensure flawless execution.

The mantra of business today is flawless execution, whether buying or selling products or services. Every organization in both the public and the private business sectors is trying to increase its velocity of business (the speed with which it meets customers' needs), while reducing costs and simultaneously ensuring that it is providing quality products or services to meet or exceed customer expectations. There is no question that the performance bar has been raised in all aspects of business. Some customers have such incredibly high performance expectations that achieving them may seem impossible. Yet what often appears impossible today becomes the performance norm tomorrow or in the not so distance future.

Clearly, in both the public and the private business sectors, we are witnessing increased use of outsourcing and performance-based contracts. Today, more than ever, buyers require customized integrated solutions to their business challenges. Often these customized solutions required multiple suppliers, each with multiple functions, to team up to seamlessly deliver solutions composed of hardware, software, and professional services. All these forces are transforming the marketplace, while posing greater risks to both parties.

Sellers are being asked to agree to increasingly demanding performance-based contracts with specific product performance requirements and service-level agreements, often with significant penalties for failure to perform. Buyers are also taking greater risks, because they are increasingly outsourcing their capabilities to other parties, thus losing some direct control over their success or failure. Business is becoming more electronically enabled, less personal, more regulated, and highly interdependent. Thus, the world we live in and the forces of emerging technologies, global economic issues, growing customer demands, and increased government regulations are shaping a new performance-based supply environment, see Figure 1-1.

Figure 1-1.
New Performance-Based Supply Environment

DEMANDING CUSTOMERS

Emerging Technologies Impact
- Rapidly changing technologies
- Enterprise-wide systems challenges
- Services & support issues

Global Economic Impact
- Unstable financial institutions
- Credit challenges
- Payment problems
- Bankruptcies

Government/ Regulatory Impact
- Focus on competition
- Use of performance-based contracts
- Increased outsourcing of professional services
- Focus on supplier ethics and compliance programs
- Increased government oversight

SUPPLIER BASE

New Performance-Based Supply Environment

Advantages
- Improved products
- More services
- Increased price competition
- Reduced cycle-time
- More integration of products and services
- Use of strategic sourcing

Disadvantages
- Credit and payment issues
- High cost of integration
- Increased customer performance demands
- Rapid obsolescence of some products
- Increased Government oversight
- Increased supply chain management challenges

3

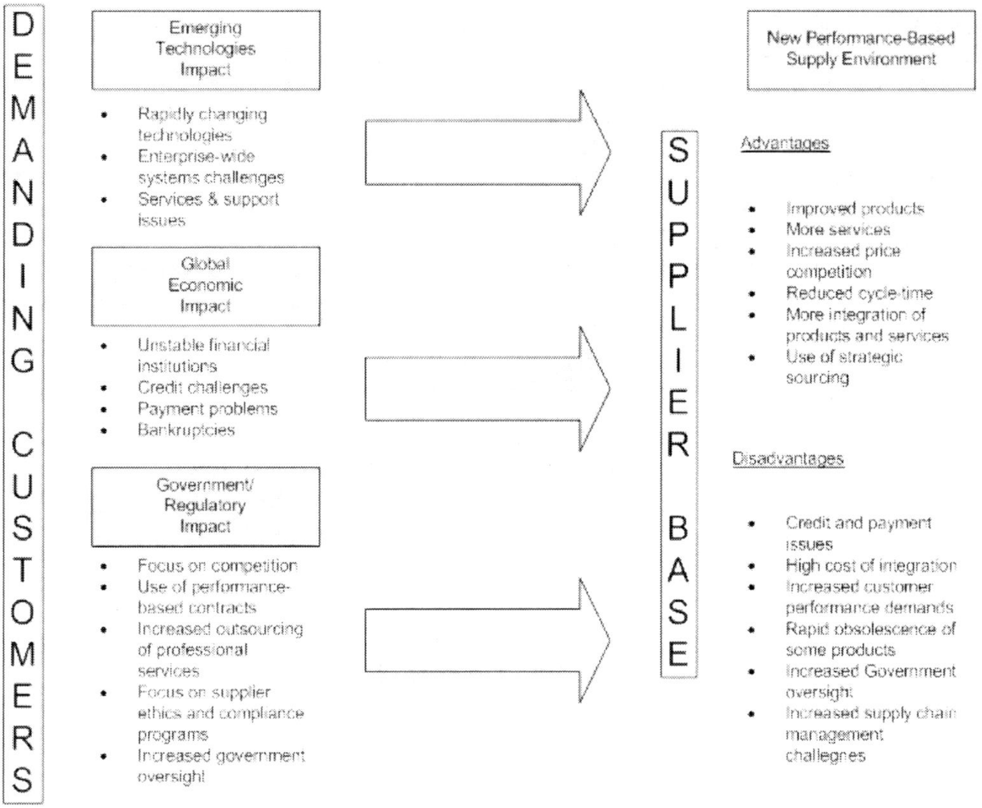

In the public business sector, composed of federal, state, and local government agencies, it is clear that all agencies are adopting more commercial buying practices in a quest to reduce acquisition cycle-time, reduce expenses, and increase customer satisfaction. Similarly, the private business sector is moving to create better, more defined, and effectively implemented business processes. Especially, in the wake of the Sarbanes-Oxley Act and the recent global economic crises, private sector companies are struggling to increase speed market, improve profitability, and increase customer confidence and loyalty. It is apparent that the public and private business sectors are in many ways converging through technology and regulations, resulting in two distinct paths: the increased use of electronic tools to rapidly procure simple off-the-shelf products and services, and the increased use of large, complex, extended enterprise supply chains to develop and deliver integrated systems and solutions.

§ 1:3   Understanding the U.S. Federal Government's supply chains

U.S. Government spending has grown significantly since 2000 (see Figure 1-2.). In fiscal year 2007, the U.S. Government spent more than $436 billion in acquiring a wide range of products, professional services, and integrated solutions from hundreds of thousands of government contractors and subcontractors. Likewise, in fiscal year 2008, the U.S. Government spent over $531 billion in procuring products and services from industry.

Figure 1-2. Government Contract Spending Grows

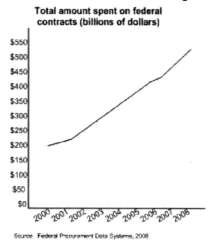

Source: Federal Procurement Data Systems, 2008

The U.S. Government spending spree was conducted by more than sixty government departments, agencies, and commissions. Over 60% of the $531 billion in FY 2008 was spent acquiring a diverse number of professional services from contractors and subcontractors, both large and small businesses.

The U.S. Government agencies have increasingly purchased professional services including: information technology (IT); systems engineering; logistics/sustainment management; program/project management; strategic sourcing; acquisition support services; accounting; and financial management services, just to mention a few.

The biggest government buyers of products, services, systems, and integrated solutions are consistently the U.S. Departments of Defense, Homeland Security, Energy, and the National Aeronautics and Space Administration, which collectively spend about 90% of the U.S. Government's annual acquisition budget. Typically, the U.S. Government awards about 80% of its acquisition budget to large businesses. In 2008, there were 7.7 million government contracts awarded (see Figure 1-3).

Figure 1-3. Government Contracts Spiral Upward

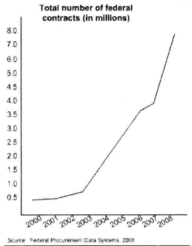

The U.S. Federal Government's supply chain varies by department or agency and by a number of very critical factors, including:

- Nature of the product or service
- Availability of the product or service
- Urgency of the requirements
- Maturity of the technology required
- Geographic location(s) required
- Quantity of products and/or services
- Overall complexity
- Life-cycle costs, and
- Other key factors including the government's budget and ability to accurately state its requirements to industry.

Simply said, the U.S. Government's supply chain typically consists of the following key elements, illustrated in Figure 1-4.

Figure 1-4. U.S. Federal Government's Supply Chain

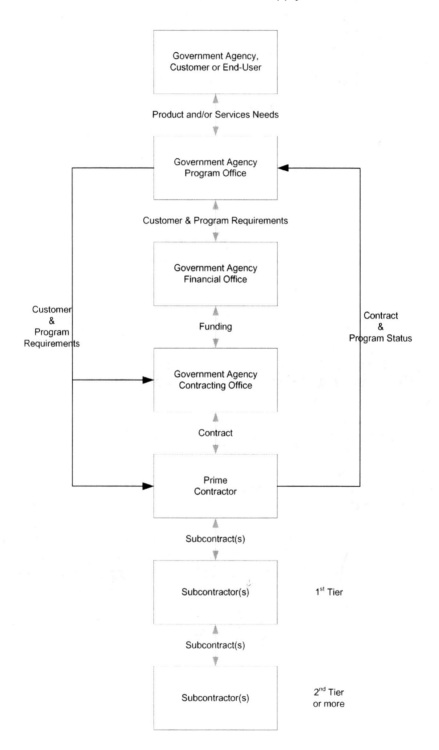

Figure 4.
U.S. Federal Government's Supply Chain

A. U.S. Federal Government Supply Chains Challenges

• The U.S. Government Is Not a Business

It is important to remember the U.S. Government is not a business. The U.S. Government operates to support the security, political, and socio-economic needs of its citizens. Toward this end, the U.S. Government acquires billions of dollars of products and services from industry, and does so in a manner which reflects the security, political, and socio-economic needs of the nation. Thus, the government does not always purchase products and services in the most cost-effective and efficient manner, because serving the broad needs of its citizens comes before getting the cheapest items.

• The Mission of the U.S. Government Is Serious and Complex

The mission of the U.S. Government is both serious and complex. Meeting the public's need for a strong economy, national defense, homeland security, energy, agriculture, commerce, transportation, labor, healthcare, system of justice, and much more are indeed serious matters. Likewise, the broad and growing needs of the U.S. public as a result of evolving global economic conditions, threats of terrorism, ever-changing technologies, potential natural disasters, and much more all impact our society, and make the mission of the U.S. Government highly complex.

• The Federal Acquisition Process Is Overly Regulated, Expensive, and Slow

The Federal Acquisition Regulation (FAR) system, which was implemented in 1984 to provide a fair and consistent purchasing process throughout the government, is overly burdensome on government agencies, government contractors, and subcontractors. However, there are a few U.S. Government agencies that are not bound by the rules and requirements contained in the 2,000 plus pages of the FAR, including the U.S. Postal Service and the Federal Aviation Administration. Typically, all of the federal government agencies bound by the FAR have developed and continually update their own FAR supplements, which may add hundreds or thousands of pages of additional requirements and/or guidelines to further tailor or customize their respective supply chain. Thus, government contractors and subcontractors must read, understand, and fully comply with thousands of pages of rules, regulations, policies, standards, and specifications, which in many cases carry the full force and effect of public law with both significant individual and organizational criminal and/or civil penalties for violations of non-compliance.

As a direct result of the overly regulated federal acquisition process, it takes government agencies far too long, and it costs far too much, to acquire most products and services. While the U.S. Government has enacted policies and requirements to streamline its acquisition process and use more commercial contracting best practices, most government agencies have not fully embraced or implemented these changes. Thus, most U.S. Government agencies still struggle to acquire needed products and services in a timely and cost-effective manner because of their tendency to over-specify their requirements, which often make their products and services unique to government agencies even when it is not truly necessary or appropriate. For example, the Government Accountability Office (GAO) recently reported that collectively the U.S. Government agencies had created more than 18,000 pages of unique requirements for commercially available off-the-shelf information technology (IT) services, which resulted in the government agencies paying far more for the same services as commercial organizations.

● Federal Government Contractors Are Increasing Their Subcontracting

In an all out effort to improve performance results, reduce costs, and transfer or mitigate risk, government contractors, who, by-in-large, tend to be a risk adverse group, are increasing their subcontracting to both large and small businesses. Government prime contractors want to create strong, cost-effective, efficient, and reliable supply chains. A supply chain is the stream of processes for moving goods and/or services from a customer order through the materials, supply, production, distribution, and delivery to the customer. However, the large businesses often struggle to meet the U.S. Government's small business subcontracting goals with the numerous specific categories stated in FAR Part 19, because of the difficulty of finding a sufficient number of small businesses with the skills, capabilities, financial support, and positive past performance record to partner with on an important government contract.

Clearly, as the level of subcontracting increases, the more vital is the prime contractor's ability to manage their supply chain to ensure on-time delivery of quality products and/or services to their government customers. Likewise, government prime contractors are required to flow-down more than fifty mandatory FAR clauses and detailed contract terms and conditions to all of their subcontractors. Plus, each agency's FAR supplement contains numerous mandatory flow-down contract clauses. Each and every one of these detailed mandatory flow-down contract clauses has a value, cost, and risk associated with them. While ultimately the government's prime contractor is held accountable for their subcontractor's performance, the use of the excessive mandatory flow clauses adds significant costs at every level of the supply chain.

● The U.S. Federal Acquisition Workforce Is Understaffed and Needs Training

Nearly every Government Accountability Office (GAO) Report of the U.S. Federal acquisition workforce, and similar studies conducted by the Professional Services Council (PSC) and Grant-Thorton, individual agency studies, or reports from the U.S. Office of Federal Procurement Policy (OFPP), have all stated the U.S. Federal acquisition workforce is understaffed at the vital mid-level ranks and is in need of more and better training. The government employee career fields which are typically cited as critical to the federal acquisition process include: contract management, program/project management, cost/price analysis, systems engineering, logistics management, accounting/auditing, and property management.

Over the past decade, many of the best and brightest people serving the government agencies in these vital acquisition-related roles have either transferred to industry, retired, or transitioned to another career field. The most important element of any supply chain or organization is the people and their collective talents/skills. Today, the U.S. Federal acquisition workforce is suffering from a shortage of talent and the need for both more and better acquisition-related formal education, cross-functional training, and on-the-job training/mentoring.

B. Recommendations for Improvement

Clearly, the current U.S. Government supply chains are vital to the operation of government and critical to its ability to support the needs of our nation. The following recommendations are provided to stimulate thinking and actions to make further improvements in the federal government's supply chain, as described in this chapter, for the benefit of the U.S. taxpayers, government agencies, government contractors, and subcontractors.

- **Simplify and Streamline the Federal Acquisition Process**

In an effort to reduce cycle-time, reduce costs, and improve customer satisfaction, the following are a few suggested actions to simplify and streamline the Federal acquisition process:

  - Rewrite the Federal Acquisition Regulation (FAR). Create a new streamlined e-FAR, web-based, with process diagrams, tools, templates, forms, best practices, and all applicable laws.
  - Implement a standardized Government-wide e-procurement software application, required for use by all federal government agencies. This would create a consistent paperless enterprise-wide e-procurement system for all federal government agencies.
  - Mandate the use of commercial item acquisition to the fullest extent possible.
  - Eliminate the federal bid protest process.
  - Reduce the mandatory FAR flow-down clauses to subcontractors.
  - Mandate the use of Alternative Dispute Resolution (ADR) techniques to resolve claims government-wide.
  - Implement government-wide strategic sourcing for all commodities and commercial off-the-shelf products and services via the General Services Administration (GSA), using commodity and/or professional services councils to consolidate demand planning and forecasting.

- **Implement Performance-Based Supply Chain Management**

Increasingly, organizations in both the public and private sector are forming strategic alliances or partnerships between or with a smaller number of suppliers, distributors, resellers, or a combination of all. Government organizations are seeking to leverage their relationships with government contractors to achieve greater discounts, reduced inventories, reduced cycle-times, and enhanced capabilities. Today, more government agencies are providing or sharing information with their business partners through extended enterprise databases. Government organizations are starting to share more forecast or demand information with their selected government contractors through secure web portals in order to reduce expenses and maximize performance results.

Information is power, and enterprise-wide software applications, which have the capability to link organizations government-wide to government contractors and in turn link them to their respective subcontractors, can form powerful extended supply chains. To create a true performance-based supply chain, government organizations must select prime contractors based in part on past-performance. Likewise, government prime contractors must select their respective subcontractor(s) on a performance basis. Once a supply chain is created via the award of contracts and subcontracts, then with the intelligent application of appropriate performance standards, measures, metrics, and financial incentives, superior results can be achieved. However, it is important to note that without on-going and effective project management, contract management, and subcontract administration by all of the supply chain partners involved, the desired outcomes will not be realized.

- **Enhance the Federal Acquisition Workforce**

The U.S. Government agencies must enhance their investment in the acquisition workforce by improving their recruiting, hiring, training, and retention of key employees. Currently, federal agencies have significant shortages of mid-level, experienced acquisition professionals, especially in the following functional areas: contract management, program/project management, systems engineering, cost/price analysis, and logistics management. The Office of Personnel Management (OPM) must work with the government agencies to improve the acquisition work environment, provide effective intern-professional development programs, provide training/education with industry programs, enhance mentor/coaching activities government-wide, and improve acquisition training.

In addition to all of the aforementioned positive actions to improve the culture, work environment, and employee development for acquisition professionals, it is also important to make salaries more competitive with the private sector. Likewise, government agencies should implement a pay-for-performance system for all acquisition professionals. Without the needed talents, which have been allowed to erode for over a decade, the government agencies will never realize the cost-savings, cycle-time reductions, and improved customer satisfaction in their respective supply chain. Remember, it is always the people and their talents that are essential to achieve success for any organization or team!

- **Create an Effective Balance of Government Surveillance and Oversight**

There is no question the government agencies have the right and responsibility as a prudent buyer of products and services to conduct appropriate surveillance and oversight of their selected contractors, especially on complex, critical, high risk contracts. However, U.S. Government agencies often overwhelm government contractors and their respective subcontractors with countless requests for information/data, certifications, reviews, audits, and investigations. The net effect is often a more risk adverse industry, which lives in fear of government audits, reviews, and investigations, which cause significant amounts of money to satisfy government auditor demands, and which do not necessarily add real-value to the products or services being acquired.

The current perception is that too many government contractors have been performing poorly as a result of reduced government surveillance and oversight during the past eight years. Thus, it is widely expected that there will be a major increase in government reviews, audits, and investigations during the Obama administration. Yet, what is really needed is an effective balance. Said differently, federal agencies should select the best qualified contractors based upon their respective past performance, pricing, technical solution, financial capabilities, and management expertise, then appropriately motivate, measure, and verify their performance in an efficient and cost-effective manner. The government should not conduct excessive audits, reviews, and investigations that drive-up costs without adding value to the supply chain.

§ 1:4 Summary

In this chapter, we have discussed the key components, structure, and major challenges currently facing the U.S. Government's supply-chains. It is vital to all U.S. taxpayers, to all government contractors and subcontractors, and to all federal government agencies that the respective supply chains created by each federal government agency operate in compliance with all appropriate U.S. laws, regulations, and policies. Likewise, it is vital to all of the parties involved in the government supply chains that the U.S. Government agencies seek and implement action plans, such as those presented in this chapter, to promote continuous improvement of their people, processes, and performance in order to use taxpayer dollars as wisely as possible.

In the next chapter, we will examine the art and science of managing subcontracts in the complex world of U.S. government contracting. Specifically, in Chapter 2 we will discuss U.S. government prime contractors challenges and best practices for improving their respective supply chain in support of demanding U.S. government agencies.

§ 1:5 Questions to consider

1. Do you agree with the discussion of our new performance-based supply environment?
2. How well do you understand the U.S. Federal government's supply chain challenges?
3. Which of the U.S. federal government supply chain recommendations for improvement do you think are most vital?

Chapter 2

U.S. Government Prime Contractors Supply Chain Challenges and Best Practices

> **KeyCite**®: Cases and other legal materials listed in KeyCite Scope can be researched through the KeyCite service on Westlaw®. Use KeyCite to check citations for form, parallel references, prior and later history, and comprehensive citator information, including citations to other decisions and secondary materials.

§ 2:1   Introduction

In 2008, the U.S. federal government awarded more than 7 million contracts, valued at over $531 Billion[1] to acquire needed products, services, systems, and integrated solutions from thousands of government contractors also referred to as prime contractors. Serving as a prime contractor is not easy business, because the U.S. federal government is very demanding. U.S. federal government prime contractors often must select and manage multiple subcontractors and comply with a tremendous number of complex laws, regulations, policies, standards, specifications, and face a growing level of government oversight-audits, reviews, and investigations. This chapter provides a detailed discussion of the critical challenges and proven best practices of U.S. federal government prime contractors in managing their respective supply chains to both comply with all the government's laws, regulations, policies, etc., but also to achieve on-time delivery of quality products and/or services, within budget, which meet or exceed the customer's requirements.

§ 2:2   U.S. government prime contractors supply chain challenges

Table 2-1. provides a list of ten of the critical challenges which U.S. federal government prime contractors often encounter in building and managing their respective supply chain with their customers and subcontractors. Following Table 2-1 is a brief discussion of each of the stated 10 critical prime contractors supply chain challenges.

[Section 2:1]

[1]U.S. Office of Federal Procurement Policy, Federal Procurement Data System, FY08 Procurement Statistics, February 2009.

(Table 2-1)

10 Critical Supply Chain Challenges Facing U.S. Government Prime Contractors
1. Financial pressures, due to global economic downturn, affecting prime contractors and subcontractors
2. Poor demand planning and requirements determination by U.S. federal government agencies
3. Insufficient government contracting and supply chain management team competencies
4. Lack of leverage of suppliers
5. Demanding U.S. government small business subcontracting goals
6. Excessive U.S. government mandatory flow-down of terms and conditions to subcontractors
7. Lack of competition in supplier selection
8. Increased government cost reduction demands
9. Excessive government detailed requirements
10. Increased U.S. government oversight-audits, reviews, and investigations

1. Financial pressures, due to global economic downturn, affecting prime contractors and subcontractors

The global economic downturn continues to manifest itself in many ways, and certainly one of them is the risk many companies are facing in terms of some of their suppliers being under significant financial pressures. Many companies in both domestic and international markets are under growing financial pressures, especially smaller companies that are not as well capitalized. A key factor in the current financial struggles of many subcontractors in both the public and private sectors is that their customers often pay even more slowly than usual as prime contractors face their own economic challenges.[1]

Cash flow is the heart of business. Financially strapped prime contractors and subcontractors may be late paying their suppliers as a result of their difficulties in: finding available loans, securing credit, paying higher interest rates, and receiving late payments from some of their customers.

A recent survey by CPO Agenda magazine found that more than three quarters of procurement executives said they were facing great pressure to reduce costs—and we're surprised the number isn't even higher. (See Figure 2-1.)[2]

[Section 2:2]

[1]Supply Chain Digest, "If Key Suppliers are Struggling Financially, What Should Procurement Organizations Do?," SC Digest, (New York: January 7, 2009).

[2]Supply Chain Digest, "For Procurement Managers, a Bit of Pay Back Time" scdigest. com, January 27, 2009.

Figure 2-1.

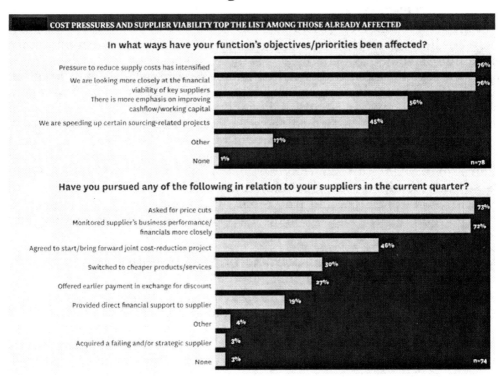

2. Poor demand planning and requirements determination by U.S. federal government agencies

It may sound amazing to some business professionals, but one of the biggest challenges government prime contractors and subcontractors encounter is that U.S. federal government agencies do not always know what they want, when they need it, and/or how many they will need! Of course, one of the golden rules to creating a cost-effective and efficient supply chain is to have an accurate demand plan/forecast of the quantity of products and/or services which the customer needs and a timeline as to when they are required. For a variety of reasons, U.S. federal government agencies have historically not done a very good job of accurately aligning their stated needs to their congressionally authorized and appropriated department budgets. As a result, government prime contractors and subcontractors often become frustrated by the inaccuracy of the government's requirements and frequent changes to the quantity, quality, and delivery schedule.

3. Insufficient government contracting and supply chain management team (SCMT) competencies

Many U.S. government prime contractors and subcontractors do not have the number of highly-skilled, well-educated, well-trained, and experienced professionals who fully understand the laws, regulations, and best practices of U.S. government contracts and supply chain management. As a result, numerous U.S. government prime contractors and subcontractors struggle to truly optimize their supply chain. Frequent company reorganizations, downsizing, and changing company policies, processes, and practices further complicate companies' ability to enhance both organizational and individual competencies in U.S. government contracting and supply chain management.

4. Lack of leverage of suppliers

One of the hallmarks of world class supply chain management companies, such as Wal-Mart, Proctor & Gamble, and IBM, is their ability to effectively leverage suppliers. Leveraging suppliers is a company's ability to negotiate discounts, obtain preferred contract terms and conditions (i.e. payment terms, cycle-time, delivery schedule, extended warranties, etc.), and form mutually successful business partnerships.[3] Unfortunately, for a variety of reasons many government prime contractors and subcontractors often struggle to form meaningful supplier relationships, thus prohibiting them from being able to effectively leverage their suppliers.

5. Demanding U.S. government small business subcontracting goals

In accordance with the Federal Acquisition Regulation (FAR) Part 19, Small Business Contracting, every U.S. federal government agency is required to establish goals to award a certain percentage of their acquisition budget to U.S. small businesses. In addition, FAR Part 19 mandates that government contracting officers require large businesses awarded specified government contracts valued above $550,000 to create a small

---

[3]Garrett, Gregory A. "Contract Negotiations," CCH Inc., (Chicago, IL 2005).

business subcontracting plan to achieve stated goals. Further, FAR Part 19 establishes numerous specific categories of small businesses, including: small disadvantaged businesses, women-owned small businesses, veteran-owned small businesses, HUB-zoned small businesses, and Alaskan and Native American-owned small businesses. Often, U.S. federal government agencies will establish an overall contract goal for prime contractors, for example 20% of the value of the contract be subcontracted to small businesses, frequently with specific subcontracting targets for each specific small business category. Achieving these contract specific small business category targets and overall small business subcontracting goals can prove very challenging in some product and service areas.

6. Excessive U.S. government mandatory flow-down of contract terms and conditions to subcontractors

As the old saying goes, "What the big print giveth, the little print taketh away." Clearly, in the world of U.S. government contracts the above statement is true as it pertains to the vast number of complex, detailed, and one-sided mandatory contract clauses, often called terms and conditions (Ts & Cs), which are required by government laws, regulations, and policies. Of course, the U.S. federal government as one of the biggest buyers of products and services in the world has a right to leverage their suppliers and protect its interest. However, the U.S. federal government extended its leverage beyond the rule of contract privity to the prime contractor's subcontractors, via U.S. government mandatory flow-down contract clauses.

Said differently, the U.S. federal government agencies are required via the FAR to ensure the mandatory flow-down of numerous, in most cases 50+, government contract clauses to subcontractors. Further, each government department or agency has developed a list of additional terms and conditions or contract clauses which must be flowed-down to subcontractors, at all levels below the prime contract. For example, a U.S. Department of Defense (DOD) prime contractor, who has received a contract above $500,000, may be required to flow-down over 50 Federal Acquisition Regulation (FAR) contract clauses and another 50+ Department of Defense Federal Acquisition Regulation Supplement (DFARS) contract clauses to their subcontractors, resulting in over 100 detailed, complex, and often expensive to implement subcontract requirements above and beyond what it normally takes to deliver the products and/or services specified.

7. Lack of competition in supplier selection

Given the numerous obstacles to successful entry into the U.S. federal government marketplace, including: complexity of requirements, entrenched incumbent competitors, unstable funding, changing requirements, numerous delays, government politics and bureaucracy, and increased government oversight-reviews, audits, and investigations, it is often difficult to maintain real competition in supplier selections. At both the prime contract level and subcontract level(s) it can prove very challenging to maintain two or more viable suppliers especially for some of the highly complex systems and integrated solutions required by the U.S. government agencies.

8. Increased government cost reduction demands

As the global economic downturn affects governments and industry worldwide, more U.S. government funding is being directed to support failing industries and financial institutions. Thus, it is widely expected that many U.S. government departments and agencies will receive less funding to support their key contracts and major programs. Clearly, the focus of the Obama administration is on healthcare, house, energy, transportation, and the environment. So, the U.S. federal government departments of Health and Human Services (HHS), Veteran Affairs (VA), Housing and Urban Development (HUD), Transportation, Energy, and the Environmental Protection Agency (EPA) are all expected to receive increased acquisition funding from the U.S. congress with support and approval by President Obama. Likewise, it is widely expected that the Departments of Defense (DOD), Department of Homeland Security (DHS), and the National Aeronautics and Space Administration (NASA) will receive less funding than in previous years. As a result, it is expected that DOD, DHS, and NASA will be highly focused on controlling expenses, especially on the design, production, and operation of major acquisition programs.[4] Government contractors will increasingly be contractually required to reduce their costs by any and all means possible, within the realm of business ethics.

9. Excessive government detailed how-to-do-it requirements

For more than 40 years, U.S. federal government agencies, especially the U.S. Department of Defense (DOD), have developed highly detailed designs, specifications, and standards to ensure they get what they want, how they want it. Unfortunately, this highly detailed and prescriptive government requirements process has often resulted in high costs, over budget, behind schedule, and sometimes poor performing products, services, systems, and integrated solutions. Further, the U.S. government's detailed specification-oriented and statement of work-driven task documents are sometimes inaccurate and/or out-dated. Finally, the U.S. government's traditional detailed "How-to-do-it" requirements process does not allow much flexibility, innovation, or cost-efficiencies to be considered or implemented by industry.

10. Increased U.S. government oversight-audits, reviews, and investigations

Today, we live in a world of mistrust or, said simply, a lack of trust in government contracting. As a result of some clear violations of U.S. government laws, regulations, and policies by some government prime contractors and subcontractors, industry is often perceived by the U.S. congress and the public to be crooks. Because of this fundamental lack of trust of industry, U.S. government prime contractors are forced to endure numerous government audits, reviews, and investigations, many with civil and/or criminal penalties associated with non-compliance. Unfortunately, because of the wrong-doings of a relatively small percentage of government prime contractors, the industry as a whole is being forced to endure an unprecedented level of government oversight lead by the Government Account-

---

[4]Garrett, Gregory A. and McDonald, Pete. "Preparing for Change: The Obama Administration Affect on Government Contractors," NCMA, Contract Management Magazine, February, 2009.

ability Office (GAO), Department Inspector General (IG) offices, Defense Contract Audit Agency (DCAA), Defense Contract Management Agency (DCMA), and many others.

§ 2:3 U.S. government prime contractors supply chain best practices

Table 2-2. provides a list of ten of the proven effective supply chain best practices as implemented by industry in either the public and/or private sector. Following Table 2-2. is a brief discussion of each of the stated 10 supply chain best practices.

(Table 2-2.)

10 Supply Chain Best Practices for U.S. Government Prime Contractors
1. Enhance cash-flow and financial management of suppliers
2. Understand government needs and contract requirements
3. Implement a supply chain management professional development program and Center of Excellence
4. Conduct strategic sourcing and spend analysis
5. Implement supplier relationship improvement programs
6. Expand the use of commercial item acquisitions
7. Enhance market research for supplier sourcing
8. Implement price-benchmarking clauses
9. Expand use of performance-based contracts
10. Benchmark supply chain management processes and performance metrics

1. Enhance cash-flow and financial management of suppliers

Many suppliers, in both the public and private sectors, are facing cash-flow issues and growing financial pressures. U.S. government prime contractors must effectively manage their invoice, payment, and cost-flow process with their government agency customers, appropriately requesting: loans, advanced payment, milestone-based payments for results achieved a.k.a. progress-payments, or cost reimbursement for allowable and allocable expenses incurred, depending upon the financial situation and the pricing arrangement agreed to in the contract. Likewise, prime contractors must do all they can afford to do to help their selected subcontractors via contract financing such as collateralized loans, improved payment terms, faster payments, progress payments, and operational assistance when necessary and appropriate. A good supplier is hard to find and if you can help them through a tough financial time, you will most likely have a strong prime-sub business relationship.

2. Understand customer needs and contract requirements

In order to become a successful U.S. government prime contractor, it is vital to understand both what are the government customer needs and what are their stated contract requirements. At times the government agencies do not properly develop their contract requirements, thus it is possible for a prime contractor to provide the government the product and services which they contractually required, yet still not meet the government's real needs. The goal of business is for a seller to meet or exceed their customer/buyer's needs, which achieving their company performance goals. Thus, it is essential for a prime contractor to ensure they understand the government's customer's needs and align the needs with the actual contract requirements.

A tool designed to help prime contractors and likewise subcontractors ensure they understand the customers needs and the key contract/subcontract requirements is the customer requirements/Deliverable Matrix (CR/DM). The CR/DM is a simple matrix jointly developed by the buyer and the seller to clearly list all of the critical customer needs and which products, services, or systems will be developed and/or delivered to meet or exceed each contract requirement. Further, top supply chain companies ensure each contract requirement is tracked via a Work Breakdown Structure (WBS), linked to a Responsibility Assignment Matrix (RAM) to assign the work to specific individuals, time-phased via a Master Integrated Schedule (MIS), and has a budget established for each contract deliverable, project, and program.

3. Implement a supply chain management professional development program and Center of Excellence

World class companied like IBM, Dell, Toyota, and others have focused on not only creating effective supply chain processes, systems, and performance-metrics, but they have also invested in their most important asset, their people. Specifically, many of the leading global companies like Toyota have made significant investments in the supply chain management education, training, cross-functional work experience for their team members. Further, a few organizations in both the public and private sectors have established a supply chain management Center of Excellence to facilitate processes, tools, training, coaching/mentoring, lessons learned, and best practices via a coordinated and integrated Knowledge Management Center. Plus, many government agencies and companies are using the numerous supply chain management education and training courses available from colleges and universities worldwide. Today, supply chain management education is offered via classroom-based instruction, computer-based instruction, and interactive online programs like the Supply Chain Management Master's Certificate Program offered by the University of San Francisco, through the University Alliance online program.

4. Conduct strategic sourcing and spend analysis

Leading purchasing organizations worldwide have learned the value and power of conducting spend analysis as a vital element of strategic sourcing. Said simply, a buying/purchasing organization should know how they are spending their money, with whom they are spending the money-byproduct or service, and what is the quality of the products and services they are receiving. Strategic sourcing is a process approach to effectively analyze the supply chain to reduce cycle-time, reduce costs, and improve product and service performance results. Many companies and government agencies have created commodity councils to aggregate their demand planning for specific commercially available raw materials, products, and/or services. Improving demand planning or product/services forecasting is an important first-step for procurement organizations to more effectively leverage their suppliers, through economic-order-quantity buying practices.

5. Implement supplier relationship improvement programs

Numerous world class companies like Wal-Mart, IBM, Honda, and others have created, implemented, and maintained highly successful supplier relationship improvement programs. Wal-Mart works with its suppliers to help them improve the quality and marketability of their products. Honda provides all of their suppliers with performance goals/targets and monthly supplier report cards. Further, Honda works with their suppliers to improve their manufacturing processes and find innovated way to reduce cycle-times and drive-out expenses.[1] IBM categorizes their suppliers based upon performance and had developed a supplier inventive/rewards program. The U.S. Department of Defense (DOD) developed and implemented the DOD Pilot Mentor-Protégé program years ago, which has helped improve the performance of many small businesses working in partnership with a successful major defense prime contractor.

6. Expand the use of commercial item acquisitions

The U.S. federal government agencies have tried to increase their use of commercial contracting practices via the implementation of the Federal Acquisition Regulation (FAR) Part 12: Commercial-Item Acquisition. FAR Part 12 provides significant process and contractual streamlining in comparison to the typical federal contracting process. The use of the Commercial-Item Acquisition process saves significant time and money for the subcontractors, prime contractors, government agencies, and U.S. taxpayers. U.S. government agencies must embrace and require the use of more commercially available products and services, versus creating unique detailed government requirements.

7. Enhance market research for supplier sourcing

Many prime contractors and U.S. federal government agencies suffer from the "incumbent contractor syndrome," which can be either positive or negative depending upon the performance of the selected contractor. Continually purchasing products and/or services from a selected contractor over an extended period of time can prove successful if the incumbent contractor is continually improving their people, processes, and performance. However, incumbent contractors have a tendency to become somewhat complacent; thus seeking higher revenues and profits without improving their people, processes, products, and/or pricing. To combat the Incumbent Contractor Syndrome, we recommend the effective use of market research to identify and select the best suppliers.

Market research can be accomplished via numerous methods, including: (1) hiring a professional market research firm (i.e. Dunn & Bradstreet, The Gartner Group, The Hackett Group, or Forrester Research), (2) conducting one-on-one market focus-group meetings with leading suppliers, (3) developing and conducting web-based market surveys, (4) conduct Internet-based searches of available suppliers, (5) contact industry trade associations for lists of available products and/or services providers, (6) review

---

[Section 2:3]

[1]Garrett, Gregory A. "Commercial Contracting Best Practices," NCMA, Contract Management Magazine, January 2008.

industry/trade magazine and catalogs, and (7) attend industry/trade association conferences and exhibitions.

8. Implement price-benchmarking clauses

A benchmarking clause is used in an outsourcing contract as a check against significant price "drift" over time. Such drift is of particular concern in longer term contracts, where major discrepancies can occur between contract prices and market pricing. Most outsourcing projects, especially longer term ones, have complex mechanisms in place for changing contract prices. These mechanisms are the primary drivers of micro-price adjustment and include: year-on-year productivity improvements, inflation adjustments, and adjustments for changes in required service volumes. The underlying commercial basis for including a benchmarking clause is not to treat it as a supplement to these mechanisms, which would cause it to become just another tool to enable an additional micro-price adjustment.[2]

9. Expand use of performance-based contracts

Said simply, a Performance-Based Contract (PBC) contains the following essential elements:

- Performance Work Statement (PWS) or Statement of Objectives (SOO)
- Performance standards, measures, and metrics
- Performance incentives (positive and negative)
- Quality Assurance Surveillance Plan (QASP)
- Appropriate pricing arrangement(s)

Without all of the above stated essential elements, a contract lacks the means to truly empowers and motivate a supplier to achieve the art of the possible. Today, too many U.S. government agencies and prime contractors still rely on out-dated, overly legalistic, highly prescriptive, and overly complex contracts containing detailed designs, specifications, and lengthy task-oriented statements of work, which often drive-up costs, extend the acquisition cycle-time, and result in poor performance results. PBCs when effectively structured and intelligently implemented can achieve superior performance results for all of the parties involved.

10. Benchmark supply chain management processes and key performance indicators

Establishing and reporting on key performance indicators (KPIs) is critical to the success of any contract. According to the recent 2007 cross-industry benchmarking studies conducted by the Center for Advanced Purchasing Studies (CAPS) research, the most popular commercial procurement KPIs include:

- Purchase spend as a percentage of sales dollars
- Purchasing operating expense as a percentage of sales dollars
- Purchasing operating expense as a percentage of purchase spend
- Purchasing operating expense per purchasing employee
- Purchasing employees as a percentage of company employees
- Purchase spend per purchasing employee

---

[2]Garrett, Gregory A. "Commercial Contracting Best Practices," NCMA, Contract Management Magazine, January 2008.

- Managed spend per purchasing employee
- Percentage of purchase spend managed/controlled by purchasing
- Percentage of companies that reported outsourcing some of their procurement activities
- Percentage of managed spend outsourced
- Percentage of purchase spend offshore
- Percentage of purchase spend onshore
- Average annual spend on training per purchasing employees
- Cost avoidance savings as a percentage of total purchase spend
- Cost reduction savings as a percentage of total purchase spend
- Percentage of active suppliers accounting for 80 percent of purchase spend
- Percentage of purchase spend with diversity suppliers
- Percentage of active suppliers who are e-procurement enabled

Most organizations understand the importance and value of conducting benchmarking of their procurement practices and performance metrics or key performance indicators. Today, many senior procurement executives, in both government and industry, are now assessing how their organization adds value to the mission-determining their value proposition. The Hackett Group, a world-class benchmarking firm, has developed a five-stage model for procurement's evolving proposition. See Table 2-3.[3]

Table 2-3.

STAGE	SUPPLY MANAGEMENT		CUSTOMER MANAGEMENT		
	1 SUPPLY AS-SURANCE	2 PRICE	3 TOTAL COST OF OWNER-SHIP	4 DEMAND MANAGE-MENT	5 VALUE MANAGE-MENT
GOAL	Right goods and services at the right time at the right price	Right goods and services AND at the right price	Shift from lowest price to lowest total cost of ownership	Reduce demand activity, complexity, and variability	Increase business value derived from spend rather than just reducing total cost/spend
PROCURE-MENT'S ROLE	Buyer Planner	Negotiator	Supply expert team leader, project manager, supplier manager	Spend/budget consultant ("money manager") and procurement relationship manager	Trusted business advisor and change agent

[3]Garrett, Gregory A. "Commercial Contracting Best Practices," NCMA, Contract Management Magazine, January 2008.

	SUPPLY MANAGEMENT		CUSTOMER MANAGEMENT		
KEY OUTPUT METRICS	Perfect Order (on-time delivery, defect-free, accurate documentation, etc.)	1. Present Value and/or spend cost savings/ avoidance 2. Performance to market	1. Cost of quality 2. Cost of capital 3. Freight, handling, duties, tariffs, taxes 4. Write-offs and disposal 5. Opportunity cost from lost profits and brand damage	1. Percent of spend/ sourcing activity with early demand influence 2. Maverick spend percentage (not channeling demand to best supply) 3. Internal customer satisfaction rating	1. Net Income, Return on Investment, Economic Value Added, Net Present Value, etc. 2. Market cap/stock price 3. Operation metrics of the spend owners
PRACTICES/ TOOLS	1. Enterprise Resource Planning 2. Supplier scheduling 3. Long term contacts, dual sourcing, etc.	1. Separation of strategic sourcing and tactical buying 2. Basic "n-step" strategic sourcing methodology 3. Price savings tracking 4. Competitive bidding techniques/ tools	1. Deep cost modeling and management 2. End-to-end functional teams (suppliers, too) 3. Supplier management, collaboration, and development 4. Working capital management 5. Complexity/ waste reduction (lean, Six Sigma, etc.) 6. Supply chain management (e.g., extended network design, multi-tier sourcing) 7. Design for cost 8. Supply risk mitigation (supplier, capacity, market, network, etc.)	1. Customer Account Management (account managers, co-location, stakeholder surveys, contract centers) 2. Demand visibility (e.g., forecasting project portfolio planning, demand planning) 3. Supply planning and demand supply matching 4. Demand shaping (joint planning/ budgeting, promotions, postponement)	1. Business process sourcing (e.g., make vs. buy, shoring) 2. Design for supply 3. Hoshin Planning and Quality Function Deployment (QFD) 4. Customer's customer focus and customer specific methodologies

§ 2:4 Summary

So in retrospect, in this chapter we have provided a detailed discussion of ten critical challenges which U.S. federal government prime contractors typically encounter in managing their respective supply chains in order to both comply with all of the government's laws, regulations, and policies, and to achieve high performance results. Further, we have offered ten supply chain best practices, which have been successfully implemented by numerous world class companies and/or leading government organizations.

Too many organizations in both the public and private sectors over promise and under deliver. Remember, the promise of successful outsourcing can only be realized through the discipline of effective supply chain management.

In chapter 3, we will discuss the suitability, advantages, and disadvantages of a variety of contractor teaming arrangements.

§ 2:5   Questions to consider

1. Which of the prime contractor critical challenges do you think are most important to remedy?
2. Which of the prime contractor proven best practices do you think are most effective?
3. How many of the prime contractor best practices has your organization implemented?

Chapter 3

Contractor Teaming Arrangements

KeyCiteᴿ: Cases and other legal materials listed in KeyCite Scope can be researched through the KeyCite service on Westlawᴿ. Use KeyCite to check citations for form, parallel references, prior and later history, and comprehensive citator information, including citations to other decisions and secondary materials.

---

§ 3:1   Introduction

Given the growing complexities of products, services, systems, and integrated solutions, in both the public and private sectors, most companies are seeking business partners to help them accomplish the work, share the risk, and achieve joint success. As a result, there is a tremendous increase in the formation of a wide-variety of business partnerships commonly called contractor teaming arrangements. It is not uncommon today to find companies working as business partners on one deal and competitors on another deal at the same time. Likewise, we increasingly encounter companies working as a U.S. government prime contractor on one contract, while on another contract serving as a subcontractor under a prime contractor, who is one of their subcontractors on another government contract. If the above stated scenario sounds complicated, then you would be correct. The focus of this chapter is to: (1) review the various business partnerships, or contractor teaming arrangements, which companies are creating to perform U.S. government contracts, (2) understand the key elements which should be included in contractor teaming agreements, and (3) discuss the lessons learned and best practices of forming business partnerships in the U.S. federal government marketplace.

§ 3:2   Contractor teaming arrangements

The Federal Acquisition Regulation (FAR) Subpart 9.6 defines a "contractor team arrangement" as an arrangement in which:

1. Two or more companies form a partnership or joint venture to act as a potential prime contractor; or

2. A potential prime contractor agrees with one or more other companies to have them act as its subcontractors under a specified government contract or acquisition program.

The FAR states the government will recognize the "integrity and validity" of contractor team arrangements so long as the relationship is "fully disclosed." Typically, contractor teaming arrangements are formed before a bid or proposal is submitted to the government contracting officer, however, the government often recognizes contractor teaming arrangements entered into after the proposal is submitted to the government.

As stated in the FAR definition of contractor team arrangements, business partnerships can take many forms, each with their respective suitability, advantages, and disadvantages. The primary contractor business partnerships include: 1) prime contractor-subcontractor teams, 2) joint ventures, 3) limited liability companies, and 4) private equity ownership agreements.

§ 3:3   Prime contractor-subcontractor teaming

The most widely used teaming structure, in both the public and private business sectors, is the prime contractor-subcontractor teaming agreement, often referred to as the prime-sub relationship. It is important to note, the rules of contract privity establish a contractual business relationship via two parties. In U.S. federal government contracting, the U.S. government agency serves as the buyer and the prime contractor serves as the seller, thus contract privity exists between the government agency and the prime contractor. Likewise, in a prime-sub relationship, the prime contractor serves as the buyer and the subcontractor serves as the seller, thus contract privity exists between the prime and the sub. Clearly, no contract privity or contractual business relationship exists between a U.S. government agency and a subcontractor. However, the U.S. federal government does exert a lot of power and influence over its selected prime contractors, thus requiring certain rights, consents, reviews, approval of subcontractors, and mandatory flow-down of key contract terms and conditions in all subcontracts.

Prime contractor-subcontractor teaming is most commonly used when each party has a well-defined scope of work, in terms of products and/or services to provide, which can be performed either separately or via an integrated effort with the prime contractor. Except when specifically prohibited by a solicitation, government agencies may properly consider the experience and past performance of subcontractors when evaluating a prime contractor's proposal.[1]

The prime contractor-subcontractor teaming relationship provides advantages to each of the parties involved. From the government's perspective, it provides a single point of contact, because the prime contractor is held accountable for the subcontractor's performance. From the prime contractor's perspective, it allows them to lead the planning and execution of the work, build strong customer relationships with the government, and

---

[Section 3:3]

[1]Humphries, Robert and Irwin, Andrew D. "Teaming Agreements/Edition III," New York, Thomson West, Briefing Papers, September 2006.

flow all revenue recognition through their company. From the subcontractor's perspective, it allows them to do the work they specialize in performing, build a strong relationship with the prime contractor, and create or expand credibility with the government.

The prime contractor-subcontractor team structure also has certain disadvantages to each of the parties. From the government's perspective, it often proves more costly as a result of the tiering of contractors' overhead costs and profits/fees. From a prime contractor's perspective, the selection and management of subcontractors can prove difficult and costly. Despite these potential pitfalls, the prime contractor-subcontractor relationship is the most commonly used teaming arrangement for businesses to work together. Clearly, the prime contractor-subcontractor teaming arrangement should be considered the preferred arrangement unless there are structural issues for the members of the team that prohibit its use.[2]

§3:4 Joint ventures

Joint ventures (JVs), often called consortia, are widely used contractor teaming arrangements. A joint venture is essentially a limited purpose partnership agreement, in which each party (two or more) are jointly and severally liable to both the customer (i.e., the government) and to third parties (i.e., subcontractors). JVs are frequently used in the construction industry and are steadily increasing in use by professional services firms worldwide.

Joint ventures as a form of contractor teaming arrangement provides advantages to each of the parties involved. From a government perspective, it allows them to secure the resources of two or more firms at the same time to perform the work they require and it may allow them to get the work for a lower price.

From a contractor perspective, as a member of a joint venture team: (1) they can exert more influence and control over contract performance to protect their interest vs. a traditional prime contractor-subcontractor relationship. (2) receive favorable joint venture income tax treatment, and (3) avoid serving as a subcontractor to its competitors.

Joint ventures as a form of contractor teaming arrangement also has certain disadvantages for each of the parties involved. From a government perspective, a JV may be viewed as lacking a clear or single point of contact, thus creating issues regarding who is really in charge and who has the authority to ensure the work is properly performed. From a joint venture team-member perspective, each company becomes jointly and severally liable to potentially multiple parties, thus creating higher financial liabilities and risk. Despite these disadvantages, many joint ventures have proven to be wildly successful in both the public and private business sectors.

§3:5 Limited liability companies

A limited liability company (LLC) is a form of business arrangement

---

[2]Garrett, Gregory A. "World Class Contracting", 4th Edition, Chicago, IL, CCH Inc., 2007.

which provides the owners with the limited financial liability of a corporation with the flow-through tax advantages of a partnership. During the past decade, in both the public and private business sectors, there has been a significant growth in the creation and use of LLCs.

The limited liability company form of contractor teaming arrangement offers several advantages. The LLC is an excellent means of structuring a teaming relationship when none of the parties is interested in a subcontractor role. The LLC is considered by both buyers and subcontractors to be a positive teaming arrangement, because the owners of the LLC share the same liability to customers and third parties as do shareholders in a major corporation.

Of course, the use of an LLC does have some disadvantages in its application. For example, the government may become confused as to: who is really in charge when there are multiple owners of the LLC, and how to conduct the evaluation of past performance of individual parties to the LLC after initial formation. Likewise, the LLC structure can lead to division amongst the owners, which may delay decision-making and create a challenging work environment.

§ 3:6 Private equity ownership agreements

When a private equity (PE) firm decides to purchase a company it typically does so, because the company current owners are looking to sell, and the PE firm believes said company has a lot of potential to grow and achieve highly profitable revenues. A typical PE firm is looking to make a relatively quick turnaround profit usually over a period of 3 to 5 years. The PE firm's involvement with the companies they acquire range quite dramatically depending upon the PE firm's capabilities and the level of support needed by the companies they acquire. Most often, PE firms help their acquired companies to grow via a combination of: improved business practices; key personnel additions and/or changes; and through the acquisition of add-on companies. PE firms typically create a new company board structure, including: members of the PE firm, leaders from the acquired company, and outside experts, selected by the PE firm or jointly selected.

Private equity ownership arrangements do offer certain advantages to all of the parties involved. From the government's perspective, PE ownership is often transparent with the exception that the company typically has access to more resources and expanded capabilities. From the acquired company's view, having a PE ownership agreement can allow a company access to increased capital to fuel product, services, and marketing expansion, plus easy access to additional business expert guidance.

Private equity ownership arrangements do present some distinct disadvantages. For example, depending upon the nature of the works which the other companies perform, who are owned by the same PE firm, an organizational Conflict Of Interest (OCI) may arise, between different companies which are owned by the same PE firm. Another potential disadvantage of PE firms is that sometimes their accessibility to credit or cash may not be available when a company needs the funding for either organic or inorganic growth. A further disadvantages, is the potential loss of top talent after the initial sale of the company to the PE firm, which can be very detrimental in the case of professional services firms, if the top talent attracts a lot of business. When our economy was booming several years ago, PE firms were rapidly expanding, however, today amidst our global economic crisis, PE firms are often struggling to make their acquisitions profitable for their investors.

§ 3:7 Contractor teaming agreements: Key elements

The exact focus and intent of a contractor team agreement does vary depending upon the role of the party. In general, contractor teaming agreements should appropriately form an agreement to partner in the event a contract is awarded by a buying organization. Said simply, it is an agreement to agree to potentially work together. Typically, prime contractors or lead parties want as much flexibility in a contractor teaming agreement as possible as to who they select to work with, how much work they are given, and when and where the work is performed. Conversely, subcontractors or minor parties want as much specificity and exclusivity in a contractor teaming agreement as possible to virtually guarantee them as much work as possible and as much control over their work as possible. As a result of these two conflicting priorities, the formation and implementation of contractor teaming agreements has been subject to a great deal of litigation during the past decade.

Table A provides a brief outline of the 12 key elements which should be contained in most contractor teaming agreements. Following Table A is a brief discussion of each of these 12 key elements of contractor team agreements.

Table A

• Purpose
• Scope of Work
• Confidentiality
• Flow-down Requirements
• Ethics
• Payment
• Bid & Proposal (B&P) Costs
• Exclusivity
• Intellectual Property Rights
• Limitation of Liabilities
• Disputes Resolutions
• Terminations

• Purpose

Every contractor teaming agreement should include a section which describes the overall nature of the products, services, systems, and/or solutions set forth in the agreements. It should at least at a high-level discuss some of the key skills and capabilities each party brings to the subject deal.

• Scope of Work

There are several ways to reflect the scope of work, including: 1) task-oriented statements of what work will be performed, 2) outcome-based or performance-based statements of the end-customer's desired results, or 3) the use of discrete and specific lists of materials, commodities, products, systems, and/or services which will be provided and by whom. The scope of work section is subject to a lot controversy and contention in the formation and execution of contractor team agreements, especially in the description of the relationship between the parties, who does what, and any implied or specific commitments. So, be very careful what wording you agree to between the parties.

● **Confidentiality**

Today most companies enter into Non-Disclosure Agreements (NDAs) before ever even considering entering into a contractor teaming agreement. Even if you have a signed NDA, it is still important to appropriately include a confidentiality clause in the contractor teaming agreement. Typically, a confidentiality clause will require the parties involved to designate in writing information that is truly proprietary. Usually, confidentiality clauses are mutual, although there may be some unique circumstances which could warrant unilateral determination of confidentiality. The confidentiality clause should contain a period of performance or length of time that the clause will stay in effect and specify whether it will survive the existence of the teaming agreement. In addition, parties to a teaming agreement will usually not be restricted into their use or disclosure of information that a) is located in the public domain, b) is already in their possession, c) is independently developed, and/or d) was properly obtained from another party.

● **Flow-down Requirements**

Pursuant to the Federal Acquisition Regulation (FAR) Part 44-Subcontracting, U.S. government prime contractors are required to flow-down specified mandatory contract clauses. If the government contract is for the acquisition of designated commercial items, then the number of mandatory flow-down clauses is significantly reduced from 50+ clauses to 10 clauses. In addition, prime contractors may require the flow-down of numerous additional contract terms and conditions to protect their interests and provide performance incentives and/or remedies for non-performance. Thus, it is important to understand all of the appropriate contract and subcontract terms and conditions.

● **Ethics**

It is critical to ensure contractors select ethical business partners who have developed and implemented effective internal ethics and compliance programs. It is vital to engage in some level of due diligence to review your partner(s) business ethics and internal compliance controls. New U.S. government requirements mandate that all contractors with over $5 million in government contracts have a code of business ethics, provide appropriate ethics training to their employees, and have an appropriate compliance or internal controls program.

● **Payment**

It is vital that all contractor teaming agreements include appropriate payment terms and conditions for each of the parties involved. It is important to address the various forms of payment which may be used based upon the potential pricing arrangements which may be used. For example, under cost-reimbursement contracts, the contractor teaming agreement should explain how each member of the team will voucher/invoice their allowable and allocable expenses and be paid their fee. Likewise, under a fixed-price type contract, it is critical that the scope of work be appropriately priced and clearly assigned to each of the respective parties. Further, any unusual payment terms and conditions should be specified, i.e., advance payments, milestone-based payments, volume-discounts, discounts for early payment, etc. Also, it is important to establish if subcontractor payments are first contingent upon the prime contractor's receipt of said payment from the government agency, prior to their payment of the subcontractor(s).

● **Bid & Proposal (B&P) Costs**

Competing for and winning a large complex U.S. government contract can require a significant Bid and Proposal (B&P) investment for all of the parties involved in a contractor teaming agreement. Usually, contractor teaming agreements require each of the parties to provide all of the necessary and appropriate resources to prepare their assigned portion of the bid/proposal and for paying for the respective B&P costs they incur. Likewise, with the growing use of oral presentations by both government agencies and prime contractors, it is important to specify that each party is responsible for preparing, delivering, and paying for their respective portion of any required oral presentations.

● **Exclusivity**

Typically contractor teaming agreements specify if any exclusivity shall exist in regards to a specific contractor being assured the assignment of certain work. When using a prime-subcontractor teaming agreement, subcontractors generally seek as much clarity regarding the scope of work and exclusivity regarding the assignment of work. Prime contractors generally seek as much flexibility as possible with their subcontractors, and prefer to avoid making any exclusive business arrangements. Clearly the type of contractor teaming agreement selected and the nature of the work significantly affect the willingness of the parties to enter into any exclusivity arrangement.

● **Intellectual Property Rights**

A contractor teaming agreement should fairly and appropriately protect the intellectual property (IP) rights of each of the parties. Typically, IP clauses limit the data rights to only the pursuit of the target contract, restrict disclosure to those who have a valid "need to know," and prevent broader distribution. In some cases, contractors must be prepared to share their IP with their teaming partners and with U.S. government agencies. However, there are times when a company must fight to protect their IP rights and restrict the use from their business partners. Both government agencies and prime contractors have been known to take advantage of small businesses by inappropriately acquiring data rights and/or violating copyrights, patents, trademarks, etc.

• Limitation of Liabilities

Frequently the parties involved in a contractor teaming agreement will choose to expressly and explicitly state their contractual and financial liability to one another. Typically parties will agree to be jointly and severally liable and any consequential damages are neither comtemplatable nor recoverable under the teaming agreement.

• Disputes Resolutions

It is essential that a contactor teaming agreement contain a dispute resolution clause, which addresses the method of dispute resolution, the choice of language, and the choice of law. The most common dispute resolution techniques include negotiations, mediation, facilitation, arbitration, binding or non-binding, and/or litigation. The choice of law relates to which substantive law will govern any dispute. The parties to the contractor teaming agreement will usually select and specify a particular state's law. Clearly, the parties involved in a contractor teaming agreement should do everything ethically possible to mitigate any disputes, and if a dispute arises, seek to promptly and dispassionately resolve their differences without entering into litigation and going to court. We recommend the parties agree to a structured and formal disputes escalation process, which begins at a mid-manager level and rises to appropriate senior executives and/or C-Suite as needed.

• Terminations

It is critical to ensure every contractor teaming agreement include a terminations clause, which permits parties to exit the relationship under certain conditions, including the following:

1. Failure to agree,
2. Failure to perform,
3. Failure to obtain required consents and approvals,
4. Financial condition (i.e., bankruptcy),
5. Government direction (i.e., suspension, debarment, Anti-Trust, etc.),
6. Passage of time (specified period of performance), and
7. Mutual agreement of the parties.

§ 3:8   Contractor teaming agreements: lessons learned and best practices

The following Table provides a summary of a few of the many lessons learned and best practices from the various parties involved in contractor teaming agreements.

Contractor Teaming Agreements	
Lessons Learned	*Best Practices*
1. Be careful what you say, and especially what you verbally promise to another party.	1. Do not make an oral binding commitment to partner or exclusivity promise unless you are 100% confident in your commitment, then promptly follow-up in writing.

Contractor Teaming Agreements	
Lessons Learned	*Best Practices*
2. Remember, Non-Disclosure Agreements (NDAs), other confidentiality agreements, and/or Memorandas of Understanding (MOU) are not a formal legal binding teaming agreement, except with regard to the treatment of confidential information.	2. Use NDAs, MOUs, or MOAs as an interim step to a formal teaming agreement.
3. Be cautious, if you are a prime contractor, to not make your teaming agreement with your potential subcontractor(s) too specific or definitive.	3. Prime contractors should view and present their teaming agreements as so-called "agreements to agree."
4. Participate in drafting the contractor teaming agreement.	4. Lead the drafting of the contractor teaming agreement to ensure it properly reflects your intent and obligations.
5. Make sure your partners have good business integrity and sound finances.	5. Conduct due diligence of potential business partners.
6. Understand that the enforceability of contractor teaming agreements may be difficult.	6. Treat contractor teaming agreements as a business framework.
7. Ensure there is an appropriate exit strategy.	7. Carefully draft a terminations/cancellation clause.

§ 3:9 Summary

So, in retrospect, in this chapter we have discussed: the numerous forms of contractor teaming arrangements typically used to win and execute U.S. government contracts, the key elements or clauses which should be included in a contractor teaming agreement, and some contractor teaming agreement lessons learned and best practices. In this world of outsourcing, contractor teaming arrangements and subsequent agreements are critical to business success.

§ 3:10 Questions to consider

1. Which of the contractor teaming arrangements discussed has your organization used to win business and execute work?
2. Which of the essential elements of contractor teaming agreements do you consider to be most important?
3. What are your lessons learned and/or best practices for developing and executing contractor teaming agreements?

Chapter 4

The Subcontract Management Process

KeyCite®: Cases and other legal materials listed in KeyCite Scope can be researched through the KeyCite service on Westlaw®. Use KeyCite to check citations for form, parallel references, prior and later history, and comprehensive citator information, including citations to other decisions and secondary materials.

---

§ 4:1 Introduction

In our world of outsourcing, the need for businesses to form partnerships, in order to deliver to their customers the products and/or professional services required, is increasingly vital to success. As a buyer (the purchasing organization of products or services), contracts are the means of obtaining the goods and services needed to conduct business. As a seller or prime contractor (the lead provider of products or services in return for compensation), contracts are the sources of business opportunities. Likewise, as a subcontractor (a company which forms a business relationship with a prime contractor) a subcontract is a means of providing products and/or services in return for compensation to a prime contractor to support the needs of a buyer. That process is called subcontract management: the art and science of managing a business relationship, between a prime contractor and subcontractor in support of a buyer, from inception through closeout.

Remember, subcontracts are first and foremost about developing and maintaining a professional business partnership between a prime contractor and a subcontractor in support of a buyer. Secondarily, subcontracts are the written documents that confirm and communicate the agreement between the prime contractor and subcontractor. To fully understand the art and science of managing subcontracts can take many years of specialized study and professional practice.

In order to manage subcontracts successfully, it is essential to describe the subcontract management actions as a process, then breakdown the subcontract management process into smaller steps that can be handled easily. The subcontract management process is composed of three distinct phases, and each phase has several key steps. This process is summarized and illustrated in Figure 4-1 and discussed briefly in the remaining sections of this chapter.

Figure 4-1

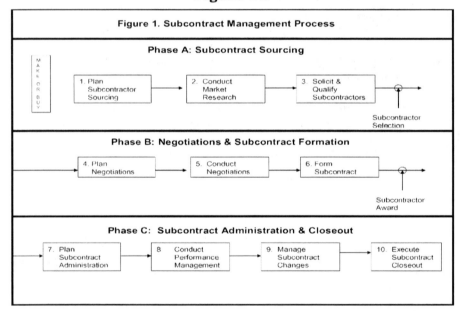

I. PHASE A: SUBCONTRACT SOURCING

§ 4:2   Step 1: Plan subcontractor sourcing

The first subcontract management challenge is to decide which goods and services to provide or perform in-house and which to outsource. This *make-or-buy or outsourcing decision* requires consideration of many factors, some of which are strategically important. The decision to outsource creates a project that will be implemented in cooperation with an outside organization that is not entirely within the prime contractor's control.

The relationship between prime contractor and subcontractor is a legal, if not economic, relationship of equals. The contract binds them to one another but does not place one under the other's managerial control. Sometimes the seller's economic position may be so powerful, however, that the *terms and conditions* (Ts and Cs) of the contract are ineffective in protecting the interests of the buyer.

For the subcontractor, the contract will present an opportunity to succeed, but it also will pose great risks. The subcontractor may find that the prime contractor has specified its need inadequately or defectively; the subcontractor's marketing department has oversold its products, services, or capabilities; faulty communication has transpired between the two parties during contract formation; or more likely, some combination of all three has occurred. In any of these cases, performance may be much more demanding than originally contemplated and may even be beyond the subcontractor's capabilities. In addition, the prime contractor may wield great economic power, which effectively outweighs the contract Ts and Cs designed to protect the subcontractor's from the prime contractor potentially unreasonable demands.

All the communication break downs, misunderstandings, conflicts, and disputes that can occur within virtually every organization also can occur between organizations, often with greater virulence and more disastrous effect. Although the contract is intended to provide a remedy to the injured party if the other fails to fulfill its contractual obligations, it is not a guarantee. Legal remedies may be uncertain and, even if attained, may not fully compensate the injured party for the other party's failure.[1]

The outsourcing decision can be a critical one for any organization. After the decision to contract for goods or services is made, the prime contractor must plan carefully and implement the decision properly.

In the course of planning for selecting the right subcontractor the prime contractor must:

- Determine how to specify its requirements or deliverables
- Identify potential sources
- Analyze the sources of uncertainty and risk that the purchase will entail
- Develop performance-based standards, metrics, and incentives
- Choose the methods for selecting a seller and for proposal evaluation, negotiations, and contract formation
- Arrange for effective administration of the contract

Developing a Statement of Work (SOW) or Performance Work Statement (PWS), or Statement of Objectives (SOO) is one of the most difficult challenges in subcontract planning. First, the prime contractor must understand its own requirements—quite a difficult task. Second, the prime contractor must be able to communicate those requirements, typically in the form of either specific deliverables or some form of a level of effort, to others outside the prime contractor's organization—an even more difficult task. Developing and communicating performance-based requirements is one of the most critical functions in subcontract management. Before final-

---

[Section 4:2]

[1]Garrett, Gregory A. "World Class Contracting," 4th Edition, CCH, Inc., Chicago, IL, 2007.

izing procurement requirements the prime contractor should conduct appropriate market research.

§ 4:3   Step 2: Conduct market research

Market research is the continuous process of collecting information to maximize reliance on the commercial marketplace and to benefit from its capabilities, technologies, and competitive forces in meeting prime contractor's needs. Market research is essential to the prime contractor's ability to buy best-value products and services that solve mission-critical problems. In the past, it was not unusual for technical staff to conduct market research about marketplace offerings, while contracting or subcontracting staff conducted market research more focused on industry practices and prices. A better approach is for the entire integrated project team to be a part of the market research effort. This enables the members of the team to share an understanding and knowledge of the marketplace—an important factor in the development of the subcontracting strategy—and a common understanding of what features, schedules, terms, and conditions are key.[1]

With regard to the more traditional market research, it is important to be acknowledgeable about commercial offerings, capabilities, and practices before structuring the procurement in any detail. Some of the traditional ways to do this include issuing "sources sought" type notices, conducting "industry days," issuing requests for information, and holding pre-solicitation conferences. But it is also okay to simply pick up the phone and call company representatives, and/or surf the internet to find potential suppliers.

Contact with suppliers for purposes of market research is essential. In fact, FAR 15.201(a) specifically promotes the exchange of information "among all interested parties, from the earliest identification of a requirement through receipt of proposals." The limitations that apply (once a procurement is underway) are that prospective contractors be treated fairly and impartially and that standards of procurement integrity (FAR 3.104) be maintained. But the real key is to begin market research before a procurement is underway.[2]

Consider one-on-one meetings with industry leaders

While many may not realize it, one-on-one meetings with industry leaders are more effective than pre-solicitation or pre-proposal conferences. It is effective to focus on commercial and industry best practices, performance metrics and measurements, innovative delivery methods for the required services, and incentive programs that providers have found particularly effective. This type of market research can expand the range of potential solutions, change the very nature of the procurement, establish the performance-based approach and represent the prime contractor's first step on the way to an "incentivized" partnership with a subcontractor.

[Section 4:3]

[1]Seven Steps to Performance-Based Services Acquisition, OFPP/GSA, Washington, D.C., 2003.

[2]Seven Steps to Performance-Based Services Acquisition, Note 2, OFPP/GSA, Washington, D.C., 2003.

§ 4:4 Step 3: Solicit and qualify subcontractors

In this step, the prime contractor must be focused on effectively communicating their product and/or services needs to potential suppliers, via clear, concise, and effective solicitation document, such as a Request for Quotation (RFQ), Request for Information (RFI), Request for Proposal (RFP), or Invitation for Bid (IFB). Within the solicitation document there are numerous critical items, which should be appropriately addressed and communicated by the prime contractor to potential subcontractors, including:

- Nature of the products and/or services needed,
- Period of performance,
- Urgency of the requirements,
- Mandatory U.S. Government flow-down terms and conditions,
- Intellectual property rights,
- Confidentiality agreement,
- Payment terms,
- Type of contract,
- Method of evaluation of errors,
- Bid/proposal instructions,
- Changes process and approval,
- Claims and methods of dispute resolution,
- Choice of law,
- Terminations,

Clearly, subcontractor qualification and selection is one of the most important decisions a prime contractor will make. Prime contract success or failure will often depend on the competence and reliability of one or more key subcontractors and their suppliers. Subcontract planners must identify potential sources of goods and services, analyze the nature of the industry and market in which they operate, develop criteria and procedures to evaluate each source, and select one for contract award. No single set of criteria or procedures is appropriate for all procurements; thus, to some extent, original analyses must be made for each contract.

Subcontractor source selection is all about the prime contractor evaluating the supplier's offers (bids, proposals, tenders, and/or oral presentation) and all of the subcontractor appropriate qualifications—past performance, use of small business, financial strength, reputation, use of break-through technologies, etc. Selecting the right source, like selecting the right dance partner, is critical to ultimate business success. The key to subcontractor source selection is to make the right partner selection as efficiently, quickly, and cost-effectively as possible. Subcontractor source selection is typically driven by the people chosen to serve on the sourcing team, the source selection process, the source selection evaluation criteria & weightings, and the key decision maker.[1]

For a prime contractor, selecting the right subcontractor(s) is extremely

---

[Section 4:4]

[1]Costello, Ann, and Garrett Gregory A., "Getting Results," CCH, Inc., Chicago, IL 2008.

important to ensure successful performance results are delivered to the customer. Too often companies are in a zeal for the deal, and they do not take sufficient time to ensure the suppliers have the necessary qualifications, including:

- Necessary financial resources,
- Key management personnel,
- Successful past performance record,
- High quality products and services,
- Fair and reasonable pricing,
- Adequate cost estimating and accounting system,
- Efficient and effective purchasing system, and
- Proven project management capabilities.

II.   PHASE B: NEGOTIATIONS & SUBCONTRACT FORMATION

§ 4:5   Step 4: Plan negotiations

After a source is selected, the parties must reach a common understanding of the nature of their undertaking and negotiate the Ts and Cs of contract performance. The ideal is to develop a set of shared expectations and understandings. However, this goal is difficult to attain for several reasons. First, either party may not fully understand its own requirements and expectations. Second, in most communication, many obstacles prevent achieving a true "meeting of the minds." Errors, miscues, hidden agendas, cultural differences, differences in linguistic use and competence, haste, lack of clarity in thought or expression, conflicting objectives, lack of god faith (or even ill will), business exigencies—all these factors can and do contribute to poor communications.[1]

Effectively planning subcontract negotiations is critical to achieving business success. The best prime contractors take the time to create a strong business case and develop a well-thought-out and approved negotiation plan, which includes:

- A prioritized list of objectives,
- A list of must haves,
- Desired schedule of product and services delivery/performance,
- Desired terms & conditions,
- Knowledge of your negotiation team member(s) strengths, weaknesses, and interests,
- Knowledge of the subcontractors negotiation team member(s) strengths, weaknesses, and interests,
- When, how, where, and who will participate in the negotiations,
- Appropriate pricing range (Worst Case; Most Likely; & Best Case).

§ 4:6   Step 5: Conduct negotiations

In the words of the best-selling author and expert negotiator Chester Karrass "In life and business, you do not get what you deserve, you get

---

[Section 4:5]

[1]Garrett Gregory A., "Contract Negotiations," CCH, Inc., Chicago, IL, 2005.

what you have the ability to negotiate. Conducting subcontract negotiations is a skill, which can only be mastered by doing. Of course, the skills for conducting negotiations can be improved: through participating in mock negotiations; work with an experienced negotiation coach, or master negotiators; and by applying numerous proven effective subcontract negotiation strategies, tactics, and countertactics.

§ 4:7 Step 6: Form subcontract

In any undertaking, uncertainty and risk arise from many sources. In a business undertaking, many of those sources are characteristic of the industry or industries involved. Because one purpose of a subcontract is to manage uncertainty and risk, the types and sources of uncertainty and risk must be identified and understood. Then buyer and seller must develop and agree to contract Ts and Cs that are designed to express their mutual expectations about performance and that reflect the uncertainties and risks of performance. Although tradition and the experiences of others provide a starting point for analysis, each subcontract must be considered unique.[1]

III. PHASE C: SUBCONTRACT ADMINISTRATION & CLOSEOUT

§ 4:8 Step 7: Plan subcontract administration

Subcontract performance is essentially doing what you said you were going to do. Subcontract administration is the process of ensuring compliance with contractual Ts and Cs during performance and up to and including subcontract closeout or termination.

After award both parties must act according to the Ts and Cs of their deal; they must read and understand their agreement, do what it requires of them, and avoid doing what they have agreed not to do.

Best Practices: In Subcontract Administration Planning

- Reading the subcontract
- Ensuring that all organizational elements are aware of their responsibilities in relation to the subcontract
- Providing copies of the subcontract to all affected organizations (either paper or electronic copies)
- Establishing systems to verify conformance with subcontract technical and administrative requirements
- Conducting performance (or kickoff) meetings with the prime contractor and subcontractor
- Assigning responsibility to check actual performance against requirements
- Ensuring that someone takes appropriate corrective action and then follows up
- Managing the invoice and payment process
- Planning for subcontract changes

[Section 4:7]

[1]Garrett Gregory A., "Contract Negotiations," Note 5, CCH, Inc., Chicago, IL, 2005.

- Establishing and maintaining subcontract documentation: diaries and telephone logs, meeting minutes, inspection reports, progress reports, test reports, invoices and payment records, accounting source documents, accounting journals and ledgers, subcontracting records, change orders and subcontract modifications, claims, routine correspondence, and e-mail.[1]

§ 4:9 Step 8: Conduct performance management

Periodically the prime contractor and subcontractor must meet to discuss performance and verify that it is on track and that each party's expectations are being met. This activity is critical. Conflict is almost inescapable within and between organizations. The friction that can arise from minor misunderstandings, failures, and disagreements can heat to the boiling point before anyone on either side is fully aware of it. When this happens, the relationship between the parties may be irreparably damaged, and amicable problem resolution may become impossible. Periodic joint assessments by subcontract managers can identify and resolve problems early and help to ensure mutually satisfactory performance.

Some world-class companies use electronic systems to assist them with subcontract monitoring, performance measurement, progress reporting, and subcontract compliance documentation.

§ 4:10 Step 9: Manage subcontract changes

Given, the difficulty of determining requirements in advance, changing customer and end-user needs, evolving technologies, and many other factors subcontract changes are very common. Thus, it is critical to ensure subcontract changes/modifications are properly managed by both the prime contractor and subcontractor(s), including:

- Ensure a Contract Changes clause is in the subcontract,
- Include the right for the prime contractor to make unilateral changes and provide the subcontractor the right to seek and equitable adjustment,
- Develop a contract changes process, which is mutually agreed to by the parties,
- Create a contract changes notification form,
- Identify those individual(s) within an organization who are empowered to approve and authorize contract changes,
- Communicate and train technical, program management, and other team members about the importance of mitigating unauthorized commitments to the subcontract agreements,
- Develop a business case for each subcontract change which addresses the cost, schedule, and technical impacts to the current subcontract agreement,
- Ensure a project manager is assigned to effectively manage the subcontract change.

[Section 4:8]

[1]Garrett Gregory A., "Contract Negotiations," Note 1, CCH, Inc., Chicago, IL, 2005.

§ 4:11   Step 10: Execute subcontract closeout

After the parties have completed the main elements of performance, they must settle final administrative and legal details before closing out the subcontract. They may have to make price adjustments and settle claims. The prime contractor will want to evaluate the subcontractor's performance. Both parties must collect records and prepare them for storage in accordance with administrative and legal retention requirements.

Unfortunately, subcontracts are sometimes terminated due to the mutual agreement of the parties or due to the failure of one or both of the parties to perform all or part of the subcontract. After a termination notice is received, the parties must still go through the same closeout actions as for a completed subcontract.

§ 4:12   Summary

This chapter has presented a holistic process model to explain the nature of subcontract management and the key activities of prime contractors and subcontractors involved in subcontract business arrangements. The subcontract management process described in this chapter is composed of three major phases and 10 key actions, which the prime contractor and/or subcontractor(s) typically accomplish. This chapter paints the big picture perspective of what subcontract management is all about and how it is vital to overall business success.

In subsequent chapters, we will discuss each of the three major phases and their respective key actions, in much more detail. With the explosive growth of U.S. government spending in housing, transportation infrastructure, healthcare, energy, education, and other areas, prime contractors will be increasingly relied upon for conducting the needed work and providing quality products and services at fair and reasonable prices. As a result, government prime contractors will be highly focused on improving their management of subcontracts and subcontractors, to ensure on-time delivery of quality products, services, and solutions at fair prices which yield profitable revenues.

§ 4:13   Questions to consider

1. In which of the three major phases of subcontract management does your organization focus most of their resources?
2. How effectively does your organization conduct subcontract management?
3. What are your organizations biggest subcontracting challenges?

Chapter 5

Subcontract Sourcing

KeyCiteʳ: Cases and other legal materials listed in KeyCite Scope can be researched through the KeyCite service on Westlawʳ. Use KeyCite to check citations for form, parallel references, prior and later history, and comprehensive citator information, including citations to other decisions and secondary materials.

---

§ 5:1   Introduction

As a prime contractor, either in the public or private business sector, the ability to: plan subcontractor sourcing; conduct market research; solicit sources of products, services, and solutions; and select the best subcontractor(s) is vital to your success. The practice of subcontractor sourcing is often referred to as: procurement planning, strategic sourcing, or subcontract source selection. It really does not matter what you call subcontractor sourcing, what matters is how well you perform the key activities which lead to your selection of the best subcontractor(s) to perform the requirements of your prime contract. In this chapter, we will examine in detail the three key steps of the subcontractor sourcing phases which are critical to the success of the subcontract management process. Specifically, we will discuss (1) develop the subcontractor sourcing plan; (2) conduct market research; (3) solicit and select the best subcontractor(s). For each key step in the subcontractor sourcing phase, we will examine the necessary process inputs, tools and techniques, and desired outputs, to serve as a practical guide to perform the work.

§ 5:2   The prime contractor's perspective of subcontractor sourcing

The subcontractor sourcing phase of the subcontract management process (see Figure 5-1), is all about the prime contractor accomplishing the following actions:

- Decide what products and services to procure from others, describe those requirements unambiguously, and estimate cost and schedule requirements.
- Identify the sources and nature of uncertainties about quality, cost, and schedule

- Define and assess the consequences of subcontractor failure to achieve performance objectives
- Determine the method of procurement
- Conduct market research to identify potential subcontractors
- Qualify potential subcontractors
- Prepare an appropriate solicitation for the needed products and/or services
- Develop the source selection process
- Evaluate bids or proposals
- Select the best subcontractor(s)

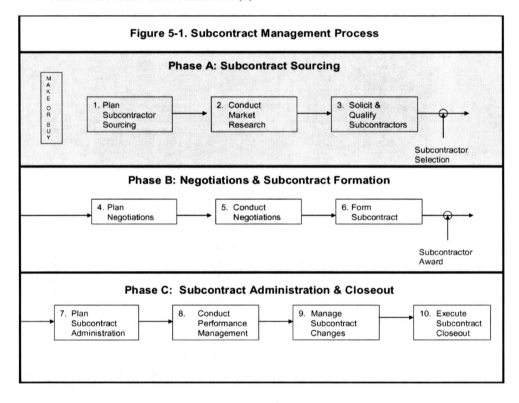

Figure 5-1. Subcontract Management Process

Phase A: Subcontract Sourcing

MAKE OR BUY

1. Plan Subcontractor Sourcing
2. Conduct Market Research
3. Solicit & Qualify Subcontractors

Subcontractor Selection

Phase B: Negotiations & Subcontract Formation

4. Plan Negotiations
5. Conduct Negotiations
6. Form Subcontract

Subcontractor Award

Phase C: Subcontract Administration & Closeout

7. Plan Subcontract Administration
8. Conduct Performance Management
9. Manage Subcontract Changes
10. Execute Subcontract Closeout

§ 5:3 Step 1: Develop a subcontractor sourcing plan

Developing a subcontractor sourcing plan is a process of determining whether to procure, how to procure, what to procure, how much to procure, and when to procure. Figure 5-2, illustrates the key inputs, tools and techniques, and desired outputs of the first step of subcontractor sourcing, namely: develop a subcontractor sourcing plan.

Figure 5-2
Step 1: Develop a Subcontractor Sourcing Plan

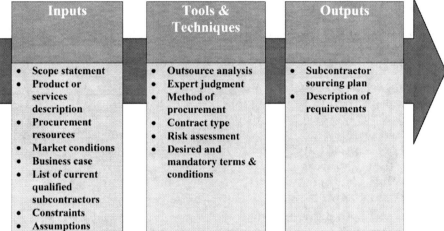

Inputs	Tools & Techniques	Outputs
• Scope statement • Product or services description • Procurement resources • Market conditions • Business case • List of current qualified subcontractors • Constraints • Assumptions	• Outsource analysis • Expert judgment • Method of procurement • Contract type • Risk assessment • Desired and mandatory terms & conditions	• Subcontractor sourcing plan • Description of requirements

Inputs

The necessary inputs to develop a subcontractor sourcing plan consists of the following items:

- *Scope statement:* The scope statement describes the current business boundaries. It provides important information about buyer needs and strategies that must be considered during procurement planning.
- *Product or services description:* The description of the project's product or service provides important information about any technical issues or concerns that must be considered during the procurement planning step. The product or services description is generally broader than a statement of work. A product description describes the ultimate end-product of the project; an SOW is a tasking document that describes the portion of that product to be provided by a subcontractor to the prime contractor.
- *Subcontract management resources:* If the organization does not have subcontract management resources, the business team leading the contract process must ensure both the resources and the expertise to support subcontract management activities are performed.
- *Market conditions:* The subcontract planning process must include consideration of what products and services are available in the marketplace, from whom, and under what terms and conditions.
- *Business case:* The prime contractor should have developed a preliminary business case, including: cost and schedule estimates, quality management plans, cash flow projections, work breakdown structure, identified risks, and planned staffing.

- *List of current qualified subcontractors:* Typically, prime contractors have developed a list of qualified suppliers based upon their financial, technical, quality, and management capabilities, plus their demonstrated past performance record. Not on the U.S. government's ineligible contractor list.
- *Constraints:* Constraints are factors that limit the prime contractors options. One common project constraint is funds availability.
- *Assumptions:* Assumptions are factors that, for planning purposes, are considered to be true, real, or certain. Assumptions made should always be documented.

Tools and Techniques

The following tools and techniques are used for developing a subcontractor sourcing plan:

- *Outsource analysis:* The decision to outsource must be made in cooperation with a multifunctional team, the precise size and identity of which depends on the nature of the undertaking and on the business and organization. The purchasing or subcontracting department should be consulted for obvious reasons, but other interested or affected functional organizations could include program management, marketing and sales, finance, engineering, human resources, quality, and legal to name a few.

  The decision to outsource or buy is essentially a decision to meld the subcontractor's organization with the prime contractor's. However, the decision casts the business professional's usual challenges of communication and control in an unusual light, because he or she must communicate and exercise control through the special medium of the contract.

  Outsource analysis must reflect the perspective of the performing organization as well as the immediate business needs. For example, purchasing a capital item (anything from a construction crane to a personal computer) rather than renting it is seldom cost-effective. However, if the performing organization has an ongoing need for the item the portion of the purchase cost allocated to the project may be less than the cost of the rental.

- *Expert judgment:* Assessing the input to the subcontractor sourcing planning process often requires expert judgment. Such expertise may be provided by any group or individual with specialized knowledge or training and is available from many sources, including other units within the performing organization, consultants and educators, professional and technical associations and industry groups.

- *Method of procurement:* The organization must decide how to conduct the procurement via: corporate purchasing card transaction; use of competitive bids process; use of competitive proposals; single source or sole source procurement.

- *Risk assessment:* Risk, which is exposure to harm, is associated with contingent events. An event is an occurrence or a nonoccurrence. Risk can take the form of either uncertainty about an event or undesirable consequences associated with the event. If an event must happen for the project to succeed, but that event's occurrence is uncertain, then risk is associated with that event. If an event must not happen for the contract to succeed, but the nonoccurrence of the event is uncertain, then risk is associated with that event. A risk assessment typically: 1) identifies potential risk factors,2) Analyzes the probability of occurrence and potential impacts, 3) Prioritizes the risks, 4) Develops risk mitigation strategies, 5) Assess the success of the risk mitigation strategies and adapt actions as needed.

- *Contract terms and conditions:* Law and custom, company experience and policy, and project-specific analyses will determine what contract Ts and Cs the buyer will prefer. Governments and large companies usually have regulations or manuals that prescribe boilerplate clauses for the most common types of contracts. In these organizations, the contract manager and subcontract managers writes the contract by simply checking off the appropriate clauses from a list (perhaps automated) for inclusion in the solicitation or subcontract document.

In smaller organizations and in larger organizations for subcontracts of an unusual nature, the Ts and Cs may have to be developed. In such cases, the subcontract clauses may have to be written or reviewed by lawyers with experience in such matters. In some industries, books are available that include samples of recommended subcontract clauses.

Today many companies have developed or purchased automated tools or other database management software to help them in developing appropriate Ts and Cs.

Outputs

The output from the developing a subcontract sourcing plan consists of the following items:

- *Subcontract sourcing plan:* This plan should describe how the remaining procurement processes (from solicitation planning through contract closeout) will be managed. The following are examples of questions to ask in developing a subcontract sourcing plan:
  - What types of subcontracts will be used?
  - If independent estimates will be needed as evaluation criteria, who will prepare them and when?
  - What actions can the project management team take on its own?
  - If standardized procurement documents are needed, where can they be found?
  - How will multiple suppliers be managed?
  - How will procurement be coordinated with other business aspects such as scheduling and performance reporting?
- *Description of requirements:* Typically, organizations will develop one of the following types of documents to describe their needs.
  - Product or service detailed description
  - Statement of Objectives (SOO)
  - Performance Work Statement (PWS)
  - Statement of Work (SOW)

§ 5:4   Step 2: Conduct market research

In order to select the best subcontractor it is vital to take the appropriate amount of time and effort to conduct market research to determine what subcontractors or suppliers of products, services, and solutions are available to meet your needs. Figure 5-3, illustrates the key inputs, proven tools and techniques, and desired outputs of the second step of subcontractor sourcing, namely conducting market research.

Figure 5-3
Step 2: Conduct Market Research

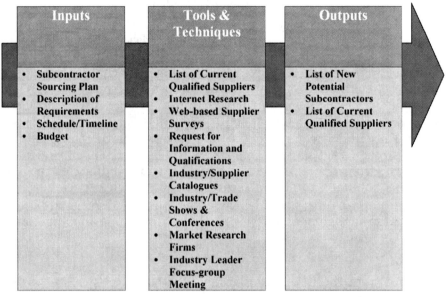

Inputs	Tools & Techniques	Outputs
• Subcontractor Sourcing Plan • Description of Requirements • Schedule/Timeline • Budget	• List of Current Qualified Suppliers • Internet Research • Web-based Supplier Surveys • Request for Information and Qualifications • Industry/Supplier Catalogues • Industry/Trade Shows & Conferences • Market Research Firms • Industry Leader Focus-group Meeting	• List of New Potential Subcontractors • List of Current Qualified Suppliers

Inputs

The necessary inputs to conduct market research consists of the following items:

- *A Subcontracting sourcing plan:* A document which describes what needs to be procured, how to procure it, when to procure it, what are the risks or procurement, who have we procured it from previously, if any, and what resources are needed to do the procurement.
- *Description of requirements:* A document which provides more details of what is needed, for example:
  - A product or service description
  - Statement of Work (SOW)
  - Statement of Objectives (SOO)
  - Performance Work Statement (PWS)
- *Schedule/Timeline:* A procurement schedule or timeline to meet the customer's needs should be included in the subcontractor sourcing plan.
- *Budget:* For needed resources both people and money, should be included in the subcontractor sourcing plan.

Tools and Techniques

The following tools and techniques are used to conduct market research to identify potential qualified suppliers of products, services, and solutions:

- *List of current qualified suppliers:* A listing of the organization's current qualified suppliers typically segmented by the products, services, and/or solutions they offer. Plus, an examination of the suppliers qualifications: financial, technical, management, quality, and past performance. Not listed on the U.S. Government's list of ineligible contractors.
- *Internet research:* Conduct internet searches of potential suppliers via various internet search engines.
- *Web-based supplier surveys:* When the purchasing organizations wants to gather a lot of information from numerous potential suppliers quickly and cost-effectively, then they may choose to develop and distribute a web-based survey to potential suppliers.
- *Request for Information & Qualifications (RFI&Q):* A common solicitation type of document used by purchasing organizations to gather information and obtain supplier qualifications for a potential future deal.
- *Industry/Supplier Catalogs:* Various professional trade catalogs, which describe products and/or services available for purchase.
- *Industry/Trade Shows & Conferences:* Attend numerous professional industry or trade shows and/or conferences, to identify best-in-class companies, products, and/or services.
- *Market Research Firms:* There are numerous outstanding professional market research firms, which are available for hire, who can gather and provide data regarding companies key information: financial capabilities, products, services, past performance, etc. Including the following firms:
  - Dunn & Bradstreet
  - Gartner Group
  - The Hackett Group
  - Forrester Research
- *Industry Leader Focus Group Meetings:* A proven method to quickly gather vital procurement information, including: best-in-class products and services, key performance standards, measures, and metrics, and appropriate quality standards.

Outputs

The desired outputs from conducting market research consists of the following items:

- *List of potential subcontractors:* Typically, the list of new potential suppliers/subcontractors would be segregated by the nature of the products, services, and/or solutions offered and possibly by the geographic location(s) of the suppliers.
- *List of current qualified subcontractors/suppliers*

## § 5:5	Step 3: Solicit and select the best subcontractor(s)

After planning the subcontractor sourcing and conducting the market research it is now time to develop an appropriate solicitation document, distribute the solicitation to your list of new potential suppliers and current qualified suppliers, and then conduct appropriate subcontract source selection: Figure 5-4, illustrates the key inputs, proven tools and techniques, and desired outputs of the third step of subcontract management; namely solicit and select the best subcontractor(s).

Figure 5-4
Step 3: Solicit and Select the Right Subcontractor

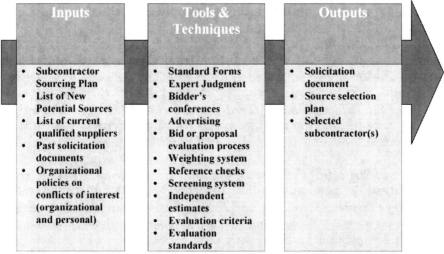

Inputs

The necessary inputs to solicit and select the right subcontractor(s) include the following items:

- *Subcontractor Sourcing Plan:* This plan, which describes how the subcontractor sourcing process will be conducted throughout the process, should be reviewed at the start of solicitation planning.
- *List of New Potential Sources*
- *List of Current Qualified Suppliers*
- *Past Solicitation Documents:* For example, (Request for Quotation (RFQ), Invitation for Bid (IFB), Request for Proposal (RFP), Request for Tender (RFT), etc.
- *Organizational Policies:* Key purchasing and subcontract management policies and procedures, including: organization conflicts of interest and personal conflicts of interest.

Tools and Techniques

The following are a list of proven tools and techniques used for developing solicitations and selecting subcontractor(s):

- *Standard forms:* These forms may include standardized versions of contracts, standardized descriptions or procurement items, or standardized versions of all or part of the needed bid documents. Organizations doing substantial amounts of procurement should have many of these documents standardized and automated.
- *Expert judgment:* As in procurement planning, expert judgment is a vital tool. Individuals with specialized knowledge or training, both in-house and outside the organization, should be consulted.

- *Bidders' conferences:* These conferences (also called contractor, vendor, or prebid conferences) are meetings with prospective subcontractors or suppliers before they prepare their proposals. They may be conducted in person, via video conference, teleconference, or net meetings. The meetings ensure that all prospective have a clear, common understanding of the procurement (both technical requirements and contract requirements). Responses to questions may be incorporated into the procurement documents as amendments.
- *Advertising:* Existing lists of potential suppliers can often be expanded by placing advertisements in general circulation publications, such as newspapers, or in specialty publications, such as professional journals. Some government jurisdictions require public advertising of certain types of procurement items; most government jurisdictions require public advertising of subcontracts on a government contract.
- *Bid or proposal evaluation process:* The use of sealed bids, two-step sealed-bids, competitive proposals, single source/selected source, or sole source evaluation process.
- *Weighting system:* After selecting the attributes for evaluation and establishing evaluation standards, the next task is to determine the importance of each attribute relative to the others. (See "Weighting System" later in this chapter for specific information.)

Assume that the prospective prime contractor of a product decides that price and quality are the attributes of interest and that quality is more than twice as important as price. Accordingly, the prime contractor assigns quality a fixed weight of 0.70 and price a fixed weight of 0.30. However, after receiving the proposals, the prime contractor discovers that the quality differences among the proposed products are small but that the differences in price are relatively large. Under these circumstances, the assigned fixed weights could result in the prime contractor paying a premium for a relatively small quality gain. When comparing the actual ranges of variance, the prime contractor may decide that price is more important than quality in making the final decision.

- *Reference checks:* Contacting previous buyers, of the potential supplier's products and services, to verify the quality of the products and services and overall performance of the supplier/subcontractor.
- *Screening system:* A screening system is used to process the information about potential sources. The prime contractor must read and analyze the information, apply the appropriate standards, and assign scores that express how well or how poorly each proposal measures up. Depending on the amount of information to be analyzed and the technical complexity of the requirement, this work might be performed by a purchasing agent or a panel of experts.

If the procurement is complex enough to warrant establishing a panel of experts, the evaluators on the panel should include someone from the prime contractor organization who will ultimately use the product or service and someone from the prime contractor purchasing office. Additional advice may be needed from accountants and attorneys. In some cases, the prime contractor may need to hire consultants to provide technical assistance. All evaluators should be thoroughly familiar with specification, statement of work, and evaluation criteria.

Before the evaluation begins, the prime contractor must decide how the evaluators will present their findings, to whom, and what kind of documentation they will prepare. The process should be kept as simple as possible. To ensure the confidentiality of information received from competing sources, many organizations require that the evaluators communicate with the sources under consideration only through the purchasing department.

- *Independent estimates:* Using consultants or outside experts to help in this process is common and can be of great value.
- *Evaluation Criteria:* Developing the evaluation criteria for subcontractor source selection requires three prerequisites. First the prime contractor must understand what goods or services it wants to buy. Second the prime contractor must understand the industry that will provide the required goods or services. And third, the prime contractor must understand the market practices of that industry. Market research provides this information.

During requirements analysis and development of the specification or statement of work, the prime contractor gains an understanding of the required products or services. Understanding the industry means learning about the attributes of the goods or services in question and the firms that make them: What feature do those goods or services have? What processes are used to produce or render them? What kinds and quantities of labor and capital are required? What are the cash requirements? Understanding the market means learning about the behavior of prime contractor and subcontractor: What are the pricing practices of the market, and what is the range of prices charged? What are the usual terms and conditions of sale?

After gaining an understanding of these issues, the prime contractor is ready to develop the evaluation criteria by selecting attributes for evaluation.

A consumer shopping for an automobile does not evaluate an automobile, per se, but rather selected attributes of the automobile, such as acceleration, speed, handling, comfort, safety, price, fuel mileage, capacity, appearance, and so forth. The evaluation of the automobile is the sum of the evaluation of its attributes.

An automobile has many attributes, but not all are worthwhile subjects of evaluation. The attributes of interest are those that the consumer thinks are important for satisfaction. The attributes that one consumer thinks are important may be inconsequential to another.

In most procurements, multiple criteria will be required for successful performance, for the following reasons: First, prime contractor usually have more than one objective; for example, many prime contractor look for both good quality and low price. Second, attributes essential for one objective may be different from those essential for others; for example, in buying an automobile, the attributes essential for comfort have little to do with those essential for quick acceleration.

To complicate matters further, some criteria will likely be incompatible with others. The attributes essential to high quality may be inconsistent with low price; high performance, for example, may be incompatible with low operating cost. Thus, for nay one source to have the maximum desired value of every essential attribute for example, highest quality combined with lowest price may be impossible. If so, the prime contractor must make trade-offs among attributes when deciding which source is best. These are considerations that make source selection a problem in *multiple attribute decision making,* which requires special decision analysis techniques.

As a rule, source selection attributes fall into three general categories relating to the sources themselves, as entities; the products or services they offer; and the prices they offer. Thus, the prime contractor must have criteria for each category that reflect the prime contractor ideas about what is valuable. The criteria concerning the sources themselves, as entities, are the *management criteria*; the criteria concerning the products or services offered are the *technical criteria*; and the criteria concerning the prices of the products or services are the *price criteria.*

Management Criteria

In the subcontracting process, the prime contractor enters a relationship with a subcontractor, and each party exchanges promises about what it will do for the other in the future. Thus, when comparing sources, the prime contractor must determine which entity would make the best partner. Management criteria relate to this set of attributes.

The specific attributes that will make for a good partner and the relative emphasis the prime contractor should place on them will depend on the prime contractor contractual objectives and the practices in the industry and marketplace. Nevertheless certain categories of attributes should always be considered, such as reputation for good performance, technical capability, qualifications of key managerial personnel, capabilities of facilities and equipment, capacity, financial strength, labor relations, and location.

Technical Criteria

In response to the prime contractor solicitation, each potential source will likely offer the prime contractor something that is somewhat different or offer the same product or services as the others but propose to use different production or performance procedures. If these differences are significant enough to affect the source's prospects for success, the prime contractor must compare them to determine their relative merits. The prime contractor must develop criteria to evaluate what each source will do or deliver and how each source will proceed with the work in other words, determine product or service quality and procedural effectiveness. These attributes are called technical criteria.

The precise nature of the technical criteria will depend on the specification or statement of work. If the solicitation specifies all aspects of product design or service performance, the prime contractor will not have to develop further criteria to evaluate what the source will do or deliver. However, the prime contractor may want to evaluate proposed production plans, policies, procedures, and techniques to decide which source is most likely to do the best job. However, if the prime contractor specifies only function or performance, it also must evaluate each proposal to determine which proposed product or service will satisfy the requirement and which will do it best. The prime contractor criteria should reflect the significant attributes of function or performance.[1]

Price Criteria

Besides evaluating management and technical attributes, the prime contractor must evaluate the reasonableness of each proposed price, in terms of realism and competitiveness:

- *Realism:* Regarding whether a proposed price is to low, realism is determined by evaluating consistency among a potential source's management, technical, and price proposals. The question is whether a source's proposed price entails too much risk given what the source's qualifications are as a company, what it has promised to do, and what methods it has proposed to use. Risk affects behavior, often in undesirable ways. If a price is too low, entailing too much risk, the subcontractor may fail to achieve project objectives. Therefore, each proposal must be analyzed to determine whether the proposed price allows for sufficient resources to do the job. The technique used to evaluate realism is cost analysis.

  The prices of commercial goods and services, however, are not necessarily determined entirely by the cost of their manufacture or performance, at least in the short term. Thus, a source may offer something for sale at prices set below cost for various sound business reasons. Still, the prime contractor must investigate if a price seems to low; otherwise, the risk of poor performance may become a reality.

- *Competitiveness:* Competitiveness refers to whether a proposed price is too high compared with what is available in the marketplace. Competitiveness is evaluated by comparing each proposed price to the others and to other pricing information. The techniques used to evaluate competitiveness is price analysis.

Qualitative vs. Quantitative Evaluation Criteria

The source selection evaluation criteria described a level of value that must be met. Some values may be stated *quantitatively*, such as size, weight, speed, mean-time-between-failure, mean-time-to-repair, and price. Other values must be stated *qualitatively*, using words rather than numbers (unless the prime contractor is willing to go to great effort to develop quantitative expressions of them). Examples include attractiveness, experience, and comfort.

Theorists of decision making sometimes refer to qualitative criteria as "fuzzy" criteria, and they have developed various ways to convert qualitative judgments to quantitative expressions. One example is the scale used to evaluate the taste of food samples. Quantitative criteria are generally easier to use, but qualitative criteria are frequently unavoidable.

Evaluation Standards

Three types of evaluation standards—*absolute, minimum,* and *relative*—

[Section 5:5]

[1]Garrett, Gregory A. "World Class Contracting," 4th Edition, CCH-Wolters Kluwer Law & Business, Chicago, IL, 2007.

express value. The main difference between these three types of standards is the amount of information required to establish them and the kind of information they provide to the prime contractor.

Absolute Standards

Absolute standards include both the maximum and the minimum acceptable values. When a prime contractor uses and absolute standard during evaluation, the performance of the source being rated is compared to the standard to determine the absolute value of its performance. For example, assume and absolute standard for price that ranges from no cost, the best value, to US $5 million, the worst value. A potential source's proposed price of US$4.5 million can be compared to the standard to determine its absolute value.

If the prime contractor utility for price is a straight-line function, a source whose proposed price is US$4.5 million could earn 10 out of 100 value points, a source whose price is US$4 million could earn 20 points, and a source whose prices is US$2 million could earn 60 points. Each point score tells the prime contractor absolutely how good or bad the price is relative to the prime contractor standard of value and relative to the other potential sources.[2]

The problem with an absolute standard is that the prime contractor needs a great deal of information to develop an absolute range of values. The prime contractor must know the highest preference level as well as the lowest. The evaluation result may not be worth the effort of developing this information.

Minimum Standards

A minimum, or ratio, standard requires only that the prime contractor know the minimum acceptable level of performance. Each potential source is compared to that minimum, and the source with the highest level of acceptable performance receives the highest score, 100 on a scale of 0 to 100. Sources that do not meet the minimum standard are eliminated. All other sources are scored in comparison to the best.

Assume that the highest acceptable price for a product or service is US$5 million. Assume that of all potential sources, the one with a price of US$2 million is considered the best. That source receives a score of 100 points. A source whose price is US$4 million could receive a score of 33 points, and one whose price is US$4.5 million could receive a score of 17 points.

The advantage of the minimum standard over the absolute standard is that the prime contractor needs less information. The obvious disadvantage is that the evaluation scores will not tell the prime contractor absolutely how good or bad each alternative is.

Relative Standards

A relative standard entails direct comparison of each potential source to the others to determine which is best and which is worst. The best source

---

[2]Garrett, Gregory A. "World Class Contracting," 4th Edition, CCH-Wolters Kluwer Law & Business, Chicago, IL, 2007.

receives the maximum number of points, 100 on a scale of 0 to 100. The worst receives no points. Having established the best and the worst alternatives, the buyer can construct a graph to determine the scores of the sources that fall between them. Those scores also can be determined mathematically.

Using a relative scale to score the same prices described in the example used for minimum standards, the US$2 million price would receive 100 points, the US$4.5 million price would receive no points, and the US$4 million price would receive 20 points.

The relative standard requires the least amount of advance information on the part of the prime contractor. Scores developed on a relative standard tell the prime contractor how good or bad each source is relative to the others but not how good or bad it is absolutely. Nevertheless, this information will be sufficient for many source selections.[3]

Weighting System

The evaluation of each source will be the sum of the evaluations of its individual attributes. The scores initially assigned to attributes during the evaluation will not reflect differences in importance among the attributes. The scores will be raw (unweighted). The decision to add the raw scores together to determine the value of the source is tantamount to a decision that each attribute is equally important. But such may not be the case. If some attributes are more important than others, the prime contractor must assign a weight to each.

Assume that a consumer decides that the relevant attributes in an automobile are acceleration, maximum speed, attractiveness, price, and fuel mileage. If any of these is more important than the others, the raw scores must be weighted to take that fact into account before adding the scores. The weighs will reflect the consumer's trade-off decisions among the various attributes and will affect the final determination of which automobile is the best.

The prime contractor may establish either *fixed weights* or *variable weights*. Fixed weights are established before receiving the proposals and do not change. Variable weighs are established only after determining the raw scores. Variable weights allow for making tradeoffs when comparing the ranges of actual performance among the alternatives.

Outputs

The following are desired outputs of the solicit and select the best subcontractor(s) step of the subcontractor sourcing phase.

- *Solicitations documents:* Solicitations documents from prospective suppliers or subcontractors. The terms *bids* and *quotation* are generally used when the source selection decision will be price driven (as when buying commercial items), whereas the term *proposal* or *tender* is generally used when nonfinancial considerations, such as technical skills or approach, are paramount (as when purchasing professional services). However, the terms are often used interchangeably and

---

[3]Garrett, Gregory A. "World Class Contracting," 4th Edition, CCH-Wolters Kluwer Law & Business, Chicago, IL, 2007.

care should be taken not to make unwarranted assumptions about the implications of the term used. Types of solicitation documents include: request for proposals (RFP), request for quotations (RFQ), and invitation for bids (IFB).

Solicitation documents should be structured to facilitate accurate and complete responses from prospective suppliers. They should always include the relevant description of the requirements, the desired form of response, and any required subcontract Ts and Cs (for example, a copy of a model subcontract's nondisclosure provisions). Some or all of the content and structure of solicitation documents, particularly for those prepared by a government agency, may be defined by regulation, including requirement for mandatory flow-down of specified contract clauses to subcontractors and suppliers at all levels of the supply chain.

- *Source selection plan:* Includes the bid or proposal evaluation process, the evaluation criteria, evaluation standards, screening system, weighting system, and key decision maker(s).
- *Selected subcontractor(s)*

§ 5:6 Subcontractor sourcing best practices:

Prime contractors should:

- Decide what products, services, or solutions you need
- Conduct market research and benchmarking of industry practices via industry leader focus groups
- Identify risks in quality, cost, and schedule (outsource analysis)
- Develop a solicitation that clearly and concisely communicates your needs in terms of performance
- Develop effective procedures for subcontractor source selection
- Obtain expert judgment internally or externally to help in solicitation planning
- Determine the appropriate type of purchasing method
- Use of risk management process to mitigate risks
- Create standard Ts and Cs that favor you
- Develop qualified supplier lists
- Conduct bidders' conferences in person, video conference, or via Net meeting
- Use draft solicitations and obtain feedback from sellers before final solicitation.

§ 5:7 Summary

The subcontractor sourcing phase of the subcontract management process is vital to the successful transaction of business involving products, services, and solutions. The prime contractor must make an informed outsourcing decision, and, if they decide to buy, then clearly and effectively communicate their needs to potential subcontractors and suppliers. Then, the prime contractor must efficiently select the best subcontractor(s) who can meet or exceed their requirements.

In the next chapter, we will discuss the negotiation and subcontract formation phase of the subcontract management process.

§ 5:8   Questions to consider

1. How well does your organization develop requirements for purchasing products, services, and/or needed solutions from outside suppliers or subcontractors?

2. To what extent does your organization conduct market research?

3. How efficiently and effectively does your organization solicit and select the best subcontractor(s)?

Chapter 6

Negotiations & Subcontract Formation

KeyCiteᴿ: Cases and other legal materials listed in KeyCite Scope can be researched through the KeyCite service on Westlawᴿ. Use KeyCite to check citations for form, parallel references, prior and later history, and comprehensive citator information, including citations to other decisions and secondary materials.

---

§ 6:1   Introduction

So, what is subcontract negotiation? According to I. William Zartman, author of The Practical Negotiator, "it is the process of unifying different positions into a unanimous joint decision, regarding the buying and selling of products and/or services." Further, Zartman states—"Negotiation is a process of making or reaching an agreement without rules about how decisions are made."[1] Based upon extensive experience and research it is clear that many business professionals fear negotiating contracts.

So, why is it many people fear negotiating contracts? The seven most typical responses include:

- It's too hostile and intimidating!
- I like to avoid conflict!
- I do not know enough about contracts!
- I do not know enough about the legal and/or technical aspects!
- I am not articulate enough!

[Section 6:1]

    [1]Zartman, I. William, ed, The Negotiation Process (Beverly Hills: Sage Publications, 1978).

- I do not want to develop a new challenging skill!

Within the Subcontract Management Process, Figure 6-1, Negotiations and Subcontract Formation is vital to success.

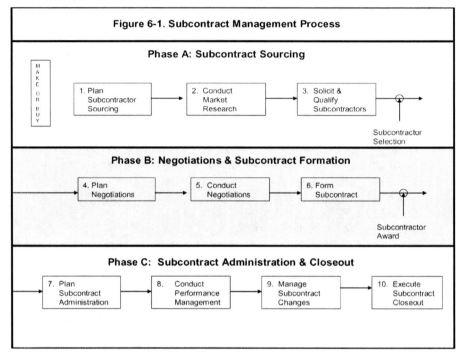

Figure 6-1. Subcontract Management Process

§ 6:2   Subcontract negotiation—A complex human activity

Negotiation is a complex human activity. Successful contract negotiators must:

- Master the art and science, or soft and hard skills, required to become a master negotiator
- Possess the intellectual ability to comprehend factors shaping and characterizing the negotiation.
- Be able to adapt strategies, tactics, and countertactics in a dynamic environment
- Understand their own personalities and personal ethics and values
- Know their products and services, desired terms and conditions, and pricing strategy
- Be able to lead a diverse multi-functional team to achieve a successful outcome

If accomplishing all of the aforementioned tasks sounds easy, then you are either a highly skilled subcontract negotiator or somewhat naïve about what it takes to become a master negotiator.

§ 6:3   Subcontract negotiation—Approaches

We all negotiate everyday—with our friends, our family, our business customers, suppliers, and/or team members. Some of us negotiate well on occasion with some of the parties in our lives. But, most of us do not negotiate consistently well with all of the parties, in both our personal and professional lives. The fact is there are two basic approaches to subcontract negotiations, the intuitive approach, and the process approach.

The intuitive subcontract negotiation approach is usually characterized as non-structured, informal, not documented, yielding inconsistent negotiation results. The intuitive subcontract negotiation approach is also affectionately known as the following:

- The no plan, no clue approach
- Fly by the seat of your pants approach
- Ad hoc approach
- Think out-of-the-box approach
- Who needs a stinking plan approach

The subcontract negotiation process approach is typically characterized as structured, planned, formal, documented, yielding more consistent negotiation results. In the world of real estate, the old saying is the three most important aspects are location, location, and location. Arguably, in the world of subcontract negotiations the three most important aspects are planning, negotiating, and documenting the deal.

§ 6:4 Subcontract negotiation—The art and science of the deal

In subcontract negotiation, getting to Yes means getting past no! As William Ury, the co-author of the best-selling book "Getting to Yes" and author of the book "Getting Past No!" states "Getting around yes, but—focusing on common interests not positions is critical to achieve successful negotiation results.[1] Creating a joint-prime contractor and subcontractor problem solving environment is vital to developing a win/win contract negotiation situation. Remember, the right solution is truly a matter of perspective for both the prime contractor and the subcontractor. Like the game of chess, contract negotiation requires strategy, tactics, countertactics, stressing one's flexibility and ability to adapt to changing situations while realizing there is more than one way to achieve success. Unlike chess, subcontract negotiations provides an opportunity for both parties to meet or exceed their respective needs.

§ 6:5 Subcontract negotiation—Objectives (interests)

Clearly, subcontract negotiations is about a prime contractor, an organization purchasing goods and/or services, selecting a subcontractor, an organization providing goods and/or services, and their respective representatives reaching a written agreement to document their relationship—who will do what, where, when, and for how much! Typically, Prime contractor's negotiation objectives include:

- Acquire necessary supplies, services, and/or solutions of the desired quality, on-time, and at the lowest reasonable price
- Establish and administer a pricing arrangement that results in payment of a fair and reasonable price

---

[Section 6:4]

[1]Ury, William, Getting Past No, (New York: Bantam Books, 1993).

- Satisfy needs of the end-user (customer)

Similarly, Subcontractor's negotiation objectives usually include:

- Grow profitable revenue (long-term vs. short-term)
- Increase market share within their respective industry
- Deliver quality supplies, services, and/or solutions—achieve customer loyalty

While each subcontract negotiation is unique and there may be some special objectives for certain deals, the previously stated subcontract negotiations objectives are relatively common for most prime contractors and subcontractors.

§ 6:6   Subcontract negotiation—A process approach for building successful business relationships

Subcontract negotiation is the process by which two or more competent parties reach an agreement to buy or sell products and/or services. Subcontract negotiations may be conducted formally or informally and may involve many people or just two—a representative for the Prime contractor and a representative for the Subcontractor. Subcontract negotiation may take a few minutes or may involve many discussions over days, months, or years.

The desired result of the subcontract negotiation process is a subcontract. Subcontract formation is the process of putting together the essential elements of the subcontract and any special items unique to a particular business agreement, see Figure 6-2.

Figure 6-2.
Subcontract Negotiation—Essential Elements[1] (for Steps 4, 5, & 6)

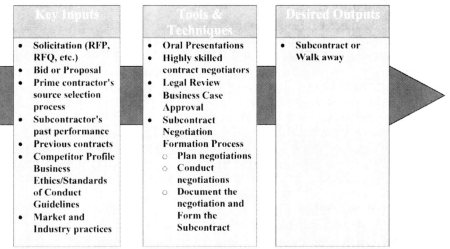

Key Inputs	Tools & Techniques	Desired Outputs

• Solicitation (RFP, RFQ, etc.)
• Bid or Proposal
• Prime contractor's source selection process
• Subcontractor's past performance
• Previous contracts
• Competitor Profile Business Ethics/Standards of Conduct Guidelines
• Market and Industry practices
	• Oral Presentations
	• Highly skilled contract negotiators
	• Legal Review
	• Business Case Approval
	• Subcontract Negotiation Formation Process
	  ○ Plan negotiations
	  ○ Conduct negotiations
	  ○ Document the negotiation and Form the Subcontract
		• Subcontract or Walk away

§ 6:7 Key inputs[1]

The key inputs to negotiations and contract formation consists of the following items:

- *Solicitation:* The solicitation is either an oral or written request for an offer (Request for Proposal (RFP), Request for Quotation (RFQ), Invitation for Bid (IFB), and so on) prepared by the prime contractor and provided to one or more potential subcontractors.
- *Bid or proposal:* The bid or proposal is either an oral or written offer by potential subcontractors to provide products or services to the prime contractor, usually in response to a solicitation. It also includes all supporting documentation, such as delivery plans, assumptions, and cost/price models.
- *Prime contractor's source selection process:* Source selection is the process by which a prime contractor selects a subcontractor or source of supply for products or services. Prime contractors typically apply evaluation criteria to select the best subcontractor to meet their needs.

This source selection process is seldom an uncomplicated one because —

Price may be the primary determinant for an off-the-shelf item, but the lowest proposed *price* may not be the lowest *cost* if the subcontractor proves unable to deliver the product in a timely manner

Proposals are often separated into technical/delivery and pricing/contractual sections, with each evaluated separately

Multiple sources may be required for critical products

Bids or proposals may be simple, requiring only one person to evaluate

---

[Section 6:6]

[1]Adapted from: World Class Contracting, by Gregory A. Garrett, CCH, Inc. 2003.

[Section 6:7]

[1]This section is a modified extract from the book World Class Contracting, by Gregory A. Garrett, CCH, Inc. 2007.

the sources and select the best alternative; they may be complex, requiring a panel of experts. In fact, some proposal evaluations may require a consultant's assistance.

☐ **Source Selection Evaluation Criteria:** Developing the evaluation criteria for source selection requires three prerequisites. First, the prime contractor must understand what goods or services it wants to buy. Second, the prime contractor must understand the industry that will provide the required goods or services. And third, the prime contractor must understand the market practices of that industry. Market research provides this information.

During requirements analysis and development of the specification or statement of work, the prime contractor gains an understanding of the required products or services. Understanding the industry means learning about the attributes of the goods or services in question and the firms that make them: What features do those goods or services have? What processes are used to produce or render them? What kinds and quantities of labor and capital are required? What are the cash requirements? Understanding the market means learning about the behavior of prime contractors and subcontractors: What are the pricing practices of the market, and what is the range of prices charged? What are the usual terms and conditions of sale?

After gaining an understanding of these issues, the prime contractor is ready to develop the evaluation criteria by selecting attributes for evaluation.

☐ **Source Selection Attributes:** A consumer shopping for an automobile does not evaluate an automobile, per se, but rather selected attributes of the automobile, such as acceleration, speed, handling, comfort, safety, price, fuel mileage, capacity, appearance, and so forth. The evaluation of the automobile is the sum of the evaluations of its attributes.

An automobile has many attributes, but not all are worthwhile subjects of evaluation. The attributes of interest are those that the consumer thinks are important for satisfaction. The attributes that one consumer thinks are important may be inconsequential to another.

In most procurements, multiple criteria will be required for successful performance, for the following reasons: First, prime contractors usually have more than one objective; for example, many prime contractors look for both good quality and low price. Second, attributes essential for one objective may be different from those essential for others; for example, in buying an automobile, the attributes essential for comfort have little to do with those essential for quick acceleration.

To complicate matters further, some criteria will likely be incompatible with others. The attributes essential to high quality may be inconsistent with low price; high performance, for example, may be incompatible with low operating cost. Thus, for any one source to have the maximum desired value of every essential attribute—for example, highest quality combined with lowest price—may be impossible. If so, the prime contractor must make trade-offs among attributes when deciding which source is best. These are considerations that make source selection a problem in *multiple attribute decision making*, which requires special decision analysis techniques.[2]

As a rule, source selection attributes fall into three general categories relating to the sources themselves, as entities; the products or services they offer; and the prices they offer. Thus, the prime contractor must have criteria for each category that reflect the prime contractor's ideas about what is valuable. The criteria concerning the sources themselves, as entities, are the *management criteria*; the criteria concerning the products or services offered are the *technical criteria*; and the criteria concerning the prices of the products or services are the *price criteria*.

- *Subcontractor's past performance:* The past performance of a subcontractor is often a critical aspect of subcontract negotiation. Has the subcontractor delivered previous products and services on time? Has the subcontractor provided high-quality products and services? Past performance can be seen as a separate evaluation factor or as a subfactor under technical excellence or management capability. Using the past performance history also reduces the emphasis on merely being able to write a good proposal.

- *Previous subcontracts:* Has the subcontractor provided products or services to this prime contractor in the past? If so, what did the previous subcontract say? How was it negotiated? Who negotiated it?

- *Competitor Profile:* The competitor profile, provides a written summary of the subcontractor's competitors and their respective strengths and weaknesses compared to the subcontractor's.

- *Business ethics/Standards of Conduct Guidelines:* Ethics is especially important, in light of numerous recent cases of corporate greed, corruption, and violations of state, federal or international laws. Every company should have mandatory business ethics policies, procedures, and well-defined standards of conduct. Even-the-Appearance of Conflicts of Interests should be avoided. All business activities should be conducted in a professional and ethical manner.

- *Market and industry practices:* Knowing what the competitors are offering (most-favored pricing, warranties, product discounts, volume discounts, and so on) is essential for a successful outcome to negotiation.

§ 6:8 Tools and techniques

The following tools and techniques are used for negotiations and subcontract formation:

- *Oral presentations:* It is usually better to orally present your bid/proposal to your customer than to merely submit it electronically (e-mail, FAX, CD-ROM) or in paper/binders. Oral presentations, when

---

[2]For more information about multiple attribute decision-making techniques, consult the following references: Ching-Lai Hwang and Kwangsun Yoon, Multiple Attribute Decision Making Methods and Applications: A State-of-the-Art Survey (Berlin: Srpinger-Verlag, 1981); Paul Goodwin and George Wright, Decision Analysis for Management Judgment (Chichester, England: John Wiley & Sons LTD., 1991); and Thomas Saaty, Decision Making for Leaders: The Analytic Hierarchy Process for Decisions in a Complex World (Pittsburgh, Pa.: RWS Publications, 1995).

preformed by a skilled, knowledgeable, and persuasive individual can help sell your products, services, and/or solution to the prime contractor. Oral presentations can be used to address questions and clarify concerns, which the prime contractor may have regarding a subcontractor's proposal.

- *Subcontract negotiation process:* The subcontract negotiation process is discussed in detail later in this chapter.
- *Highly skilled negotiators:* Conducting subcontract negotiation is a complex activity that requires a broad range of skills. Providing negotiators with the best available training in subcontract negotiation is vital. Top negotiators help their organizations save money and make higher profits.

§ 6:9   Case study: Northrop Grumman Corporation

For more than 25 years, Northrop Grumman Corporation (NGC) has had an excellent reputation in building or developing highly skilled subcontract negotiators and negotiation teams. NGC has traditionally ensured their sales managers, subcontract managers, and subcontract administrators receive appropriate and timely negotiation training, via in-house professional seminars, university-based courses, and attendance at educational conferences and seminars. In addition, NGC has for many years developed and maintained a seasoned and highly-skilled major negotiations team, which is tasked to tackle the largest and most important subcontract negotiations.

- *Legal review:* A legal review should be conducted, if not as a regular part of the subcontract negotiation process, then at least for all key subcontracts.

§ 6:10   The subcontract negotiation process

The subcontract negotiation process is composed of three phases planning negotiations, conducting negotiations, and documenting the negotiations. Table A describes an effective, logical approach to plan, conduct, and document subcontract negotiations based on the proven best practices of world-class organizations.

Table A
Subcontract Negotiation Process

Step 4: Plan Negotiations	Step 5: Conduct Negotiations	Step 6: Form Subcontract
1. Prepare yourself and your team	11. Determine who has authority	21. Prepare the negotiation memorandum
2. Know the other party	12. Prepare the facility	
3. Know the big picture	13. Use an agenda	22. Send the memorandum to the other party
4. Identify objectives	14. Introduce the team	
5. Prioritize objectives	15. Set the right tone	23. Offer to write the subcontract

Step 4: Plan Negotiations	Step 5: Conduct Negotiations	Step 6: Form Subcontract
6. Create options	16. Exchange information	24. Prepare the subcontract
7. Select fair standards	17. Focus on objectives	25. Prepare negotiation results summary
8. Examine alternatives	18. Use strategy, tactics, and countertactics	
9. Select your strategy, tactics, and counter-tactics	19. Make counteroffers	26. Obtain required reviews and approvals
10. Develop a solid and approved team negotiation plan	20. Document the agreement or know when to walk away	27. Send the subcontracts to the other party for signature
		28. Provide copies of the subcontract to affected organizations
		29. Document lessons learned
		30. Prepare the subcontract administration plan

§ 6:11 Step 4: Plan negotiations

The following ten actions should be performed to properly plan the negotiation:

1. *Prepare yourself and your team:* Ensure that the lead negotiator knows their personal and professional strengths, weaknesses, and tendencies as well as those of other team members. (Many self-assessment tools are available, including the Myers-Briggs Type Indicator® assessment. It can provide helpful insight on how an individual may react in a situation because of personal or professional tendencies.) Preparing a list of the strengths and weaknesses of team members can be an important first step in negotiation planning. (See Form 6-1)

Form 6-1
Team Members Strengths, Weaknesses and Interests

Team Member	Team Member
Name	Name
Job Title	Job Title
Phone No.	Phone No.
Fax No.	Fax No.
E-Mail:	E-Mail:

Team Member	Team Member
Strengths 1	Strengths 1
2	2
3	3
Weaknesses 1	Weaknesses 1
2	2
3	3
Interests 1	Interests 1
2	2
3	3

Date Prepared:_____   Lead
Negotiator:_____

2. *Know the other party:* Intelligence gathering is vital to successful negotiation planning. Create a checklist of things to know about the other party to help the team prepare for negotiation. (See Form 6-2.) Listed below are a few suggested questions which you should discuss with your team members to ensure you understand as much as possible about your organization and the other side.

Form 6-2
Things to Know About the Other Party

Prime contractor and Subcontractor
- ☐ What is the organization's overall business strategy?
- ☐ What is its reputation?
- ☐ What is its current company business environment?
- ☐ Who is the lead negotiator?
- ☐ Who are the primary decision makers?
- ☐ What are their key objectives?
- ☐ What are their overall subcontract objectives?
- ☐ What are their personal objectives?
- ☐ Who or what influences the decision makers?
- ☐ What internal organization barriers do they face?

Subcontractor Only
- ☐ When does the prime contractor need our products or services?
- ☐ How much money does the prime contractor have to spend?
- ☐ Where does the prime contractor want our products and services delivered?
- ☐ What benefits will our products and services provide?
- ☐ What is our company's past experiences with this prime contractor?

Date Prepared:_____ Lead Negotiator:_____

3. *Know the big picture:* In the words of Stephen R. Covey, author of *The Seven Habits of Highly Effective People,* "begin with the end in mind." Keep focused on the primary objectives. Be aware that the ability of either party to be flexible on some issues may be limited because of internal policies, budgets, or organizational politics.

One of the proven best practices to keep the negotiation focused is using interim summaries. The key is not to get caught up in small, unimportant details that take the negotiation off track.

4. *Identify objectives:* Know what both you and the other party want to accomplish. (See Form 6-3.) Successful negotiators know that nearly everything affects price, as illustrated in Figure 6-3: changes in schedule, technology, services, terms and conditions, customer obligations, subcontract type, products, and other subcontracting elements affect subcontract price.

(Figure 6-3)

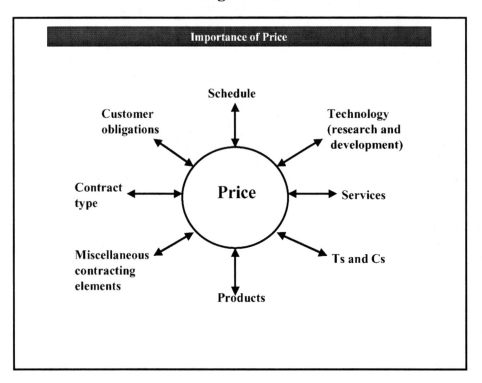

You can easily identify a novice or apprentice negotiator because they always want to discuss price first. An experienced negotiator knows you should agree to all of the terms and conditions (Ts and Cs) first. Price is the last item a master negotiator will discuss and agree to with the other side. Master negotiators know what the big print giveth and the little print taketh away.

Form 6-3
Objectives Identification

Subcontractor Objectives	Prime contractor Objectives
Personal 1	Personal 1
2	2
3	3
4	4
5	5
Professional 1	Professional 1
2	2
3	3
4	4
5	5
6	6
7	7

Date Prepared:_____   Lead
                                      Negotiator:_____

5. *Prioritize objectives:* Although all terms and conditions are important, some are clearly more important than others. Prioritize your objectives to help you remain focused during negotiation. (See Form 6-4.) Figure 6-4 shows that various terms and conditions affect cost, risk, and value.

(Figure 6-4)

Importance of Ts and Cs

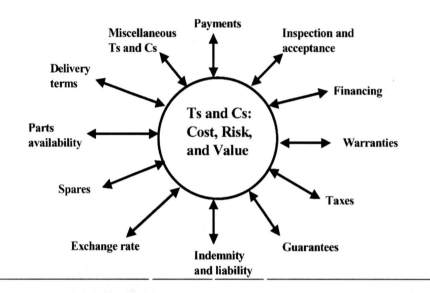

It is important for subcontract negotiators to truly understand and appreciate that all terms and conditions (Ts and Cs) contained in the deal have a cost, risk, and value associated with them and their specific wording. The exact wording of the deal is critical in subcontract negotiations.

Form 6-4
Objective Prioritization

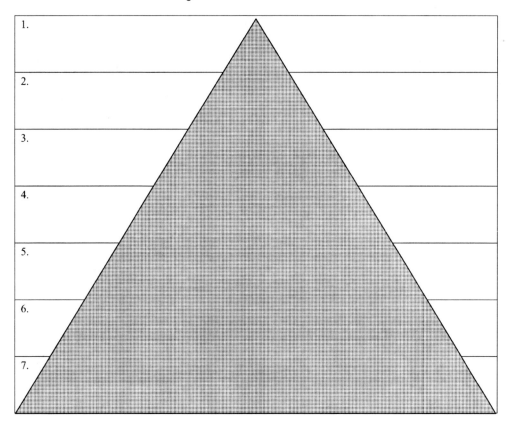

Date Prepared:————————   Lead
                                  Negotiator:————————

6. *Create options:* Creative problem solving is a critical skill of successful negotiators. Seek to expand options; do not assume that only one solution exists to every problem. Conducting team brainstorming sessions to develop a list of options to achieve negotiation objectives is a proven best practice of many world-class organizations. (See Form 6-5.)

Form 6-5
Create Options for Achieving Negotiation Objectives

Subcontractor Objectives	Possible Options	Prime contractor Objectives

Date Prepared:————————   Lead
                                  Negotiator:————————

7. *Select fair standards:* Successful negotiators avoid a contest of wills by turning an argument into a joint search for a fair solution, using fair standards independent of either side's will. Use standards such as the—

- Uniform Commercial Code
- United Nations Convention on Subcontracts for the International Sale of Goods
- American Arbitration Association standards
- ISO 9000 quality standards
- State, local, and federal laws
- Market or industry standards

8. *Examine alternatives:* Prepare in advance your alternatives to the important negotiation issues or objectives. Successful negotiators know their best-case, most-likely, and worst-case (walk-away) alternatives for all major objectives. (See Form 6-6.)

Form 6-6
Objectives and Alternatives-Worst Case, Most Likely, and Best Case

Objective:		
Worst Case	**Most Likely**	**Best Case**

(Plot your most likely position)

Date Prepared:—————————   Lead Negotiator:—————————

9. *Select your strategy, tactics, and countertactics:* Negotiation strategies provide the overall framework that will guide how you conduct your negotiation. Negotiation strategies can be divided into two types: win-lose and win-win.

The win-lose negotiation strategy is about winning today, despite the potential long-term effect tomorrow and beyond. Common characteristics of the win-lose strategy include concealing one's own position and interests, discovering the other party's position and interests, weakening the other party's resolve, and causing the other party to modify its position or accept your position on all key issues. Although the win-lose negotiation strategy is not a politically correct approach, it is a commonly used negotiation strategy worldwide.

The win-win negotiation strategy is about creative joint problem solving, which develops long-term successful business relationships. The win-win negotiation strategy, however, may sometimes be difficult to accomplish.

Among the obstacles to developing the win-win business environment are previous adverse prime contractor-subcontractor relations, lack of training in joint problem solving and conflict resolution, and complex and highly regulated contracting procedures in some organizations, especially large companies and government agencies.

Winning or losing a subcontract negotiation is, indeed, a matter of perspective, which is based on your knowledge, experience, and judgment. The only way to know whether you have won or lost a negotiation is to compare the results to your negotiation plan. Did you get what you wanted? Is what you got closer to your best-case, most-likely, or worst-case alternative? Clearly, without a subcontract negotiation plan, you have no basis against which to evaluate the negotiation outcome.

To achieve your desired subcontract negotiation results, you need not only a strategy, but also tactics and countertactics, which are a means to a desired end.

10. *Develop a solid and approved team negotiation plan:* The conclusion of subcontract negotiation planning should be the summary and documentation of all planned actions. If necessary, have the negotiation plan reviewed and approved by higher management to ensure that all planned actions are in the best interests of the organization. (See Form 6-7.)

Form 6-7
Sample Negotiation Planning Summary

Negotiation Information

Location	Date	Time
1	1	1
2	2	2
3	3	3

Key Objectives (Plot your most likely position)

1. Price	Worst Case		Best Case
	$10.5M	$12.0M $12.5M	

2. Payments	Worst Case		Best Case
	After Delivery	Progress payments	Advance payments

3. Warranty period	Worst Case		Best Case
	36 months	18 months 12 months Industry average	
4.	Worst Case	Best Case	
5.	Worst Case	Best Case	
6.	Worst Case	Best Case	
7.	Worst Case	Best Case	
8.	Worst Case	Best Case	
9.	Worst Case	Best Case	
10.	Worst Case	Best Case	
11.	Worst Case	Best Case	

12.	Worst Case	Best Case
		_____

Possible Tactics and Countertactics

Objective	Planned Tactics—Prime subcontractor	Planned Countertactics—Subcontractor

Subcontract Price

Range	
Best Case	
Most Likely	
Worst Case	

Date Prepared:_____   Lead Negotiator:_____

Approved by:_____   Date Approved:_____

§ 6:12   Step 5: Conduct negotiations

The following activities are necessary to conduct the negotiation:

11. *Determine who has authority:* If possible, before the negotiation, determine who has the authority to negotiate for each party. At the start of the negotiation, ensure that you know who has that authority, who the lead negotiator is for the other party, and what limits, if any, are placed on the other party's authority.

12. *Prepare the facility:* Most prime contractors want to conduct the negotiation at their offices to provide them with a sense of control. If you are the subcontractor try to conduct the negotiation at your location or at

a neutral site, such as a hotel, conference center, via conference call, or Net-meeting.

Other key facility considerations include the—

- Size of the room
- Use of break-out rooms
- Lighting
- Tables (size, shape, and arrangement)
- Seating arrangements
- Use of audiovisual aids
- Schedule (day and time)
- Access to telephone, fax, e-mail/Internet access, restrooms, food, and drink

13. *Use an agenda:* A proven best practice of successful negotiators worldwide is creating and using an agenda for the negotiation. Provide the agenda to the other party before the negotiation begins. (See Form 6-8.) An effective agenda helps a negotiator to—

- Set the right tone
- Control the exchange of information
- Keep the focus on the objectives
- Manage time
- Obtain the desired results

Form 6-8
Negotiation Agenda

Subcontract

Title		Date
Location		Time

Topics of Action		**Time**
☐ Introduce team members		_____
☐ Provide overview and discuss purpose of negotiation		_____
☐ Exchange information on key interests and issues		
• Quantity of products		_____
• Quality of products and services		_____
• Past performance		
• Delivery schedule		
• Maintenance		
• Training		
☐ Have a break		
☐ Review agreement on all key interests and issues		
☐ Agree on detailed terms and conditions		
☐ Agree on price		_____

☐ Review and summarize meeting	_____
	_____
	_____
	_____
Date Prepared:_____ Lead Negotiator:_____	

14. *Introduce the team*: Introduce your team members, or have team members make brief self-introductions. Try to establish a common bond with the other party as soon as possible.

15. *Set the right tone:* After introductions, make a brief statement to express your team strategy to the other party. Set the desired climate for subcontract negotiation from the start.

16. *Exchange information:* Conducting subcontract negotiation is all about communication. Be aware that information is exchanged both orally and through body language, visual aids (pictures, diagrams, photographs, or videotapes), and active listening.

17. *Focus on objectives:* Never lose sight of the big picture.

18. *Use strategy, tactics, and countertactics:* Do what you said you were going to do, but be flexible to achieve your objectives. Anticipate the other party's tactics, and plan your countertactics. Adjust them as necessary.

19. *Make counteroffers:* A vital part of conducting the negotiation is providing substitute offers, or counteroffers, when the other party does not accept what you are offering. Document all offers and counteroffers to ensure that both parties understand any changes in the terms and conditions.

When offers and counteroffers are done right—they are part art and science. A subcontractor should know the approximate range (monetary amount) the prime contractor intends to spend. Plus, a well prepared subcontractor should know approximately what their competitors are likely to offer and the approximate price. Likewise, well informed and prepared Prime contractor's know what approximate range (monetary amount) the subcontractor's are likely to seek. When well prepared Prime contractors and Subcontractors enter into the exchange of offers and counteroffers there should exist a negotiation zone (see Table C).

Table C

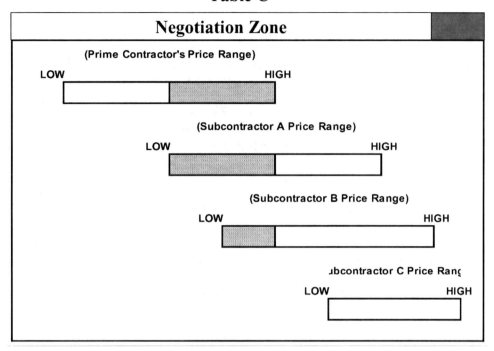

Given a competitive source business environment, subcontractors must ensure their initial offer is not so high that they will be eliminated from the competition. However, a subcontractor must also ensure they maintain a healthy profit margin and still have room in their offer to give further price reductions if necessary to capture the business. Clearly, every subcontractor must perform a balancing act between their desire to win business vs. their need to reduce/mitigate risks, while maximizing revenue and profit.

As illustrated in the Negotiation Zone, (Table C), every Prime contractor has a monetary range they expect to spend for their required products and/or services, which vary (low to high) based upon numerous variables typically contained within subcontract terms and conditions. Further, as depicted in Table C each Subcontractor (A, B, or C) has a monetary range, typically described in their approved business case, within which they can make offers and counteroffers, based upon their costs, risks, desired profit margin, and preferred terms and conditions.

Once both parties have made their initial offer, then the fun really begins. How do you determine how much to move? Do you alter your terms and conditions in conjunction with changes in pricing? Do you offer a different type of pricing arrangement i.e. Fixed-Price to Time & Materials or Cost-Plus-Fixed Fee (see Table D Advantages, Disadvantages & Suitability of Various Subcontract types)? Should you refuse to move to force the other party to counteroffer? The answers to all of the above questions is-it depends! That is why, experienced highly skilled master subcontract negotiators are a valuable asset to every organization involved in detailed, complex, and expensive subcontract negotiations (see Form 6-9).

Table D
Advantages, Disadvantages, and Suitability of Various Subcontract Types

Type	Essential Elements and Advantages	Disadvantages	Suitability
Firm Fixed Price (FFP)	Reasonably definite design or performance specifications available. Fair and reasonable price can be established at outset. Conditions for use include the following: • Adequate competition • Prior purchase experience of the same, or similar, supplies or services under competitive conditions. • Valid cost or pricing data • Realistic estimates of proposed cost. • Possible uncertainties in performance can be identified and priced. • Subcontractors willing to accept subcontract at a level that causes them to take all financial risks • Any other reasonable basis for pricing can be used to establish fair and reasonable price.	Price not subject to adjustment regardless of subcontractor performance costs. Places 100% of financial risk on subcontractor.	Commercial products and commercial services for which reasonable prices can be established.

Type	Essential Elements and Advantages	Disadvantages	Suitability
Fixed Price with Economic Price Adjustment (FP/EPA)	Unstable market or labor conditions during performance period and contingencies that would otherwise be included in subcontract price can be identified and made the subject of a separate price adjustment clause. Contingencies must be specifically defined in subcontract. Provides for upward adjustment (with ceiling) in subcontract price. May provide for downward adjustment of price if escalated element has potential of failing below subcontract limits. Three general types of EPAs, based on established prices, actual costs of labor or material, and cost indexes of labor or material.	Price can be adjusted on action of an industry-wide contingency that is beyond subcontractor's control. Reduces subcontractor's fixed-price risk.	Commercial products and services for which reasonable prices can be established at time of award.

Type	Essential Elements and Advantages	Disadvantages	Suitability
Fixed Price Incentive (FPI)	Cost uncertainties exist, but there is potential for cost reduction or performance improvement by giving subcontractor a degree of cost responsibility and a positive profit incentive.	Requires adequate subcontractor accounting system. Prime contractor must determine that FPI is least costly and award of any other type would be impractical.	Development and production of high-volume, multi-year subcontracts.
	Profit is earned or lost based on relationship that subcontract's final negotiated cost bears to total target cost.	Prime contractor and subcontractor administrative effort is more extensive than under other fixed-price subcontract types.	
	Subcontract must contain target cost, target profit, ceiling price, and profit-sharing formula.	Used only with competitive negotiated subcontracts.	
	Two forms of FPI: firm target (FPIF) and successive targets (FPIS).	Billing prices must be established for interim payment.	
	FPIF: Firm target cost, target profit, and profit-sharing formula negotiated into basic subcontract; profit adjusted at subcontract completion.		
	FPIS: Initial cost and profit targets negotiated into subcontract, but final cost target (firm) cannot be negotiated until performance. Contains production point(s) at which either a firm target and final profit formula, or a FFP subcontract, can be negotiated.		
	Elements that can be incentives: costs, performance, delivery, quality.		

Type	Essential Elements and Advantages	Disadvantages	Suitability
Cost-Reimbursement Subcontracts (Greatest Risk on Prime contractor)			
Cost	Appropriate for research and development work, particularly with nonprofit educational institutions or other nonprofit organizations, and for facilities subcontracts. Allowable costs of subcontract performance are reimbursed, but no fee is paid.	Application limited due to no fee and by the fact that the prime contractor is not willing to reimburse subcontractor fully if there is a commercial benefit for the subcontractor. Only nonprofit institutions and organizations are willing (usually) to perform research for which there is no fee (or other tangible benefits)	Research and development; facilities.
Cost Sharing (CS)	Used when prime contractor and subcontractor agree to share costs in a research or development project having potential mutual benefits. Because of commercial benefits accruing to the subcontractor, no fee is paid. Subcontractor agrees to absorb a portion of the costs of performance in expectation of compensating benefits to subcontractor's firm or organization. Such benefits might include an enhancement of the subcontractor's capability and expertise or an improvement of its competitive position in the commercial market.	Care must be taken in negotiating cost-share rate so that the cost ratio is proportional to the potential benefit (that is, the party receiving the greatest potential benefit bears the greatest share of the costs).	Research and development that has potential benefits to both the prime subcontractor and the subcontractor.

Type	Essential Elements and Advantages	Disadvantages	Suitability
Cost-Reimbursement Subcontracts (Greatest Risk on Prime contractor)			
Cost Plus Incentive Fee (CPIF)	Development has a highly probability that is feasible and positive profit incentives for subcontractor management can be negotiated.	Difficult to negotiate range between the maximum and minimum fees so as to provide an incentive over entire range.	Major systems development and other development programs in which it is determined that CPIF is desirable and administratively practical.
	Performance incentives must be clearly spelled out and objectively measurable.	Performance must be objectively measurable.	
	Fee range should be negotiated to give the subcontractor an incentive over various ranges of cost performance.	Costly to administer; subcontractor must have an adequate accounting system.	
	Fee is adjusted by a formula negotiated into the subcontract in accordance with the relationship that total cost bears to target cost.	Used only with negotiated subcontracts.	
	Subcontract must contain target cost, target fee, minimum and maximum fees, fee adjustment formula.	Appropriate prime subcontractor surveillance needed during performance to ensure effective methods and efficient cost controls are used.	
	Fee adjustment is made at completion of subcontract.		

Type	Essential Elements and Advantages	Disadvantages	Suitability
Cost Plus Award Fee (CPAF)	Subcontract completion is feasible, incentives are desired, but performance is not susceptible to finite measurement. Provides for subjective evaluation of subcontractor performance. Subcontractor is evaluated at stated time(s) during performance period. Subcontract must contain clear and unambiguous evaluation criteria to determine award fee. Award fee is earned for excellence in performance, quality, timeliness, ingenuity, and cost-effectiveness and can be earned in whole or in part. Two separate fee pools can be established in subcontract: base fee and award fee. Award fee earned by subcontractor is determined by the prime contractor and is often based on recommendations of an award fee evaluation board.	Prime contractor's determination of amount of award fee earned by the subcontractor is not subject to disputes clause. CPAF cannot be used to avoid either CPIF or CPFF if either is feasible. Should not be used if the amount of money, period of performance, or expected benefits are insufficient to warrant additional administrative efforts. Very costly to administer. Subcontractor must have an adequate accounting system. Used only with negotiated subcontracts.	Level-of-effort services that can only be subjectively measured, and subcontracts for which work would have been accomplished under another subcontract type if performance objectives could have been expressed as definite milestones, targets, and goals that could have been measured.

Type	Essential Elements and Advantages	Disadvantages	Suitability
Cost Plus Fixed Fee (CPFF)	Level of effort is unknown, and subcontractor's performance cannot be subjectively evaluated. Provides for payment of a fixed fee. Subcontractor receives fixed fee regardless of the actual costs incurred during performance. Can be constructed in two ways: Completion form: Clearly defined task with a definite goal and specific end product. Prime contractor can order more work without an increase in fee if the subcontract estimated costs is increased. Term form: Scope of work described in general terms. Subcontractor obligated only for a specific level of effort for stated period of time. Completion form is preferred over term form. Fee is expressed as percentages of estimated cost at time subcontract is awarded	Subcontractor has minimum incentive to control costs. Costly to administer. Subcontractor must have an adequate accounting system. Subcontractor assumes no financial risk.	Completion form: Advanced development or technical services subcontracts. Term form: Research and exploratory development. Used when the level of effort required is known and there is an inability to measure risk.

Type	Essential Elements and Advantages	Disadvantages	Suitability
Time and Materials			
Time and Material (T&M)	Not possible when placing subcontract to estimate extent or duration of the work, or anticipated cost, with any degree of confidence. Calls for provision of direct labor hours at specified hourly rate and materials at cost (or some other basis specified in subcontract). The fixed hourly rates include wages, overhead, general and administrative expenses, and profit. Material cost can include, if appropriate, material handling costs. Ceiling price established at time of award.	Used only after determination that no other type will serve purpose. Does not encourage effective cost control. Requires almost constant surveillance by prime contractor to ensure effective subcontractor management. Ceiling price is required in subcontract.	Engineering and design services in conjunction with the production of suppliers, engineering design and manufacture, repair, maintenance, and overhaul work to be performed on an as-needed basis.

Form 6-9, provides a simple, yet, effective means of documenting offers and counteroffers exchanged during subcontract negotiations. Remember, the number of offers and counteroffers exchanged is not as important as the value of the concessions made.

Form 6-9
Offers and Counteroffers Summary

Subcontractor	Prime contractor
Offer	Counteroffer
Offer	Counteroffer
Offer	Counteroffer

Subcontractor	Prime contractor
Offer	Counteroffer

Date Prepared:_____   Lead
Negotiator:_____

20. *Document the agreement or know when to walk away:* Take time throughout the negotiation to take notes on what was agreed to between the parties. If possible, assign one team member to take minutes. To ensure proper documentation, periodically summarize agreements on all major issues throughout the negotiation. At the end of the negotiation, summarize your agreements both orally and in writing. (See Form 6-10.) If a settlement is not reached, document the areas of agreement and disagreement. If possible, plan a future meeting to resolve differences.

Remember: Do not agree to a bad deal—learn to say, "No thank you," and walk away.

Form 6-10
Negotiation Results Summary

Subcontract Title	Date of Subcontract
Parties Involved	Date(s) of Negotiation

Brief Product/Service Description	Location
Agreed to Price	
Key changes from Approved Proposal	

Date Prepared:_____ Lead Negotiator:_____

§ 6:13   Step 6: Form subcontract

The following activities are conducted to document the negotiation and form the subcontract.

21. *Prepare the negotiation memorandum (minutes or notes):* Document what was discussed during the negotiation. After having the memorandum word processed, spell checked, and edited, have it reviewed by someone within your organization who attended the negotiation and someone who did not. Then determine whether they have a similar understanding.

22. *Send the memorandum to the other party:* As promptly as possible, provide a copy of your documented understanding of the subcontract negotiation to the other party. First, e-mail or fax it to the other party. Then send an original copy by either overnight or 2-day mail. Verify that the other party receives your negotiation memorandum by following up with an e-mail or telephone call, or send by registered mail, return receipt requested.

23. *Offer to write the subcontract:* As the subcontractor, offer to draft the agreement so that you can put the issues in your own words. Today, most subcontracts are developed using electronic databases, which facilitate reviews, changes, and new submissions.

24. *Prepare the subcontract:* Writing a subcontract should be a team effort with an experienced subcontract management professional at the lead. Typically, automated standard organizational forms, modified as needed, are used with standard terms and conditions that were tailored during negotiation. At other times, a subcontract must be written in full. Ensure that no elements of the subcontract are missing. (See Form 6-11.) After the initial subcontract draft, obtain all appropriate reviews and approvals, preferably through electronic data.

Form 6-11
Essential Subcontract Elements Checklist

Project Name	Prepared by (Print)	Date Prepared
Customer	Telephone/Fax	e-mail

☐ Deliverables and prices (provide a listing of deliverables and their prices)

- ☐ Deliverable conformance specifications
- ☐ Requirements in statement of work (determine SOW requirements not listed as deliverables)
- ☐ Delivery requirements (list delivery requirements, deliverable packaging and shipping requirements, and service performance instructions)
- ☐ Deliverable inspection and acceptance
- ☐ Invoice and payment schedule and provisions (include in subcontract tracking summary)
- ☐ Representations and certifications
- ☐ Other terms and conditions

25. *Prepare negotiation results summary:* Prepare an internal-use-only summary of key negotiation items that have changed since originally proposed. Many organizations have found such a summary to be a valuable tool for explaining changes to senior managers.

26. *Obtain required reviews and approvals:* Depending on your organizational procedures, products, services, and other variables, one or more people may be required to review and approve the proposed subcontract before signature. Typically, the following departments or staff review a subcontract: project management, financial, legal, procurement or subcontract management, and senior management. Increasingly, organizations are using automated systems to draft subcontracts and transmit them internally for the needed reviews and approvals.

27. *Send the subcontract to the other party for signature:* Send a copy of the subcontract to the other party via e-mail or fax, and then follow up with two mailed original copies. With all copies include an appropriate cover letter with a return mail address and time/date suspense for prompt return. Verify receipt of the subcontract by phone or e-mail. Today, many organizations, as well as the laws of many nations, recognize an electronic signature to be valid.

28. *Provide copies of the subcontract to affected organizations:* The subcontract is awarded officially after it is executed, signed by both parties, and delivered to both parties. Ensure that all other affected organizations or parties receive a copy.

29. *Document lessons learned:* Take the time to document everything that went well during the subcontract negotiation process. Even more important, document what did not go well and why, and what should be done to avoid those problems in the future.

30. *Prepare the subcontract administration plan:* At the end of the subcontract negotiation process, follow a proven best practice by having the team that negotiated the subcontract help the team that is responsible for administering it develop a subcontract administration plan.

The following Table E, provides a checklist of proven effective subcontract negotiation Best Practices. How many of the actions listed in Table E do you and your organization both know and do! Remember, knowing what to do is good, but, doing it is better!

Table E
Checklist of Prime contractor—Negotiation Best Practices

(The Prime contractor Should:)

- [ ] Know what you want-lowest price or best value
- [ ] State your requirements in performance terms and evaluate accordingly
- [ ] Conduct market research about potential sources before selection
- [ ] Evaluate potential sources promptly and dispassionately
- [ ] Follow the evaluation criteria stated in the solicitation: management, technical, and price
- [ ] Use absolute, minimum, or relative evaluation standards to measure performance as stated in your solicitation
- [ ] Develop organizational policies to guide and facilitate the source selection process
- [ ] Use a weighting system to determine which evaluation criteria are most important
- [ ] Use a screening system to prequalify sources
- [ ] Obtain independent estimates from consultants or outside experts to assist in source selection
- [ ] Use past performance as a key aspect of source selection, and verify data accuracy
- [ ] Conduct price realism analysis
- [ ] Create a competitive analysis report
- [ ] Use oral presentations or proposals by subcontractors to improve and expedite the source selection process

(The Prime contractor and Subcontractor Should:)

- [ ] Understand that negotiation is a process, usually involving a team effort
- [ ] Select and train highly skilled negotiators to lead the negotiation process
- [ ] Know market and industry practices
- [ ] Prepare yourself and your team
- [ ] Know the other party
- [ ] Know the big picture
- [ ] Identify and prioritize objectives
- [ ] Create options-be flexible in your planning
- [ ] Examine alternatives
- [ ] Select your negotiation strategy, tactics, and countertactics
- [ ] Develop a solid and approved team negotiation plan
- [ ] Determine who has the authority to negotiate
- [ ] Prepare the negotiation facility at your location or at a neutral site
- [ ] Use an agenda during contract negotiation
- [ ] Set the right tone at the start of the negotiation
- [ ] Maintain your focus on your objectives
- [ ] Use interim summaries to keep on track
- [ ] Do not be too predictable in your tactics
- [ ] Document your agreement throughout the process
- [ ] Know when to walk away
- [ ] Offer to write the contract
- [ ] Prepare a negotiation results summary

☐   Obtain required reviews and approvals
☐   Provide copies of the contract to all affected parties
☐   Document negotiation lessons learned and best practices
☐   Prepare a transition plan for contract administration
☐   Understand that everything affects price
☐   Understand the Ts and Cs have cost, risk, and value
☐   Tailor Ts and Cs to the deal, but understand the financial effects on price and profitability
☐   Know what is negotiable and what is not

Desired Outputs

- *Subcontract:* The output from negotiations and subcontract formation may be the subcontract, which is both a document and a relationship between parties.

   Or it may be best to—

- *Walk away:* Do not agree to a bad deal. No business is better than bad business.

§ 6:14   Summary

Outsourcing is essential to business in both the public and private sectors. As stated in Chapter 1, many simple and smaller value business transactions are routinely done via self-service electronic catalogs procurement cards, or e-auctions. However, most large complex business to business transactions still require more formal subcontract negotiations and formation. Clearly, less face-to-face or in-person interaction is required, in today's business, because of the numerous advances in communication technologies—video conferences, net meetings, teleconferences, e-mails, e-documents, electronic signatures, and electronic funds transfers. However, the need for highly-skilled negotiators who understand the process and have mastered all of the inputs, tools and techniques, and outputs is more important now than ever before!

Negotiation and subcontract formation is vital to the success of prime contractors and subcontractors worldwide. When skilled negotiators follow a proven process approach, successful business agreements are reached. Through effective subcontract formation practices, win-win subcontracts are developed and documented, yielding beneficial results for both parties.

Remember, in the words of Dr. Chester Karrass, author, consultant, and master negotiator, "You don't get what you deserve, you get what you have the ability to negotiate." The primary focus of this chapter is mastering the subcontract negotiation process, the use of a logical, organized, documented, step-by-step approach to build successful business relationships. The highly effective subcontract negotiation process discussed in this chapter has been taught to more than 20,000 business professionals worldwide via the National Contract Management Association (NCMA), The George Washington University School of Business, The Keller Graduate School of DeVry University, Villanova University On-Line Masters Certificate Program in Contract Management, the University of California at Los Angeles, the U.S. Naval Postgraduate School, just to name a few, with outstanding results. I hope that you will consider using the subcontract negotiation process, forms, and best practices discussed in this chapter.

In the next chapter, we will closely examine the importance of subcontract administration and closeout.

§ 6:15   Questions to consider

1. Does your organization have a logical, documented, and proven successful subcontract negotiation process?
2. Do you consistently achieve your desired negotiation results?
3. Has your organization walked-away from any potential bad deals in the past year? If so, how many and why?

Chapter 7

Subcontract Administration & Closeout

KeyCite®: Cases and other legal materials listed in KeyCite Scope can be researched through the KeyCite service on Westlaw®. Use KeyCite to check citations for form, parallel references, prior and later history, and comprehensive citator information, including citations to other decisions and secondary materials.

---

§ 7:1   Introduction

Subcontract administration is the process of ensuring that each party's performance meets contractual requirements. On larger projects with multiple product and service providers, a key aspect of subcontract administration is managing the interfaces among the various providers. Because of the legal nature of the contractual relationship, the project team must be acutely aware of the legal implications of actions taken when administering the subcontract.

The principal objective of subcontract administration is the same for both parties—to ensure the fulfillment of the contractual obligations by all the parties to the contract. If the parties are individuals, this task is a matter of self-discipline. However, when organizations are involved, the problem is more complicated. Organizations must perform as systems, integrating the efforts of many people who compose the components of the organization. Thus, for organizations to function efficiently requires communication and control, which is the primary task of subcontract administration, see Figure 7-1, The Subcontract Management Process.

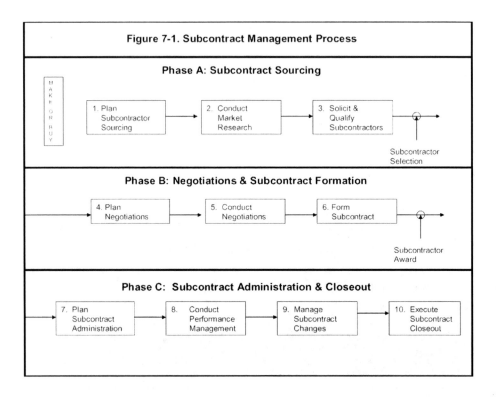

Figure 7-1. Subcontract Management Process

Phase A: Subcontract Sourcing

MAKE OR BUY

1. Plan Subcontractor Sourcing
2. Conduct Market Research
3. Solicit & Qualify Subcontractors

Subcontractor Selection

Phase B: Negotiations & Subcontract Formation

4. Plan Negotiations
5. Conduct Negotiations
6. Form Subcontract

Subcontractor Award

Phase C: Subcontract Administration & Closeout

7. Plan Subcontract Administration
8. Conduct Performance Management
9. Manage Subcontract Changes
10. Execute Subcontract Closeout

§ 7:2 Step 7: Plan subcontract administration

Effective subcontract administration is critical to effective project management, because an organization's failure to fulfill its contractual obligations could have legal consequences. Thus, someone must observe performance of contractual obligations. That person is the contract manager, who must always be aware of the legal consequences of an action or a failure to act and who must take steps to ensure that required actions are taken and prohibited actions are avoided. In a real sense, a subcontract manager is a project manager, and the principles of project management apply to his or her work. No matter where subcontract management reports subcontract administration needs to be accomplished, but, clearly some functional areas care more about subcontract performance and administration than others.

Each party to the subcontract should appoint a subcontract manager, who monitors not only his or her own organization but also the other party to ensure that both parties are keeping their promises. The subcontract manager must maintain these two perspectives throughout subcontract performance. Subcontract administration is largely commitment management, as illustrated by Figure 7-2, Subcontract administration & Closeout Process.

Figure 7-2—Prime Subcontract administration & Closeout Process (Steps 7—10)

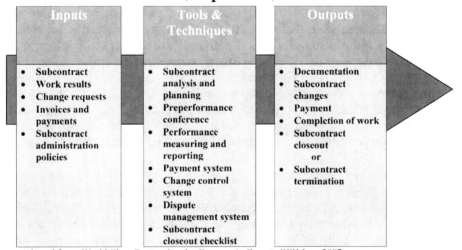

Adapted from: World Class Contracting, by Gregory A. Garrett, CCH Inc., 2007

Subcontract administration includes applying the appropriate project management processes to the contractual relationships and integrating the output from these processes into the general management of the project.

Inputs

Inputs to subcontract administration consists of the following items:

- *Subcontract:* The subcontract document is the primary guide for administering the subcontract.
- *Work results:* The results of performing the requirement will affect the administration of the contract.

- *Change requests:* Change requests are a common element of most subcontracts. An effective process for managing change must be in place to ensure that all requests are handled smoothly. Changes may be called amendments, modifications, add-ons, up-scopes, or down-scopes. Changes are opportunities either to increase or decrease profitability for the subcontractor. Changes are a necessary aspect of business for prime contractors, because of changes in their needs.
- *Invoices and payments:* An efficient process must be developed for handling invoices and payments throughout subcontract administration. Few areas cause more concern to subcontractors than late payment. Prime contractors can realize savings by developing an efficient and timely payment process, because subcontractors are often willing to give discounts for early payment.
- *Subcontract administration policies:* Although the specific policies that will apply to subcontract administration depend on the contracting parties, four policies are key: compliance with contract terms and conditions, effective internal and external communication and control, effective control of contract changes, and effective resolution of claims and disputes. * These policies will be discussed further in this chapter in "Subcontract administration Policies."

- **Tools and Techniques**

The following tools and techniques are used for subcontract administration:

- *Subcontract analysis and planning:* Before the award of a subcontract, each party should develop a subcontract administration plan and assign the responsibility of administering the subcontract to a subcontract manager. To whom should the job be assigned? A project manager could do double duty as subcontract manager. However in most large companies, subcontract administration is a specialized function, usually performed by someone in the subcontracting department, because doing the job will require special knowledge and training.

  Subcontract administration is an element of both contract management and project management. If the project is under a subcontract, then project management and subcontract administration will overlap considerably, depending on how the company defines those terms. If the project is not under a subcontract but subcontracts to obtain goods and services essential to project implementation, subcontract administration will be a smaller element of project management.

  Assume for the moment that a project is under a subcontract and that the project manager and subcontract manager are different people. What should their relationship be? Although organizations divide the responsibilities differently in general the project manager will have overall responsibility for executing the project, and the subcontract manager will oversee the contractual aspects of the project. The subcontract manager's special knowledge and training about contracts will be an asset to the project manager. Whether the contract manager reports to the project manager or to someone else will depend on whether the work is organized along project, functional, or matrix lines of authority.

In anticipation of subcontract award, the project manager and subcontract manager should analyze the terms and conditions of the prospective contract and develop a work breakdown structure that reflects both the technical and administrative aspects of contract performance. They should then determine which departments of the organization will be affected by those terms and conditions.

Many functional managers will be affected by subcontract terms and conditions. Consider, for example, the following clause from a services subcontract:

Fitness of Employees

Subcontractor shall employ on or in connection with the Project only persons who are fit and skilled for the Project. Should any objectionable person be employed by Subcontractor, Subcontractor shall, upon request of ABC Company, cause such person to be removed from the Project.

Clauses of this type are not unusual in services contracts, particularly when the work will be performed at the prime contractor's facility. The clause is not unreasonable, and to many it would even seem innocuous. Not so, however, because this clause has potentially great significance to a company's human resources department and for labor relations in general. The human resources department may have specific procedures for removing an employee from an assignment. Therefore, the project manager and subcontract manager should contact that department to discuss the contract and the appropriate personnel procedures to be followed.

The project manager and subcontract manager must meet with the managers of all affected functional areas to inform them of the subcontract, the terms and conditions related to their operations, and subcontract administration policies and procedures. In some companies, the functional managers will already know about the subcontract and will have made preliminary preparations for performance. In others, they will not have been informed and may be completely unprepared for what they must do.

The project manager and subcontract manager should try to reach agreement on intermediate performance goals with each manager who has performance responsibility. Intermediate goals will enable the subcontract manager and the functional manager to measure progress, detect significant performance variances, take corrective action, and follow up. Of course, performance goals must reflect contract performance obligations.

The project manager, subcontract manager, and other business managers also must decide how and when to measure and report actual performance. The techniques, timing, and frequency of measurement and reporting should reflect the nature and criticality of the work. A reasonable balance must be struck between excessive reporting and no measurement or reporting of any kind. Functional managers may see these requirements as nuisances that are of little value to themselves.

The realities of subcontract administration, however, are often quite different from the ideal situation. First, most companies devote more effort to source selection and contract formation than to subcontract administration. Project commencement often depends on subcontract award, so more resources are devoted to startup than to oversight. Second, in performing these tasks, the project manager and subcontract manager will face all the challenges that confront all project managers, but their responsibility may not come with formal authority. In many companies, functional managers simply do not appreciate the importance of subcontracts and subcontract administration and will resent the imposition of what they see as additional performance burdens. Third, the project manager and subcontract manager may not have the luxury of working on only one project or subcontract at a time. Nevertheless, a reasonable effort must be made to ensure that all personnel recognize their responsibilities under the subcontract and attempt to ensure that those responsibilities are fulfilled.

- *Preperformance conference:* Before performance begins, the prime contractor and the subcontractor should meet to discuss their joint administration of the subcontract. The meeting should be formal; an agenda should be distributed in advance, and minutes should be taken and distributed. Each party should appoint a person who will be its organization's official voice during contract performance. At the meeting, the parties should review the contract terms and conditions and discuss who will do what. They also should establish protocols for written and oral communication and for progress measurement and reporting and discuss procedures for managing change and resolving differences. Prime contractor and subcontractor department managers who will have performance responsibilities should attend the preperformance conference or, at the least, send a representative. Important subcontractors also should be represented. The meeting should be held at the performance site, if possible.

- *Performance measuring and reporting*: During subcontract administration, the project manager, subcontract manager, and responsible business managers must observe performance, collect information, and measure actual contract achievement. These activities are essential to effective control. The resources devoted to these tasks and the techniques used to perform them will depend on the nature of the subcontract work, the size and complexity of the subcontract, and the resources available. Performance measuring and reporting will be discussed further in this chapter in "Performance Measurement and Reporting."

- *Payment system:* Every subcontract must establish a clear invoicing and payment system or process. The prime contractor and subcontractor must agree to whom invoices should be sent and what information is required. Subcontractors must submit proper invoices in a timely manner. Prime contractors should pay all invoices promptly. Subcontractors should insist that late payment penalty clauses be included in all contracts.

- *Change control system:* As a rule, any parties that can make a subcontract can agree to change it. Changes are usually inevitable in contracts for complex undertakings, such as system design and systems integration. No one has perfect foresight; requirements and circumstances change in unexpected ways, and contract terms and conditions must often be changed as a result. (Details are presented later in this chapter in "Change Management")

- *Dispute management system:* No one should be surprised when, from time to time, contracting parties find themselves in disagreement about the correct interpretation of contract terms and conditions. Most such disagreements are minor and are resolved without too much difficulty. Occasionally, however, the parties will find themselves entangled in a seemingly intractable controversy. Try as they might, they cannot resolve their differences. If the dispute goes unresolved for too long, one or both of the parties may threaten, or even initiate, litigation.

Litigation is time consuming, costly, and risky. No one can ever be entirely sure of its result. It rarely results in a truly satisfactory resolution of a dispute, and it sours commercial relationships. For these reasons, it should be avoided. One goal of business managers and subcontract managers should be to resolve disputes without litigation whenever possible.

The keys to effective dispute resolution are as follows:

☐ Recognize that contract documents are not perfect
☐ Keep larger objectives in mind
☐ Focus on the facts
☐ Depersonalize the issues
☐ Be willing to make reasonable compromises

When disputes become intractable, seeking the opinion of an impartial third party can sometimes help. When this approach is formal, and the third party's decision is binding on the parties, it is called *arbitration*. Some companies include a clause in their contracts that makes arbitration the mandatory means of resolving disputes. Such a clause might read as follows:

Disputes

Should any dispute occur between the parties arising from or related to this Agreement, or their rights and responsibilities to each other, the matter shall be settled and determined by arbitration under the then current rules of the American Arbitration Association. The arbitration shall be conducted by a single arbitrator, the decision and award of the arbitrator shall be final and binding, and the award so rendered may be entered in any court having jurisdiction thereof. The language to be used in the arbitral proceeding shall be English.

In an international contract, the "Disputes" clause may be modified to provide for an international forum. The clause might read—

The arbitral tribunal shall be composed of three (3) arbitrators who shall be appointed by the Chairman of the Royal Arbitration Institute of the Stockholm Chamber of Commerce.

The arbitration process will be more formal than ordinary negotiation between the parties (which may be represented by attorneys), but it will be less formal than court proceedings.

- **Subcontract closeout Checklist**

Outputs

The following outputs result from subcontract administration:

- *Documentation:* Documentation is essential to provide proof of performance, management of changes, justification for claims, and evidence in the unlikely event of litigation.

The most important documentation is the official copy of the contract, contract modifications, and conformed working copies of the contract. Other important forms of documentation include the following items:

☐ *External and internal correspondence:* All subcontract correspondence should be electronically maintained by the contract manager in a central, chronological reading file, with separate data files for external and internal correspondence. Each piece of correspondence should be dated and assigned a file number. The project manager or subcontract manager should initial and date each piece of correspondence to acknowledge that it was read. Ideally, only one person should be authorized to correspond regarding contractual aspects with the other party to the contract. However, if more than one person on the project team is authorized to correspond with the other contract party, copies of all correspondence must be sent to the subcontract manager for filing. All mail, e-mail, or faxes requiring an answer must be addressed promptly, preferably in writing; this is a fundamental rule of effective subcontract administration.

☐ *Meeting minutes:* Minutes should be recorded for all meetings between the subcontractor and the prime contractor. The minutes should state the date, time, and location of the meeting and identify all attendees by name, company or organization, and title. They should describe all issues discussed, decisions made, questions unresolved, and action items assigned. Copies of the minutes should be provided to each attendee and to others interested in the meeting but unable to attend. Minutes of internal meetings must be kept only for purposes of project management, not for contract management.

☐ *Progress reports:* Progress reports should be electronically filed chronologically, by subject. The project manager and subcontract manager should initial and date each progress report to acknowledge that they have read it and are aware of its contents.

☐ *Project diaries:* On large projects, the project manager and subcontract manager should keep a daily diary, in which they record significant events of the day. They should update their diaries at the end of each workday. The entries should describe events in terms of who, what, when, where, and how. Preferably, the diary should be kept in a perfect-bound book with prenumbered pages or electronically in a shared-data file.

A diary supplements memory and aids in recalling events. A diary is also useful as an informal project history when a new project manager or contract manager must take over. It can be of great assistance in preparing, negotiating, and settling claims or in the event of litigation. However, a diary may become evidence in court proceedings, so a diarist should be careful to record only facts, leaving out conclusions, speculations about motives, and personal opinions about people or organizations.

☐ *Telephone logs:* Another useful aid to memory is a telephone log, which is a record of all incoming and outgoing calls. It identifies the date and time of each call, whether it was incoming or outgoing, and if outgoing, the number called. It lists all parties to the call and includes a brief notation about the discussion.

☐ *Photographs and videotapes:* When physical evidence of conditions at the site of performance is important, a photographic or videotape record can be helpful. This record will greatly facilitate communication and will provide an excellent description of the exact nature of the site conditions. Whenever a contract involves physical labor, the project manager, subcontract manager, or other on-site representative should have a camera and film available for use.

The purpose of documentation is to record facts and reduce reliance on human memory. Efforts to maintain documentation must be thorough and consistent.

- *Subcontract changes:* As a result of changes in the prime contractors' needs, changes in technologies, and other changes in the marketplace, prime contractors need flexibility in their subcontracts. Thus changes are inevitable. Subcontractors must realize that changes are not bad, that they are in fact good, because changes are often an opportunity to sell more products or services.

- *Payment:* Cash is important—subcontractors want their money as quickly as possible. Prime contractors should seek product or service discounts for early payments. Likewise, subcontractors should improve their accounts receivable management and enforce late payment penalties.

- *Completion of work:* This last step is the actual accomplishment by the subcontractor of the prime contractor's requirement for products, services, systems, or solutions.

§ 7:3 Step 8: Conduct performance management

Observing, collecting information, and measuring progress will provide a basis for comparing actual achievement to planned achievement. Generally, observing and collecting information cover three categories of concerns: cost control, schedule control, and compliance with specifications and statements of work. Cost control and schedule control are usually integrated; the latter category is often addressed in quality assurance and control. However, a fourth category—compliance with paperwork requirements, that is, the administrative aspects of performance—is recommended. Observation in this area may be direct or indirect.

Direct Observation

Direct observation means personal, physical observation. The project manager, subcontract manager, or a representative is physically present at the site of the work during its performance to see how it is progressing. This approach is practical when the work is physical in nature and performed at a limited number of sites. Construction projects, for example, are good candidates for direct observation.

Direct observation by the project manager or subcontract manager is of limited use, however, if the work is largely intellectual in nature or if it is too complex for physical inspection alone to provide enough information to measure progress. In such cases, direct observation must be supplemented with or replaced by indirect observation.

Indirect Observation

Indirect observation includes testing, progress reports from many observers, and technical reviews and audits. Indirect observation is appropriate whenever direct observation would provide insufficient or ambiguous information. For example, determining by personal observation whether, at a given point in time, actual project costs are greater than, equal to, or less than budgeted costs would be difficult. Likewise, for projects involving an intellectual effort, such as system design, personal observations at the offices where the work is performed are unlikely to reveal whether the work is on, ahead of, or behind schedule.

In these circumstances, the project manager and subcontract manager must devise an indirect way to collect information. For some small, noncritical subcontracts, a telephone call may be all that is necessary to find out whether everything is proceeding according to plan. For large, complex subcontracts, however, the project manager or subcontract manager may require extensive reports, regular progress meetings, formal testing, and technical reviews and audits.

Sometimes a subcontract will specify such requirements, as in the following excerpt from a clause in a consultant agreement:

Reports

Consultant shall provide ABC Company with monthly progress reports during the term of this Agreement, describing the status of the work, and shall participate in monthly status review meetings with ABC Company, at such times and locations reasonably specified by ABC Company. Additional meetings will be held if reasonably requested by either party.

Note that the clause does not describe specific information that must be included in the monthly report to describe the status of the work, so the subcontractor may determine the information to be provided and its format. If the project manager or subcontract manager has specific information requirements, they should be described in the subcontract.

Reports

Generally, indirect observations are presented in reports that may be written or oral and may include raw data, informational summaries, analyses, conclusions, or a combination thereof. In the "Reports" clause, the monthly report is likely to be a collection of statements describing the subcontractor's conclusions about the work's status. The conclusions may or may not be supported by raw data and an account of the subcontractor's analysis. Often, this kind of report is adequate; other times, it is not.

Progress meetings are simply oral reports of progress. They have some advantages and some disadvantages. Listeners are able to ask questions about the information, analyses, and conclusions reported and have discussions with the reporter. However the listeners may not have time during the meeting to ponder the information provided and make their own analyses before the meeting ends.

Reports rarely provide real-time data. They do not describe how things are now; rather they provide a picture of some past point in time. How old the data are will depend on the nature and frequency of the report and on the reporter's capabilities. A cost and schedule performance report that is submitted on July 1 and depends on accounting data may actually describe cost and schedule status as of May 30, depending on the capabilities of the subcontractor's accounting system.

Reported conclusions about project status are valid only if the information on which they are based is accurate and the analyst is competent, realistic, and honest. Subcontractors are renowned for their optimism during the period before a crisis emerges. Facts can be presented in ways that permit almost any conclusion to be drawn from them.

In deciding to rely wholly or in part on reports (including meetings), the project manager or subcontract manager also must decide what information each report must contain. Following are some issues that should be addressed:

- What aspects of performance should the report address?
- What information should the report include—conclusions about performance, analyses, raw information, or some combination thereof?
- How frequently must the report be submitted and at what points in time?
- What is the cut-off point ("as of" date) for information to be included in the report?
- In what format should the report be submitted?
- To whom should the report be submitted, and to whom should copies be sent?

Identification and Analysis of Performance Variances

Observed and collected information about project performance must be analyzed to determine whether the project is proceeding as planned. The analyst compares actual performance to performance goals to determine whether any variances exist. An analyst who discovers a variance between actual and expected performance must determine several things: Is it significant? What was its cause? Was it a one-time failure, or is it a continuing problem? What type of corrective action would be most effective?

Variance analysis must be timely, particularly when the information is obtained through reports. That information is already old by the time it is received. Delays in analyzing its significance may allow poor performance to deteriorate further, perhaps beyond hope of effective corrective action. Acting promptly is particularly important during the early phases of subcontract performance, when corrective action is likely to have the greatest effect.

It is not uncommon for project managers and subcontract managers to collect reams of information that sit in their in-baskets and file cabinets, never put to use. When a project has gone badly, a review of information in the project files frequently shows that there were warning signs— reports, meeting minutes, letters, memos—but that they were unnoticed or ignored. Often, several people, perhaps a variety of business managers, share the responsibility for monitoring performance. In these instances, the project manager and subcontract manager must take steps to ensure that those people promptly analyze the information, report their findings, and take corrective action.

Corrective Action

When the project manager and subcontract manager discover a significant variance between actual and expected performance, they must take corrective action if possible. They must identify the cause of the problem and determine a solution that will not only eliminate it as a source of future difficulty, but also correct the effect it has already had, if possible. If the effect cannot be corrected, the parties may need to negotiate a change to the subcontract, with compensation to the injured party, if appropriate.

Follow-Up

After corrective action has been taken or is under way, the project manager and subcontract manager must determine whether it has had or is having the desired effect. If not, further action may be needed. Throughout this corrective action and follow-up process, the parties must keep each other informed about what is going on. Effective communication between the parties is essential to avoid misunderstandings and disputes when things are not going according to plan. The party taking corrective action must make every effort to let the other party know that it is aware of the problem and is addressing it seriously. Sometimes this step is more important than the corrective action itself.

§ 7:4   Step 9: Manage subcontract changes

With change comes the risk that the parties will disagree on the nature of their obligations to one another. This situation is particularly likely to occur in subcontracts between organizations in which many people on both sides are in frequent contact with one another. These people may make informal, undocumented arrangements that depart from the subcontract terms and conditions. Thus, performance may be at variance with expectations, which can lead to misunderstandings and disputes.

Even when the parties formally agree to make changes, they may disagree about who should bear the burden of the effect on cost and schedule. Changes can affect budgets and schedules in unexpected ways, leading to serious disputes. A risk also exists that a proposal for a formal change may provide one party with an opportunity to renegotiate the entire subcontract based on issues not connected with the change.

Best Practices: Seven Actions to Improve Change Management

These considerations demand careful management of change. Best practices in change control include the following:

- Ensure that only authorized people negotiate or agree to subcontract changes
- Make an estimate of the effect of a change on cost and schedule, and gain approval for any additional expense and time before proceeding with any change
- Notify project team members that they must promptly report (to the project manager or subcontract manager) any action or inaction by the other party to the subcontract that does not conform to the subcontract terms and conditions

- Notify the other party in writing of any action or inaction by that party that is inconsistent with the established subcontract terms and conditions
- Instruct team members to document and report in writing all actions taken to comply with authorized changes and the cost and time required to comply
- Promptly seek compensation for increases in cost or time required to perform, and negotiate claims for such compensation from the other party in good faith
- Document all changes in writing, and ensure that both parties have signed the subcontract; such written documentation should be completed before work under the change begins, if practical.

Managing change means ensuring that changes are authorized, their effect is estimated and provided for, they are promptly identified, the other party is properly notified, compliance and impact are reported, compensation is provided, and the entire transaction is properly documented.

Subcontract Change Clauses

Subcontracts frequently include a clause that authorizes the prime contractor to order the subcontractor to conform with certain changes made at the prime contractor's discretion. Such clauses are called *change clauses*. The following clause is an example:

Changes

ABC Company reserves the right at any time to make changes in the specifications, drawings, samples, or other descriptions to which the products are to conform, in the methods of shipment and packaging, or in the time or place of delivery. In such event, any claim for an adjustment shall be mutually satisfactory to ABC Company and Subcontractor, but any claim by Subcontractor for an adjustment shall be deemed waived unless notice of a claim is made in writing within thirty (30) days following Subcontractor's receipt of such changes. Price increases or extensions of time shall not be binding upon ABC Company unless evidenced by a purchase order change issued by ABC Company. No substitutions of materials or accessories may be made without ABC Company's written consent. No charges for extras will be allowed unless such extras have been ordered in writing by ABC Company and the price agreed upon.

This clause does not expressly tie the amount of the subcontractor's claim to the effect of the change on its cost or time requirements. Moreover, there is no express mention of reductions in price or time. However, the clause does say that any claim must be "mutually satisfactory" to both parties. It is unclear what, if any, legal significance there is in these subtle differences in language.

The clause requires that "notice of a claim" by the subcontractor be made in writing within 30 days of the subcontractor's receipt of the change order.

Documentation of Change

Whenever the parties make a change in the subcontract, it is important that they maintain the integrity of that document as trustworthy evidence of the terms and conditions of their agreement. Logically, a change will add terms and conditions, delete terms and conditions, or replace some terms and conditions with others. Thus, when modifying the subcontract, the parties should decide what words, numerals, symbols, or drawings must be added, deleted, or replaced in the subcontract document.

Parties to a subcontract will often discuss the change they want to make but fail to describe the change in the context of their subcontract document. After a few such changes, the document will no longer accurately describe the current status of their agreement, and the parties may dispute what the current terms really are. Such an occurrence should surprise no one, human communication and memory being what they are.

The best way to avoid this problem is to draft the language of the change carefully in the context of the subcontract document, ensuring that the new language describes the intent of the parties. This action should be taken before making any attempt to estimate the cost and schedule effect of any change or to perform the work. People sometimes argue that expediency demands that the work proceed before reaching agreement on the precise language of the change. However, this practice is likely to create confusion over just what changed and how. If the parties cannot reach agreement on the language of the change in a reasonable time, they probably are not in agreement about the nature of the change and should not proceed.

Modification of the Subcontract Document

One party will have the original copy of the subcontract. The other party will usually have a duplicate original. These originals should remain with the subcontract manager, or in the subcontracts department or legal office.

When parties agree to change the subcontract, they should never alter the original documents. Instead, they should prepare modification documents that describe the subcontract changes. These changes can generally be described in two ways: First, the modification document can include substitute pages in which deleted original language is stricken out and new or replacement language is inserted in italics. Second, minor changes can be described in "pen and ink" instructions that strike out certain words and add others.

Copies of each modification should be distributed promptly to all project team members who have a copy of the original document. The project manager, subcontract manager, and other key team members should maintain a personal conformed working copy of the subcontract. This copy should be kept in a loose-leaf binder or electronic database so that pages can be replaced easily. The conformed working copy should be altered as necessary to reflect the current status of the agreement between the parties. Changes should be incorporated promptly. Each team member should always keep the conformed working copy readily available and bring it to meetings. The subcontract manager should periodically check to ensure that each team member's conformed working copy is up-to-date.

Effect of the Change on Price and Schedule

After the parties are in precise agreement as to how the subcontract was modified, they should try to estimate the cost and schedule impact of the change. They can do this independently, but the most effective approach is to develop the estimate together, as a team, working out the details and their differences in the process. If the parties are open and honest with one another, this approach can save time and give them greater insight into the real effect of the change on cost and schedule. A well-developed work breakdown structure and project schedule graphic can be of enormous value to this process. Work may proceed based either on an estimate of the cost and schedule impact, with a limit on the parties' obligations, or on a firm-fixed adjustment.

If the parties work out their estimates independently (the traditional approach), an agreement will entail a certain amount of bargaining. This approach can lead to time-consuming haggling and even to deadlock, and such delays can be costly when a change is needed during performance.

Another approach is for the parties to agree that the subcontractor can proceed with the work as changed and submit a claim later. This method can spell trouble for both parties, however, particularly if the adjustments are unexpectedly high. For the prime contractor, it can mean unpleasant surprises about the effect on prices and schedules for changed work. For the subcontractor, it can mean a dismayed prime contractor and delays in settling claims. For both, it can mean a damaged relationship. Working out the cost and schedule impact before committing to the change is better for both parties.

If the subcontractor must proceed with the work before the change can be fully negotiated, the parties should agree to limits on their mutual obligations in relation to the change. It is common practice for parties to agree on cost and schedule ceilings when work must begin before agreement is complete. Obviously, such limits should be documented in writing.

Authorization of Performance Under the Change

After the parties have agreed to the change and to either an estimate of the impact on cost and schedule or a final price adjustment, the prime contractor should provide the subcontractor with written authorization to proceed with the work as changed. The easiest way to accomplish this objective is to prepare, sign, and distribute a modification document. If this approach will take too long, a letter or other form of written documentation will suffice. The authorization should include a description of the change, its effective date, and a description of any limits on the obligations of the parties.

Submission, Negotiation, and Resolution of Claims

If price and schedule adjustments are not negotiated before authorizing performance under the change, the parties must negotiate such matters after performance. As a rule, the prime contractor should try to limit any price adjustments to the cost increases caused by the change, plus reasonable allowances for overhead and profit, and any additional time required to perform the work as changed. However, if the change reduces the cost or time of performance, the prime contractor should seek a reduction in price or schedule.

The project manager and subcontract manager should keep detailed records of all costs incurred in complying with changes. They must document the effect of changes on the time required to perform. The party submitting the claim should be able to make a reasonable demonstration of a cause-and-effect relationship between the change and the increased or decreased cost and time requirements. Ideally, the parties will have reached an advance agreement about the nature and extent of claim documentation. The objective of negotiation should be to seek a reasonable settlement that will fairly compensate the subcontractor for performing additional work or fairly reduce the prime contractor's price when work is deleted.

Effective Resolution of Claims and Disputes

The inherent shortcomings of language as a medium of communication, the organizational nature of the subcontracting process, and the dynamic nature of subcontract relationships all contribute to the potential for disagreements between the parties. In fact, like changes, disagreements are virtually inevitable. They should be expected as a normal part of subcontract management. The larger and more complex the project, the greater the potential for misunderstanding and disagreement.

However, the parties must not allow disagreements and disputes to prevent the execution of the subcontract. They must commit themselves to resolving disputes that will arise between them in an amicable way. Although claims and disputes cannot be avoided, they can be resolved effectively, fairly, and without rancor and litigation. Experienced parties to a subcontract will anticipate claims and disputes and recognize that they do not necessarily indicate incompetence or ill will but, rather, reflect the fact that human foresight, planning, and performance are imperfect.

Professional subcontract managers understand that subcontract disputes must be resolved dispassionately. They also recognize that personalities may affect disputes. But they know that the objective is final disposition in an inexpensive, expeditious, and less formal manner, before disputes fester and infect the contractual relationship.

Each party to the subcontract has the power to litigate if it believes it has been wronged. Ultimately a losing proposition for all involved, litigation is costly and time consuming, and its results are uncertain. Negotiation and arbitration are preferable to litigation, and the parties to the subcontract should strive to use those techniques to the fullest extent practical.

§ 7:5   Step 10: Execute subcontract closeout

A subcontract can end in one of three ways: successful performance, mutual agreement, or breach of subcontract. Most subcontracts end by successful performance. However, under some circumstances, the parties may agree to end their subcontract even though the original objectives were not met. They may reach this agreement through negotiation or arbitration. In a breach of subcontract, one or both of the parties fail to keep their promises; this could result in arbitration or litigation. Subcontract closure by mutual agreement or breach of subcontract is called *subcontract termination.*

Subcontract closeout refers to verifying that all administrative matters are concluded on a subcontract that is otherwise physically complete. In other words, the subcontractor has delivered the required supplies or performed the required services, and the prime contractor has inspected and accepted the supplies or services.

Many subcontractors have a policy that their subcontract manager sign a subcontract completion statement confirming that all administrative actions were performed. Standard times for closing out a subcontract vary depending on many factors.

Occasionally, subcontracts take on lives of their own. For instance, "administrative convenience," "extensions of time" or "additional goods and services" are often added to an existing agreement that may have been completely executed by the subcontractor. Closing out the completed subcontract and opening a new one may be more appropriate in such cases, especially when new or different terms and conditions might lead to confusion.

Subcontract closeout includes the following actions:

- *Completion of work:* A subcontract is physically complete when one of two events has occurred:
  - ☐ All required supplies or services are delivered or performed, inspected, and accepted, and all existing options were exercised or have expired
  - ☐ A subcontract completion notice was issued by one party to the other
- *Subcontract documentation:* The purpose of closeout is to ensure that no further administrative action is necessary on the subcontract. Part of this task is to check that all paperwork was submitted. The following forms, reports, and payments may be outstanding after a subcontract is physically complete:

  For the prime contractor—
  - ☐ Closeout report
  - ☐ Certificate of completion or conformance
  - ☐ Subcontractor's release of claims

  For the subcontractor—
  - ☐ Closeout report
  - ☐ Proof of prime contractor's final payment
  - ☐ Release of performance bonds and letter of credit
- *Termination notice* (for termination only): A written or oral notification to cancel the subcontract due to cause or default of subcontract, or for convenience, is issued in the event of subcontract termination.
- *Compliance verification:* Administrative tasks, incidental to subcontract performance, may have to be accomplished before closing out the file. Final payment cannot be authorized until the subcontractor has accomplished all administrative tasks, such as—
  - ☐ Return, or other disposition, of prime contractor-furnished property
  - ☐ Proper disposition of intellectual property
  - ☐ Settlement of subcontracts
  - ☐ Fulfillment of procedural requirements of termination proceedings (for termination only)
- *Subcontract documentation:* Several types of documentation must be dealt with at this time:

☐ *Outstanding claims or disputes:* Some issues related to basic subcontract performance may not be resolved, and the prime contractor may not have raised some issues. All outstanding issues must be addressed at this time. To avoid reopening a closed file, some subcontractors make a standard practice of requesting a signed statement from the prime contractor that all subcontract terms and conditions were met. Some unscrupulous prime contractors have attempted to coerce subcontractors into abandoning outstanding claims in return for getting paid amounts that are not in dispute. Such actions are bad faith on the part of the prime contractor.

☐ *Payments:* Final payments or outstanding underpayment should be collected by the subcontractor. The prime contractor's payment office should make payment based on the subcontractor's invoice and its receipt of a receiving report. On more complex requirements, subcontract managers generally have a more active role in these tasks. Underpayment can be the result of many factors, including liquidated damages, adjustments after an audit, and retroactive price reductions.

☐ *Files:* The project manager or subcontract manager must keep a log of closed-out files containing information, such as the date the file was closed out, date the file was transferred physically to a storage center, location of the storage center, and filing location provided by the storage facility. Some information in subcontract files must be kept for a certain number of years. Such information should be specified in the subcontract.

☐ *Subcontract completion statement:* The subcontract manager should prepare a subcontract completion statement.

- *Subcontract closeout checklist:* A checklist can be a useful tool during subcontract closeout.
- *Termination* (for termination only): Termination is the administrative process exercising a party's contractual right to discontinue performance completely or partially under a subcontract. The three types of terminations are termination for cause or default, termination by mutual agreement (for convenience), and no-cost settlement. (See "Termination Types" later in this chapter for further discussion.)
- *Documented lessons learned:* At the completion of each subcontract, the project manager, subcontract manager, and project team should jointly develop a lessons-learned summary, which should describe the major positive and negative aspects of the subcontract. The lessons-learned summary focuses on sharing best practices with other company project teams, warning others of potential problems, and suggesting methods to mitigate the risks effectively to ensure success.

Termination Types

Termination with respect to a subcontract refers to an ending before the closure of the anticipated term of the subcontract. The termination may be by mutual agreement or may be by one party's exercising its remedies due to the other party's omission or failure to perform a contractual or subcontract law duty (default).

Termination by Mutual Agreement

Both parties may agree at any time that they do not wish to be bound by the subcontract and terminate their respective rights and obligations stemming from the subcontract.

Termination for Cause or Default

The right to terminate a subcontract may originate from either the general principles of subcontract law or the express terms of the subcontract. Subcontracts may be terminated for default for the following reasons:

- *Failure to tender conforming supplies or services:* If the subcontractor fails, or is unable, to cure a nonconforming tender, the subcontractor is in default and the subcontract can be terminated or other remedial action can be taken.
- *Failure to complete performance substantially within the time specified in the subcontract:* Usually, the prime contractor does not consider or have the legal right of termination for default actions when only minor corrective work remains on the subcontract.
- *Repudiation of the subcontract by the subcontractor:* A repudiation, or anticipatory breach, occurs when a subcontractor or prime contractor clearly indicates to the other party that it cannot or will not perform on the subcontract. Examples indicating that an anticipatory repudiation may exist include a letter stating an intention of nonperformance or job abandonment.
- *Failure to perform any other terms of the subcontract:* A failure to comply with bonding requirements, progress-schedule submission requirements, or fraud statutes would constitute a failure to perform other subcontract terms.

Although authority to terminate may be expressly provided to both parties, subcontract managers must exercise this authority in good faith based on conditions of the termination clause or a material breach of subcontract terms. The decision is highly discretionary, based on the business judgment of the subcontract manager and business advisors.

Factors to be considered before terminating a subcontract for default include—

- Subcontract terms and conditions and applicable laws and regulations
- Specific failure of the prime contractor or subcontractor and the excuses made by the breaching party for such failure
- Availability from other sources
- Urgency of the need and time that would be required by other sources as compared with the time in which completion could be obtained from the current subcontract
- Degree of essentially of the subcontractor, such as unique subcontractor capabilities
- Prime contractor's availability of funds to finance repurchase costs that may prove to be uncollectible from the defaulted subcontractor, and the availability of funds to finance termination costs if the default is determined to be excusable
- Any other pertinent facts and circumstances

Termination for Convenience

It is the right of the parties, usually the prime contractor, to terminate a subcontract unilaterally when completing the subcontract is no longer in the prime contractor's best interest. This has long been recognized in U.S. government subcontracts, and the consequences are defined by law. This type of termination of government subcontracts has been the subject of many U.S. court and legal decisions. In U.S. government subcontracts, the prime contractor has the right to terminate without cause and limit the subcontractor's recovery to the—

- Price of work delivered and accepted
- Costs incurred on work done but not delivered
- Profit on work done but not delivered if the subcontract incurred no loss
- Costs of preparing the termination settlement proposal

In commercial subcontracts, the concept of prime contractor's best interest is not used. Termination occurs only as a result of default due to breach of subcontract or due to mutual agreement. Recovery of anticipated profit is generally precluded.

No-Cost Settlement

Used without normal termination procedures, no-cost settlement can be considered when—

- The subcontractor has indicated it will accept it
- No prime subcontractor property was furnished under the subcontract
- No outstanding payments or debts are due the subcontractor, and no other obligations are outstanding
- The product or service can be readily obtained elsewhere

Note that termination for convenience is not a commercial contracting concept. Thus, if a subcontract contains a statement allowing parties to terminate the subcontract unilaterally, the parties should exercise extreme caution in defining specific remedies and consequences of such action.

Best Practices: 30 Actions to Improve Results

Prime contractor and Subcontractor

- Read and analyze the subcontract
- Develop a subcontract administration plan
- Appoint a subcontract manager to ensure that your organization does what it proposed to do
- Develop and implement subcontract administration policies or guidelines for your organization
- Comply with subcontract terms and conditions
- Maintain effective communication and control
- Control subcontract changes with a proactive change management process
- Resolve claims and disputes promptly and dispassionately
- Use negotiation or arbitration, not litigation, to resolve disputes
- Develop a work breakdown structure to assist in planning and assigning work
- Conduct preperformance conferences
- Measure, monitor, and track performance

- Manage the invoice and payment process
- Report on progress internally and externally
- Identify variances between planned versus actual performance
- Be sure to follow up on all corrective actions
- Appoint authorized people to negotiate subcontract changes and document the authorized representatives in the subcontract
- Enforce subcontract terms and conditions
- Provide copies of the subcontract to all affected organizations
- Maintain conformed copies of the subcontract
- Understand the effects of change on cost, schedule, and quality
- Document all communication—use telephone and correspondence logs
- Prepare internal and external meeting minutes
- Prepare subcontract closeout checklists
- Ensure completion of work
- Document lessons learned and share them throughout your organization
- Communicate, communicate, communicate!
- Clarify team member roles and responsibilities
- Provide leadership support to the team throughout the subcontract management process
- Ensure that leadership understands the subcontract management process and how it can improve business relationships from beginning to end.

§ 7:6 Straight talk: Suggestions for significant improvement

The primary focus of nearly every subcontract management organization is get deals signed. With the majority of subcontract management resources and talent, from both the prime contractors and subcontractors, are dedicated to preparing solicitations, bids or proposals, reviewing bids or proposals, and negotiating and awarding subcontracts. Unfortunately, in both the public and private business sectors too little time and resources are allocated to properly manage subcontracts after they have been awarded. As a result, subcontract administration is often either poorly performed by individuals not properly trained, not performed at all, or only performed by exception, i.e. when a problem arises someone must be assigned to fix the problem. Those organizations which do have full-time subcontract administrators often have them heavily overbooked often managing far too many subcontracts for them to provide sufficient proactive subcontract management. Most organizations do not really appreciate the value-added of professional subcontract administration, via timely subcontract interpretation, effective subcontract change management, timely subcontract invoicing and payment, effective dispute resolution, and efficient subcontract closeout.

§ 7:7 Summary

The subcontract administration and closeout phase is simply a matter of both parties doing what they promised to do. The on-going challenge is maintaining open and effective communication, timely delivery of quality products and services, responsive corrective actions to problems, and compliance with all other agreed-on terms and conditions. After the project has been successfully completed, proper procedures are put into place to close out the subcontract officially. In these instances where the subcontract is terminated due to cause of default, action is taken to legally cancel the subcontract.

Remember the power of precedent. Your organization is always evaluated based on your past performance and the precedents it sets. Your subcontract management actions taken years ago affect your organization's reputation today. Likewise, the subcontract management actions that you take today form your organization's reputation for tomorrow.

§ 7:8   Questions to consider

1. How well does your organization staff the right quality and quantity of resources to perform subcontract administration?
2. Who has the lead role for subcontract administration and closeout in your organization?
3. How well does your organization manage subcontract changes?
4. How well does your organization manage subcontract closeouts?

Chapter 8

U.S. Government Contracting And Subcontracting: Policies, Regulations, & Reviews

---

KeyCite[R]: Cases and other legal materials listed in KeyCite Scope can be researched through the KeyCite service on Westlaw[R]. Use KeyCite to check citations for form, parallel references, prior and later history, and comprehensive citator information, including citations to other decisions and secondary materials.

---

§ 8:1   Introduction

Realizing the significant increases in U.S. federal government spending during the past decade, and the huge spending spree of new Obama administration, U.S. Government contracting and subcontracting is now under intense scrutiny. In this chapter we will discuss: the Obama administration effect on government contractors; Contractor Purchasing System Reviews (CPSRs); and government audits and other reviews. Clearly, the opportunities and risks involved with serving as a government prime contractor and/or subcontractor are rising to a new level. Thus it is imperative for prime contractors and subcontractors to understand the U.S. government's key acquisition policies, regulations, reviews, audits, and what it takes to ensure compliance.

§ 8:2   Preparing for change: The Obama administration effect on government contractors

With the new Obama administration, government contractors are already seeing substantial changes, with increased focus on performance results, controlling costs, competition, transparency, oversight, and ethics/compliance programs. While the Bush administration largely focused on

making Government agencies more accountable, the new Obama administration is heavily focused on industry, primarily improving government
contractor performance. For example, both the Democratic Congress and
the new administration perceives there has been too much coddling of
government contractors, especially large defense contractors. To address
this concern, the heavily Democratic congress has significantly increased
funding for government contractor audits and special investigations to be
conducted by the Defense Contract Audit Agency (DCAA), Government Accountability Office (GAO), Defense Contract Management Agency (DCMA),
and various department Inspector General (IG) offices. "Toward the end,
the 2008 Defense Appropriations Act required new audits of coalition
logistical support and reconstruction contracts. Along the same lines, the
final report by the congressional Commission on Wartime Contracting due
in the summer of 2010 can be expected to highlight perceived instances of
waste and mismanagement.[1]

Controlling Costs and Increasing Competition on Government Contracts

During the presidential campaign, Senator Obama announced a number
of initiatives regarding the importance of controlling costs and increasing
competition on government contracts. One suggested approach was to prohibit contractors with tax delinquencies from receiving government
contracts. Also, both Senators Obama and McCain supported the reduction
or even elimination of cost-plus contracts in favor of fixed-price contracts,
in an effort to control the costs of large complex programs. One reform that
already made it to the 2009 Defense Appropriations Act requires sole
source awards based on "unusual and compelling urgency" to be limited in
duration but in no event to exceed one year. Complementing this requirement, the Obama administration has required all agencies to separately
justify their non-competitive awards to the Office of Management and
Budget, Office of Federal Procurement Policy. The Obama administration
has announced an across the board initiative to increase competition on all
contracts, with the emphasis on fixed-price contracts. It is expected the
Obama administration will reinforce the need and value of performance-
based contracting, with the appropriate and intelligent use of contract
incentives and award fees.[2]

In an effort to support the new Obama administration the Government
Accountability Office (GAO) has created a Web site, http://www.gao.gov/tra
nsition_2009, which includes a list of 13 urgent issues facing the new
administration and the 111th Congress. The GAO web site lists numerous
opportunities to cut government costs, such as improving the Department
of Defense weapon systems acquisition process, applying best practices to
strategic sourcing, promoting competition for contracts, improving the use

---

[Section 8:2]

[1]Garrett, Gregory A., and McDonald, Pete "Preparing for Change: The Obama
Administration Effect on Government Contractors," NCMA, Contract Management
Magazine, February 2009.

[2]Garrett, Gregory A., and McDonald, Pete "Preparing for Change: The Obama
Administration Effect on Government Contractors," Note 1, NCMA, Contract Management
Magazine, February 2009.

of award fees and incentives, improving the Department of Homeland Security acquisition management, improving oversight of oil and gas royalties, reducing improper federal payments, and owning instead of leasing property.

The Need for Transparency

Another new Obama administration reform which is widely affecting government contractors is the movement toward "greater transparency." In brief, this means more government oversight of contractors, both on an individual and organizational basis, via the increased focus on the potential for Personal Conflicts of Interest (PCI) and Organizational Conflicts of Interest (OCI). Plus, greater transparency will include more reviews and audits by government agencies on government contractors, including: Contractor Purchasing Systems Reviews (CPSRs), Earned Value Management Systems (EVMS); Integrated Baseline Reviews (IBRs); Cost Estimating and Accounting System reviews; Government Property (GP) management systems reviews; DCAA audits; IG inspections; and so on. Effective December 21, 2008, there are new requirements for government contractors contained within the Federal Acquisition Regulation (FAR). The new regulations require government contractors to do the following:

1. provide timely disclosure to the government of certain violations of criminal law, False Claims Act violations and any significant overpayment by the government;
2. have a written code of business ethics and conduct and provide education and training to its employees; and
3. establish specific internal controls to prevent and detect improper conduct in connection with government contracts.

For this reason, compliance programs will become even more important for government contractors.[3]

What to Expect Going Forward

Apart from the heightened scrutiny for all government contractors, we expect an intense focus on major defense and homeland security contractors. Clearly, defense and homeland security spending is likely to experience significant programmatic changes as the new Obama administration addresses domestics concerns, as well as the global financial crisis. Accordingly, defense and homeland security programs will be forced to adjust to budget realignments and forces structure trade-offs (some programs may be cancelled outright).

Moreover, the Department of Defense and Department of Homeland Security will not be the only agencies to undergo internal competition for diminished budget resources. In short, there will probably be an increase in terminations for convenience, especially in the Departments of Defense, Homeland Security, Energy, and NASA where the majority of funding is spent acquiring products, services, and integrated solutions from government contractors.

In addition, we expect the Obama administration to focus on rebuilding

---

[3]Garrett, Gregory A., and McDonald, Pete "Preparing for Change: The Obama Administration Effect on Government Contractors," Note 1, NCMA, Contract Management Magazine, February 2009.

the federal government's workforce, thus, reducing the practice of competitive sourcing which is currently implemented via the Office of Management and Budget (OMB) Circular A-76. Further, the Obama administration has already requested the Office of Management and Budget, Office of Federal Procurement Policy (OFPP) to evaluate the definition of the term "inherently governmental function" to possibly include key acquisition workforce functions such as: acquisition planning, strategic sourcing, source selection, contract administration, project planning, system engineering, cost/price/analysis, contract auditing, and program management. Currently, tens of thousands of government contractors are filling these key acquisition roles, because the government does not have the expertise required to get the needed work accomplished. Therefore, we expect the Obama administration to focus on significantly increasing the hiring, training, and retaining of federal government employees across the civilian service system, with special emphasis on key acquisition positions which perform inherently governmental functions.[4]

Where is the money being spent?

The Obama administration and the U.S. Congress have already, via the 2009 American Recovery and Reinvestment Act $787 billion spending law, authorized huge increases in funding for numerous U.S. Government departments and agencies, including:

- U.S. Department of Education
- U.S. Department of Labor
- U.S. Department of Health & Human Services
- U.S. Department of Housing & Urban Development
- U.S. Department of Energy
- Environmental Protection Agency
- U.S. Department of Transportation
- U.S. Department of State
- Many others[5]

Preparing for the Obama Administration

As the saying goes, "It is best to live in interesting times," clearly the next several years will be very interesting times for government contractors, especially so for major defense contractors. Accordingly, we suggest government contractors focus on the following five actions to prepare for the new Obama administration:

1. Improve performance results on government contracts and programs, especially on-time delivery within budget, and meet or exceed government requirements.
2. Be well prepared for increased government oversight on all business systems, policies, and practices.
3. Increase the use of competition in internal purchasing system and practices;

---

[4]Garrett, Gregory A., and McDonald, Pete "Preparing for Change: The Obama Administration Effect on Government Contractors," Note 1, NCMA, Contract Management Magazine, February 2009.

[5]Federal Procurement Data System, OFPP, Report, Washington, D.C., March 2009.

4. Enhance ethics and compliance programs, especially PCI and OCI aspects; and
5. Improve the education and training of accounting, contract management, pricing, supply chain management, and project/program management personnel to address the requirements and elevated scrutiny from government agencies and Congress.[6]

§ 8:3 Contractor Purchasing System Reviews (CPSRs): regulatory authority and background

Contractor Purchasing System Reviews (CPSRs) are governed by the Federal Acquisition Regulation (FAR) Part 44.3 the contracting officer or Administrative Contracting Officer (ACO) "shall" determine whether a CPSR is needed for a particular prime contractor based on, but not limited to:

- The past performance of the contractor and
- The volume, complexity, and dollar value of its subcontracts

If a contractor's sales to the Government (excluding competitively awarded firm-fixed-price and competitively awarded fixed-price with economic price adjustment contracts and sales of commercial items pursuant to FAR Part 12) are expected to exceed $25 million during the next 12 months, then the ACO must perform a review to determine whether a CPSR is necessary. The term "sales" includes receipts from prime contractors, subcontracts under Government prime contracts, and modifications. Generally, a CPSR is not performed for one specific contract. The head of the agency responsible for contract administration may raise or lower the $25 million review level if it is in the Government's best interest to do so.

In deciding whether to conduct a CPSR, the ACO is going to be assessing the risk posed by the contractor's system. In doing so, the ACO will consider a number of factors:

- The contractor's CPSR history
- How previous CPSR recommendations were addressed (or not)
- Dates of previous CPSRs
- The mix of contracts performed by the contractor
- Direct material and material overhead as a percentage of total sales
- The percentage of total sales represented by Government sales
- Previous DCAA audit reports
- Information obtained from contracting officers and other officials
- Education, training and experience of the contractor's procurement personnel
- The contractor's efforts to conduct internal audits and other types of self-assessments
- The contractor's position in the industry
- Reorganizations, mergers and divestitures
- Significant increase or decreases in sales

Once the initial determination has been made to conduct such a review, the ACO must make a similar determination at least every three years.

---

[6]Federal Procurement Data System, OFPP, Report, Note 1,Washington, D.C., March 2009.

§ 8:4   CPSR's extent of review

A CPSR reviews a prime contractor's purchasing system, but shall not include subcontracts that the contractor awarded in support of Government prime contracts that were competitively awarded firm-fixed price, competitively awarded fixed-price with economic price adjustment, or awarded for commercial items pursuant to FAR Part 12. Special attention shall be given to:

- The degree of price competition obtained by the prime
- Pricing policies and techniques, including methods of obtaining accurate, complete, and current cost or pricing data and certifications as required
- Methods of evaluating a prospective sub's responsibility under FAR Part 9, including methods intended to avoid awarding subcontracts to suspended or debarred entities
- Treatment given to affiliates and other concerns that work closely with the prime
- Policies and procedures relating to small business subcontracting
- Planning, award and post-award management of major subcontracting programs
- Compliance with CAS in awarding subcontracts
- Appropriateness of the types of contracts used
- Management and control systems, including internal audit procedures, to administer progress payments to subs

The government will also look for:

- Non-compliance with public laws
- Non-compliance with regulations
- Non-compliance with prime contract requirements
- Failure to establish sound policies and procedures in subcontracting
- Failure to implement sound business practices

§ 8:5   Effect of an approved purchasing system

If the ACO approves a prime's purchasing system, the approval will list the plant or plants covered by the approval. If an approval is granted, the prime will no longer be required to provide advance notice to the Government in awarding subcontracts under fixed-price contracts, but will still be required to provide advance notice under cost-reimbursement prime contracts. Also, the prime will not be required to obtain the Government's consent to subcontracts in fixed-price contracts and for specified subcontracts in cost-reimbursement contracts. This exemption would not apply to any subcontracts that are under an ACO's "surveillance" pursuant to FAR 44.304.

§ 8:6   Effect of disapproval of the purchasing system

Disapproval means that there are major weaknesses in the contractor's system. Even if a contractor has an approved system, approval can be withdrawn any time the ACO determines that the contractor's system has deteriorated or that withdrawal is necessary to protect the Government's interest. FAR 44.305-3. The regulation stipulates that approval can be withheld or withdrawn when there is a recurring noncompliance with requirements, including, but not limited to:

- Cost or pricing data
- Implementation of CAS
- Advance notification
- Small business subcontracting

The contractor normally will have 15 days in which to develop a plan to address the reasons for disapproval.

Without an approved subcontracting system, a firm will be unable to award a subcontract without obtaining prior approval from the Government. In addition to adding time (and expense) to your company's business processes, there are a variety of other problems that can flow from disapproval, such as:

- Losing out on competitive proposals
- Poor past performance reports
- Disallowance of certain costs paid to subs
- Loss of revenue
- Increased Government oversight
- Increased overhead
- Delayed billings and collections

§ 8:7 How to approach a CPSR

- View it as an opportunity, not as a problem
- Don't be reactive—instead, conduct your own risk assessment to determine how well your company is doing
- Develop new a new processes, policies and procedures where necessary
- Train your procurement staff and your end-users
- Brief upper management on what is at stake and what you are doing
- Make sure your people understand all of the positive things that can come out of a CPSR, especially how it can maintain or improve your relationship with the Government

§ 8:8 U.S. government audits and other reviews, and oversight actions of contractors

One of the distinctive features of federal contracts is the audit clause that gives the contracting officer and the Comptroller General the right to review certain prime contractor books and records. The clause (FAR Subsection 52.215-2) in part states the following:

a. *Examination of costs.* If this is a cost-reimbursement, incentive, time-and-material, labor-hour, or price redeterminable contract, or any combination of these, the prime contractor shall maintain and the contracting officer, or an authorized representative of the contracting officer, shall have the right to examine and audit all records and other evidence sufficient to reflect properly all costs claimed to have been incurred or anticipated to be incurred directly or indirectly in performance of this contract. This right of examination shall include inspection at all reasonable times of the contractor's plants, or parts of them, engaged in performance of the contract

b. *Cost or pricing data.* If the prime contractor has been required to submit cost or pricing data in connection with any pricing action relating to this contract, the contracting officer, or an authorized representative of the contracting officer, in order to evaluate the accuracy, completeness, and currency of the cost or pricing data, shall have the right to examine and audit all of the prime contractor's records, including computations and projections, related to (1) the proposal for the contract, subcontract, or modification; (2) the discussions conducted on the proposal(s), including those related to negotiating; (3) pricing of the contract, subcontract, or modification; or (4) performance of the contract, subcontract or modification.

c. *Comptroller General.* The Comptroller General of the United States, or an authorized representative, shall have access to an the right to examine any of the contractor's directly pertinent records involving transactions related to this contract or a subcontract hereunder.[1]

The federal government contract audit agencies, the largest of which is the Defense Contract Audit Agency (DCAA), are responsible for providing financial and accounting advice to federal government procurement officials. Procurement officials may also call upon agency inspectors general (IGs) or CPA firms under contract to perform this service. The contracting officer may request field pricing support, which includes a government evaluation of any offeror's proposal prior to negotiation of a contract or modification (FAR Subsection 15.404-2). The contract auditor also serves as the contracting officer's representative in the review of prime contractor accounting records and provides advisory comments and recommendations to the contracting officer. While the contract audit opinions are advisory, internal government follow-up procedures have been established to assure appropriate consideration and action taken on audit recommendations.

To provide the contracting officer with financial and accounting advice, the contract auditor performs various reviews, such as the following:

- *Preaward survey.* Financial capability and accounting system surveys are performed to assess the prospective prime contractor's financial soundness, as well as the adequacy of the accounting system to accumulate the type of cost information required by the contract.
- *Forward pricing proposals evaluation.* The contract auditor evaluates cost estimates in the prime contractor's contract-pricing proposal for allocability, reasonableness, and allowability. These government audits may be directed at specific procurement actions or may involve prospective cost rates that may be used to estimate costs on future procurement actions.
- *Postaward review of cost or pricing data.* This is the government's terminology for reviews intended to test compliance with PL 87-653, commonly known as The Truth in Negotiation Act. This legislation states that the prime contractor shall provide the government with accurate, current, and complete cost or pricing data when negotiating

[Section 8:8]

[1]American Institute of Certified Public Accountants, Inc. "Audit & Accounting Guide for Federal Government Contractors," New York, 2008.

contracts subject to PL 87-653. To the extent that the prime contractor does not comply with the provisions, thereby increasing the contract price, the government is entitled to a corresponding price reduction for the so-called "defective pricing."

- *Incurred cost audit.* This government audit focuses on the allowability of direct and indirect costs billed to the government on contracts providing for cost reimbursement or settlement of final prices based on costs incurred.

- *Cost accounting standards compliance and adequacy reviews.* The purpose of the compliance review is to determine whether the prime contractor's accounting practices conform to the standards promulgated by the CASB. The adequacy reviews are designed to determine whether the description of the cost-accounting practices contained in the company's CAS Disclosure Statement is accurate, current, and complete.

- *System reviews.* These audits cover systems related to federal contract pricing, costing, and billing, such as estimating systems, labor reporting systems and billing systems.

- *Terminated contract audits.* When a contract or subcontract is partially or completely terminated, the termination contracting officer shall submit all contractor settlement proposals over $100,000 to the appropriate audit agency for examination and recommendations concerning the allocability, allowability, and reasonableness of costs. (FAR Subpart 49.107).

- *Claim audits.* These audits include evaluations of requests for equitable adjustments and claims to be resolved under the Contract Disputes Act of 1978, as amended (41 U.S.C. 601 to 603).

- *Operations audits and other financial reviews.* Generally, these audits activities involve evaluating those management and operational decisions made by the prime contractor that affect the nature and level of costs being proposed and incurred on government contracts. These reviews usually result in the government auditor providing the company with recommendations on how to improve controls, and the economy and efficiency of prime contractor operations.

In summary, the fundamental purpose of a government contract audit is to determine the allowability (including reasonableness and allocability) of costs contained either in a proposed price or in a statement of costs incurred during contract performance. FAR Part 31 provides the authoritative criteria for making this determination. Furthermore, contracts provide broad access rights, and statutory inspectors general and DCAA have authority to subpoena certain contractor books, records, and other supporting documentation.[2]

Allowability and Allocability of Costs

The concept of allowability of costs is derived primarily form the procurement regulations. For most federal agencies, FAR Part 31 contains the criteria for determining allowability, and many agencies supplement these basic criteria with FAR supplements that specify more precise rules for

---

[2]American Institute of Certified Public Accountants, Inc. "Audit & Accounting Guide for Federal Government Contractors," Note 7, New York, 2008.

the respective agencies. A cost is considered allowable when it is reasonable and allocable and not prohibited by the provisions of FAR or contractual terms and conditions.

For many prime contractors, the standards promulgated by the Cost Accounting Standards Board (CASB) provide the guidance for determining the allocability of costs to government contracts. FAR Part 31 also contains some basic guidance relating to allocability. Once the cost is determined to be allocable, the contract cost principles (FAR Part 31) provide the guidance for identifying which of these costs are eligible for reimbursement. Generally accepted accounting principles (GAAP) apply where FAR or CAS fails to address a specific element of cost.

A significant portion of the contract pricing under negotiated procurements is cost-based. Furthermore, the accounting method used in pricing negotiated contracts is full-absorption costing. Therefore, all allowable and allocable costs ordinarily should be identified in conformity with applicable procedures so that reimbursement may be obtained.

The government does not require prime contractors to restructure their accounting systems to accommodate the full absorption concept. Therefore, memorandum records may be used to make the allocations. For example, some companies do not include general and administrative (G&A) expenses in work-in-process inventory. Prime contractors are permitted to use memorandum records to make the allocation because those costs are allocable and allowable. However, the memorandum records are subject to audit and, therefore, should be reconcilable to the formal accounting records.[3]

Subcontracts Audits

Companies serving as subcontractors, at all tiers, are generally subject to the same terms and conditions that apply to the federal prime contractors. The prime contractor, or higher-tier subcontractor, is responsible for administering the respective subcontracts. This includes performing audits of subcontract prices and compliance with contractual requirements, such as CAS, cost and pricing data, and progress payment provisions.

Understandably, subcontractors are often reluctant to allow prime contractors to review their books and records. The government, in recognizing this sensitivity, may perform these reviews in lieu of the prime contractor. However, the prime contractor still remains contractually liable for its subcontractors' compliance with applicable procurement rules and regulations. The government has the right to reduce the prime contract price for subcontractor violations. The prime contractor is then faced with obtaining indemnification from the subcontractor for losses suffered as a result of the subcontractor's failure to comply with any procurement regulation.

Unique to government contracts is that prime contracts meeting certain dollar thresholds must contain a positive plan for awarding subcontracts to small business concerns (FAR Subpart 19.7). Additionally, the Small

---

[3]American Institute of Certified Public Accountants, Inc. "Audit & Accounting Guide for Federal Government Contractors," Note 7, New York, 2008.

Business Act of 1953, as amended, established direct procurement responsibilities for each procuring agency with socially and economically disadvantaged firms under Section 8(a) of the act. The program is more commonly known as the 8(a) program. Actually, the procuring agency enters a tripartite agreement with the Small Business Administration and the socially and economically disadvantaged firm. These 8(a) procurements are, by definition, negotiated (FAR Subpart 19.8).[4]

Oversight Activities

There are two important oversight functions related to federal government contracting: the Government Accountability Office (GAO) and the Offices of the Inspector General (OIGs). The GAO is an agent of Congress and conducts reviews necessary to evaluate all the activities in the executive departments, including procurement. GAO's focus is to ascertain whether the executive agencies are properly implementing the laws passed by Congress. The GAO's examination authority is granted through the audit and records-negotiation clause (FAR Subsection 52.215-2 paragraph [d]). The OIG's examination authority is derived from the Inspector General Act of 1978, as amended. The OIG operates as an oversight function within the agency for which it was established. In connection with its review of the procurement process, OIG has been granted administrative subpoena authority to assure access to the books and records of government contractors. Note that, for some government agencies, the OIG has contract audit responsibility.[5]

§ 8:9 Summary

In this chapter, we have reviewed the U.S. government's increasing role in establishing new acquisition policies, expanding regulations, conducting reviews, and performing audits on government prime contractors and subcontractors. Specifically, we have reviewed: (1) the Obama administration effect on government contractors; (2) understanding and preparing for Contractor Purchasing System Reviews (CPSR); and (3) understanding the numerous U.S. Government Audits, other reviews, and oversight actions the government may conduct on contractors. To achieve success as a government prime contractor and/or subcontractor you must know the rules of the game, be fully compliant with the U.S. government's laws and regulations, and know how to maximize your opportunity while mitigating the risk of doing business with the government.

§ 8:10 Questions to consider

1. Has your organization been impacted by the Obama administration's new acquisition policies or regulatory changes?
2. How efficient and effective is your organization's purchasing system?
3. Which U.S. government audits have you participated in, either giving and/or receiving?

---

[4]American Institute of Certified Public Accountants, Inc. "Audit & Accounting Guide for Federal Government Contractors," Note 7, New York, 2008.

[5]American Institute of Certified Public Accountants, Inc. "Audit & Accounting Guide for Federal Government Contractors," Note 7, New York, 2008.

Chapter 9

Mitigating the Risk of Litigation Risk

By Robert Burton, Paul Debolt, and Terry Elling[1]

KeyCiteᴿ: Cases and other legal materials listed in KeyCite Scope can be researched through the KeyCite service on Westlawᴿ. Use KeyCite to check citations for form, parallel references, prior and later history, and comprehensive citator information, including citations to other decisions and secondary materials.

---

§ 9:1 Importance of managing litigation risk throughout the procurement lifecycle

Litigation is expensive and time consuming. It is a distraction from a company's core business activities. But litigation is also a risk that each government contractor faces in relationships throughout the supply chain (from subcontractors and vendors to the government), which requires planning and preparation. Too often, government contractors who believe a case will never go to litigation end up struggling to gather their resources for just that eventuality. Had they identified and managed their litigation risk better, beginning as early as contract formation, the company would have been in a dramatically better position to either recover monies owed them or to defend against government claims.

Litigation is extremely expensive compared to other business activities and, except in limited circumstances, a contractor that prevails will not be able to recover its litigation costs.[1] Under the applicable Federal Acquisi-

---

[1]Partners in the Government Contracts practice group at Venable LLP, 575 7th Street NW, Washington DC, 20004 (http://www.venable.com). The authors gratefully acknowledge the assistance of Dismas Locaria and James Chiow, Associates at Venable LLP, in the preparation of this chapter.

[Section 9:1]

[1]For example, a small business may be able to recover some its litigation costs in successfully litigating claims against the federal government at the Board of Contract Appeals or the U.S. Court of Federal Claims under the Equal Access to Justice Act (5 U.S.C. § 504; 28 U.S.C. § 2812). Similarly, a contractor that successfully protests a solicitation or award

tion Regulation (FAR) cost principles, costs incurred in the defense of government claims or the prosecution of claims against the government are unallowable.[2] Similarly, costs incurred in the protest of a government solicitation or contract award are unallowable unless the costs of defending against a protest are incurred pursuant to a written request from the contracting officer.[3]

Litigation is also extremely disruptive to a company's day-to-day business activities. Over the course of a single case, parties will have to collect and produce thousands, if not millions, of pages of documents. In light of the proliferation of the types and amounts of electronic media used by companies, document production can be a very expensive endeavor. Moreover, courts will usually require a company to incur the time and expense associated with the production of relevant electronic media (*e.g.*, e-mails, electronic versions of documents, spreadsheets, databases, program management files).

In addition to physically producing their documents, parties will be obliged to provide written responses to requests for production of documents, interrogatories and requests for admissions. Further, companies will have to make individuals available for depositions. These depositions may involve individuals that were involved in the day-to-day management of the contract under dispute; the financial people responsible for tracking the programs costs; or even a company's chief executive officer (CEO). Alternatively, an opposing party may request that your company designate an individual to speak on behalf of the corporation on a host of topics. Finally, to resolve a suit successfully, a company must undertake a substantial amount of factual development and analysis. This fact gathering and analysis focuses on past problems rather than present or future business operations. Litigation is very rarely a profit center.

As a result, before entering into a business relationship with the government or another contractor, companies must assess the risk associated with the relationship. Typically, there are at least three types of risk that must be assessed in considering the possibility of litigation that may arise in the course of government procurements (both before and after award): (1) performance risk; (2) contractual risk; and (3) financial risk.

- **Performance Risk** is the risk that contract award or performance will be adversely affected if a contractor fails to anticipate potential litigation. For example, failing to document discussions with the government concerning a contractor's understanding of a statement of work (and to preserve the documentation) may undercut the contractor's ability to provide supplies or services in the manner in which it intended if the government subsequently disagrees and claims an understanding that is different from the contractor's.

- **Contractual Risk** is the risk that a contractor's rights and duties under the terms of its contract or subcontract will be adversely

---

to the Government Accountability Office may be able to recover its fees and costs under the Competition in Contracting Act (31 U.S.C. § 3554(c)). Recovery of litigation costs even in these settings, however, may be subject to caps on hourly rates and other limitations and, in practice, contractors rarely recover all of their costs associated with litigation.

[2]FAR 31.205-47(f)(1).

[3]FAR 31.205-47(f)(8).

affected. Failing to confirm or correct the contractor's understanding of a solicitation or a contract's scope of work and terms will usually result in any doubts being resolved in favor of the government as the contractor usually bears the risk of confirming these matters prior to award or, at a minimum, prior to problems arising, as a matter of law.

- **Financial Risk** is the risk that a contractor will not optimize its profit or suffer unanticipated losses. Failing to anticipate potential pre- and post-award litigation may result in a contractor losing its ability to protest or defend a contact award, or to successfully prosecute a claim that arises in the course of performance. All of these possibilities may result in lost revenue and profit.

Not assessing litigation risk and having the right policies and practices in place will compromise your chances of success if you are forced to pursue or defend a bid protest or claim. Thus, these risks must be addressed at the outset of every contractual relationship.

§ 9:2 Managing risk during the formation of a government contract

The time that it makes the most sense to identify risk and take affirmative steps to manage the identified risks is prior to contract award, when a contractor's ability to shape or clarify a contract's terms and conditions is greatest. However, to fully and accurately identify the risks in a solicitation, a contractor must have a thorough understanding of the type of procurement as well as the scope of the project.

a. Determining and Mitigating Risk in Contractual Terms

To limit risk at the contract's outset, contractors must have a thorough understanding of the contract type.[1] The two types of contracts predominantly used by the government are either fixed-price or cost-reimbursement contracts. Within each of these categories, there are a number of variations that may impact the ultimate risk borne by the contractor.[2] Pursuant to a fixed-price contract, the contractor bears the risk of performing the contract at the fixed price the government has agreed to pay. In contrast, the government bears the risk of performance under a cost-reimbursement contract.

Irrespective of the procurement vehicle used, contractors must read the solicitations and ensure that they understand the project's scope of work. Frequently, many performance problems arise because the contractor failed to fully analyze the scope of the contract. Prior to submitting a proposal or signing a contract, contractors should ask themselves:

[Section 9:2]

[1]Contractors must be very careful of agreeing to one type of contract and entering into a different type of contract with its subcontractors that may impact its overall ability to manage the contract. For example, a company that enters into a firm-fixed price contract with the government and then, in turn, enters into cost-reimbursement or time and material contracts with its subcontractors may find that it will be unable to control subcontractor costs to the extent necessary to maintain profitability on the prime contract.

[2]Insert discussion of varying types of contracts; fixed-price contracts with economic price adjustment, fixed-price incentive contracts, fixed-price contracts with price-redetermination; firm-fixed price level of effort contracts.

- What does the contract require us to do?
- Who will judge whether we successfully meet the terms of the contract?
- Does the individual that will evaluate our performance have a stake in the outcome of the contract?[3]
- What standards will the individual use to determine whether our performance was successful?
- What are the terms of the contract?
- What contract terms have been incorporated by reference?
- To the extent a dispute arises, what law will apply to the resolution of the dispute and what forum will handle the resolution of the dispute, *i.e.*, a court or an arbitrator?
- What notice must the company give the other party if a dispute arises under the contract?
- If a dispute arises, does the contractor have an obligation to continue performance?
- Does the contract obligate the contractor to indemnify my company for the violation of a patent? Does my company have to indemnify the government or the other contractor if the company violates a patent?
- What type of warranty will the company receive or be required to provide under the contract?
- Are there clauses that must be flowed-down to our subcontractors?
- Are there contract terms that may apply by "operation of law" even if the government failed to include them in the written contract?

Prime contractors can make a number of mistakes at the outset of the contract that potentially increase the risk of performance or that may increase costs or have adverse contractual consequences. For example, government contracts often contain a boilerplate clause such as "this contract is subject to all applicable rules and regulations." In other instances, the contracts incorporate an entire host of regulations and standards by reference. Before signing the contract, a company should expend the effort to determine the regulatory framework under which it will perform the contract. Contractors can mitigate this risk by commenting on or submitting questions.

Subcontractors also make a number of mistakes at the contract's outset. A common mistake occurs when subcontractors fail to analyze all of the terms and conditions that are "flowed down" by the government prime contractor. Today, many large government prime contractors incorporate a very large numbers of FAR, DFARS, and other clauses into virtually all of their subcontracts through incorporating, by reference, a website that lists their standard terms and conditions. Unfortunately, these often detailed

---

[3]This issue can be very problematic in contracts where there are multiple stakeholders that have different policy goals and objectives. For example, under environmental remediation contracts, the contractor's performance may have to be approved by the U.S. Department of Energy, the U.S. Environmental Protection Agency, a state department of health as well as a Management and Operations contractor. As we have seen over the years, each of these entities have a different interpretation of the myriad of regulations that may apply to a project. Likewise, there is no guarantee that these entities have a uniform understanding of the contract.

terms and conditions are not provided with every subcontract or purchase order and, in their haste to close a deal, the subcontractor simply does not review the clauses even though they are readily available on the internet. Moreover, these "standard" terms and conditions may include a number of certifications and representations that can result in civil or even criminal liability if they are violated. An example that has led to many problems for subcontractors supplying material and components for major weapons systems involves compliance with the Berry Amendment's requirement that only domestic specialty metals be used in these systems. The failure to confirm and analyze these requirements, which were largely "incorporated by reference" into subcontracts and purchase orders, led to prosecutions or government claims against a number of many commercial suppliers/subcontractors of items such as metal fasteners and parts.

Whether your company is a government prime or subcontractor, there are a number of steps you can take at the outset to reduce the risk inherent in your contract.

- First, the contractor should determine whether any contract terms can be interpreted in more than one way. If they can, the contractor has an obligation to seek clarification of the ambiguous terms.[4]
- Second, contractors must identify the standards and regulations incorporated into the contract.
- Third, the contractor must identify the areas where it lacks relevant experience and whether it will need to acquire that experience through a teaming agreement of subcontract arrangement.

b. Determining and Mitigating Performance and Financial Risk

Another common source of risk that can be determined and addressed at the outset of a program relates to the financial and performance assumptions. Overly-optimistic financial and performance assumptions, in particular, are areas that can doom a contract to a poor outcome if not carefully considered prior to contract or subcontract award.

For example, if a company historically has had an overhead rate of forty-eight (48) percent, senior management should aggressively challenge an assumption in a bid or proposal that that performance efficiencies will somehow reduce the overhead rate to thirty-two (32) percent and therefore support a potentially unrealistic price. Likewise, if a proposal relies on a cutting-edge technology, management should ensure that the assumptions relating to the maintainability and operability of the project are not overstated.

Other bid or proposal terms and assumptions, which should trip alarms and increase scrutiny, include the following items:

- **Schedule**—A contractor must ensure that it has resources, financial and otherwise, to maintain the contract's required delivery or completion schedule. Be very wary of assumptions that rely on dramatic improvement in your company's or in your subcontractor's "efficiency"

---

[4]Under no circumstances should the contractor plan to use its more favorable interpretation of the ambiguous term during its performance of the contract. This type of "gamesmanship" with the hope of building in a change order during performance almost always fails.

to meet schedule requirements. When a critical-path or similar schedule methodology is available, look carefully for performance paths that have no "lag time" or that rely on a number of tasks being completed before a critical activity can be started.

- **Cost**—Where a company's bid relies upon a number of vendors or subcontractors, determine whether the vendors' prices are confirmed and will remain binding for a reasonable time after contract award; failure to do so can be disastrous if you win a bid, only to find that your actual costs will be substantially higher than planned. Where a bid calls for pricing for a number of years, or for a base period and option periods, carefully examine annual escalation rates and projected cost increases for reasonableness.

- **Assumption of Performance Risk**—Carefully review the solicitation's specifications or statement of work to determine which party (*i.e.*, the government or the contractor) bears the risk of not being able to satisfy the contract's performance requirements. For example, unless a contract is truly a "build to print" project where the government provides detailed design specifications, the contractor typically assumes the risk that it will be able to achieve the specification's performance requirements (and assumes risk of nonpayment and liability to the government for default and excess reprocurement costs).

Some of the techniques that a contractor can use to reduce this risk include rejecting unrealistic assumptions and revising its bid based upon a more realistic assessment of the performance, contractual and financial risks under a contract. Any assumptions upon which a proposal is based must be grounded on a complete and careful evaluation of the solicitation's terms, conditions, and specifications. It may be possible to include contingencies in a proposal or to take exception to terms and conditions that a contractor determines are unrealistic, but it can be difficult to do this under government contracts because many terms and conditions are required by law or may require that the solicitation be amended (which many government contracting agencies may be reluctant to do). To identify these issues, companies should involve a company's legal counsel in key decisions and proposal submissions to better identify the pre-award risks under a solicitation.

§ 9:3 Managing risk during performance of a government contract

Once a company has been awarded a government contract, it must continually monitor the performance, contractual and financial risks that arise in the course of contract performance. To do this, contractors must have controls in place that accurately track every aspect of its performance. Of particular importance are tools that track cost and schedule.

a. Risks in Taking Direction From Unauthorized Government Representatives.

One of the most important principles for a government contractor to understand to protect itself from all of the risks attendant to performing a government contract is to ensure that the government representative with whom it is dealing has the *actual* authority to bind the government. It is an axiom of government contract law that only actual authority binds the government. "Where a party contracts with the government, apparent authority of the government's agent to modify the contract is not sufficient; an agent must have actual [express or implied] authority to bind the government."[1]

In Winter v. Cath-dr/Balti Joint Venture, the underlying contract explicitly set forth the limit of the authority of the government representative. Specifically, the government representative did not have the authority to obligate the government.[2] Although the court in Winter acknowledged that the "government [was] not without blame" it held that no implied authority could exist where the contract language and incorporated references were so clear.[3] Thus, there was no express or implied authority and apparent authority was held insufficient to bind the government.

The issue of authority frequently arises with government program managers, inspectors and contracting officer representatives. To protect your company, if you are unsure whether a government official has the authority to issue contractual direction, you should not follow the instructions until you have verified the instructions with the contracting officer. If the contracting officer approves of the direction orally, you should send a confirming letter or e-mail that documents the instructions. Failure to follow this process will usually result in the loss of a contractor's ability to recover any increased costs the contractor incurs in complying with the unauthorized direction (and sometimes *demands*) of a government official that lacks contractual authority to bind the government.[4]

b. Managing Risks of Contract Changes.

Even when dealing with authorized government representatives, a contractor must implement procedures to identify and manage changes to the contract in order to mitigate risks. Most importantly, the contractor must ensure it can recover increased costs or show it is entitled to a revision of the contract schedule or other terms. In contrast to most commercial contracts, the government has the ability to order changes to a

---

[Section 9:3]

[1]Winter v. Cath-dr/Balti Joint Venture, 497 F.3d 1339, 1343.

[2]497 F.3d 1339, 1343–1348.

[3]497 F.3d 1339, 1346.

[4]Moreover, most government contracts require the contractor to expressly waive any rights to invoke the jurisdiction of local courts where the contracts are performed and contractors agree to accept the exclusive jurisdiction of a contract appeals board and the United States Court of Federal Claims. The underlying contracts may also contain unambiguous clauses providing (1) that the contract will be construed and interpreted in accordance with U.S. law; and (2) that the Contracting Officer is the only person with authority to bind the government. Government representatives' appointment letters also contain clear prohibitions against obligating government funds and otherwise restrict those employees' authority. With such clear provisions, neither the Federal Circuit nor any other court is likely to find that the government is bound by a government employee's actions, absent government ratification. Ratification occurs when the government knows that an employee exceeded his or her authority, but a person with proper authority subsequently authorizes the action.

contract unilaterally.[5] While the formal changes clauses vary with the type of contract, the clause generally requires the contractor to continue with performance of the contract and to submit a request for an equitable adjustment seeking relief from any increased costs in performance as well as any required changes to the contract's performance schedule.

To recover for changes to the contract, the contractor first must have a thorough understanding of what the contract required. Then, the contractor must give prompt notice of the change so that the Contracting Officer has an opportunity to determine whether the directed course of action constitutes a change. If the government decides to require the contractor to continue performance with the government's interpretation of the contract, the contractor generally has 30 days to submit its claim for equitable adjustment. To capture the costs, the contractor should establish a separate charge number for the changed work. Failure to segregate and to provide an accurate accounting of the direct costs of a change will compromise the contractor's ability to recover any increased costs at a later date.

Contractors should also implement policies to identify changes and to ensure that they meet any contractual notice requirements. All government contracts require contractors to provide notice of a change to the contract. Although there is no particular format that this notice must follow, it must include, at a minimum:

- The date, nature, and circumstances of the conduct or government direction that the contractor regards as a change;
- The name, position, and office of the government officials that are involved in, or know of, the change;
- An identification and description of any documents and oral communications relating to the change;
- If the change is in the form of an acceleration of the delivery or performance schedule, the circumstances under which the acceleration arose; and
- A description of the particular elements of the contract for which the contractor believes it is entitled to an adjustment (e.g., line items, labor or material required to complete the change; description of any delays or disruptions caused by the change; what adjustments to delivery schedule, price, or other contract terms must be made to accommodate the change).[6]

Failure to make a timely notice of a change may severely undercut or even defeat a contractor's ability to pursue a claim successfully, especially where the government argues it lost the opportunity to direct the contractor not to perform the change.

c. Managing the Risk of Potential Litigation

All contractors should ensure that their existing company policies, procedures and internal controls will not undermine their ability to prosecute a claim (or defend against a government claim). These policies include records retention, telecommunications usage (including e-mail), ethics and compliance and former employee responsibilities. Contractors must not

---

[5]*See* FAR 52.243-5 (Changes and Changed Conditions).

[6]*See* FAR 52.243-7 (Notification of Changes).

only have these policies in place and ensure that they are consistent with law and with the terms and conditions of their government contracts—*they must actually follow them!*

In too many companies, these items frequently exist in name only and are not followed in practice. Many employees believe that these programs distract from their focus on day-to-day business without providing any benefit to the bottom line. While the benefits of these programs may not be readily apparent on a daily basis, any company that has implemented and followed these policies will see substantial benefits should litigation arise under their contracts.

Some of the issues that should be the focus of document retention policies include:

- How long documents will be retained;
- Whether or not documents can be taken off the premises by an employee; and
- How to handle documents when employees leave the company.

Of all the documents created by companies, e-mails are by far the most dangerous. In addition to the expense associated with collecting and analyzing these materials, people, for whatever reason, write e-mails as if they will never be seen by anyone outside the company. Employers must instruct and remind their employees that business e-mail accounts should be used for business purposes. In addition, employees should keep their work-related e-mails factually accurate. Clarity of e-mail is extremely important, as e-mails can be easily misconstrued and taken out of their original context when reviewed years later by individuals uninvolved in the original communication. Employees should also not engage in attacks on their colleagues or their counterparts in the government or with other companies. Likewise, employees should not write e-mails that say things like "we are really screwing this project up. I hope we can get well on change orders."

Another common mistake made by contractors is that they always want to know why there was a problem with the performance of a specific program. While all contractors should seek to reinforce the practices where they are successful and improve in those areas where their performance fell short of the mark, "red team", "tiger team", or "gold team" reviews generate a wealth of information regarding the problems on a program that frequently provide the opposition with ample fodder for discovery. Some of the issues that we have seen "red teams" identify as problems include: lack of program direction; poor program management; absence of cost controls; lack of a detailed work breakdown structure; failure to identify critical path activities; lack of skilled personnel; and overly optimistic schedule or cost assumptions.

It is obvious that a catalogue of these types of problems can undercut even the best legal argument. Attorneys love cases where they can state that their client does not have to say a word. If the court wishes to know why the contract failed, we can simply listen to the words of the contractor's [pick your color] team. The people on these teams must be sensitive to potential litigation and avoid the use of phrases that will render any claim or future litigation dead on arrival.

Contractors and their employees must also be sensitive to protecting their attorney-client and other privileged communications. Many documents (including e-mails and electronic documents) are privileged and do not have to be provided to adverse parties, including the government, if they are prepared by or for an attorney to assist in investigating a matter, formulating legal advice, or other purposes. In order retain this privilege, the documents and information they contain must be kept confidential, and the privilege will be lost if they are disclosed to third parties outside of the company. Accordingly, contractors must ensure that any potentially privileged documents are clearly marked as "Attorney-Client Privileged" and are safeguarded so that they are not disclosed, even inadvertently, to anyone outside the company.

With regard to privileged documents, attorneys with the Department of Justice (DOJ) and at other agencies have long treated a company's decision not to turn over attorney-client privileged protected documents as a failure to fully cooperate in the investigation. In response to concerns by Congress and industry, the DOJ has issued updated guidelines regarding the waiver of the attorney-client and work product privileges.

In the Filip Letter, the DOJ provides prosecutors with five guidelines to be followed in evaluating whether a company has cooperated in an investigation:

- Cooperation will be measured by the relevant facts and evidence disclosed by the corporation and not by the waiver of the attorney-client or work product privileges.
- Federal prosecutors will not demand the disclosure of confidential attorney-client communications or an attorney's mental impressions as a condition for credit.
- Federal prosecutors will not consider whether the corporation has advanced attorneys' fees to its employees.
- Federal prosecutors will not consider whether the corporation has entered into a joint defense agreement.
- Federal prosecutors will not consider whether the corporation has retained or sanctioned employees.[7]

Despite the new guidance contained in the Filip Letter, federal prosecutors may continue to seek waivers of the attorney-client and attorney work product privileges. Accordingly, contractors should consider the following:

- When conducting internal investigations, business organizations should consider that the government may ask for copies of any investigation reports, witness statements, and related documents.
- If the organization wishes to cooperate fully with the government's investigation, but also wants to avoid disclosing internal legal advice and other attorney work product, take reasonable steps, such as those outlined below, to ensure that documents such as investigation reports and witness statements do not include any privileged material. Preparing documents in this fashion may enable the company to provide the government the facts it needs to complete its investigation.
- Include only information that is "factual" in nature in such documents, and consider not reducing initial observations and information to writing until after key facts can be confirmed.

---

[7]*See* Letter, July 9, 2008, Deputy Attorney General ("DAG") Mark Filip to U.S. Congress.

- Avoid including attorney impressions, conclusions, or legal advice in such documents.
- The government is unlikely to waive prosecution or adverse administrative action in exchange for privileged information where the facts appear to establish a violation. This factor favors not waiving the attorney-client and work product privileges so that the company's legal advice and strategies remain confidential throughout the course of any investigation as well as any ensuing judicial or administrative proceedings.

§ 9:4 Managing risk when litigation appears possible

The first step that a contractor must take when litigation appears imminent is to ensure that any evidence relating to that dispute is preserved. Failure to preserve evidence at the contract's outset may result in allegations that a contractor has destroyed evidence. This so-called "spoliation of evidence" is taken very seriously by the courts and can result in a host of sanctions against the party responsible for destroying the evidence. These sanctions can include an order preventing the contractor from presenting favorable evidence in the areas to which the destroyed evidence relates. In extreme cases, for example when evidence has been intentionally destroyed, a claim may be dismissed by the court or board of contract appeals.

"Spoliation is the destruction or significant alteration of evidence, or failure to preserve property for another's use as evidence in pending or *reasonably foreseeable* litigation."[1] The guiding principle behind the sanctions regime is to ensure that spoliators do not benefit from their conduct. Courts have the inherent authority to sanction spoliation of evidence and may choose from a range of options from making an adverse inference to declaring a default judgment and imposing costs and attorney fees. Once the spoliation has occurred, the courts gives greater leniency where there is disclosure of the spoliation, no future spoliation, and where the impact can be mitigated through other evidence.

The primary step taken by most companies to avoid spoliation of evidence is for the Chief Counsel or another senior official within the company to instruct the employees working on the project to take steps to preserve documents relating to the dispute. As part of this notice procedure, companies must notify their IT support group not to overwrite back-up tapes that may contain documentation relevant to the dispute. This notice should include a brief description of the sorts of documents (including e-mails and electronic documents) that should be retained and identify an official in the company that should be provided with a description and the location of all such documents.

Early on and as part of the document collection process, contractors must take steps to create a list of individuals that have worked on the project or contract over the years. People frequently move between jobs or

---

[Section 9:4]

[1]United States Medical Supply Company, Inc., v. United States, 77 Fed.Cl. 257, 263 (2007) (citing West v. Goodyear Tire & Rubber Co., 167 F.3d 776, 779 (2d Cir. 1999)) (emphasis added).

provide matrix support for a particular aspect of the project, and these individuals often create their own personal files of documents relating to the case that contain harmful information.

In addition to collecting documentation, contractors need to establish an internal structure with responsibility and authority to manage the potential litigation, be it a claim, protest, etc. As part of this process, the company's counsel should prepare a memorandum to give to potential witnesses that outlines their role in the factual investigation. In addition, it should state unequivocally that legal counsel seeks their assistance so that it may provide legal advice to the corporation. The memorandum should also make it clear that, to the extent outside counsel is conducting the fact-finding, counsel represents the corporation and not the individual. Failure to properly describe the scope of the representation may result in the disqualification of counsel from defending or prosecuting the case.

The best way to manage risk during litigation is to focus on the litigation. Too many companies view litigation as a minor inconvenience that will go away if ignored. While a company certainly can decide not to pursue litigation as a Plaintiff, once a party becomes a Defendant, the issue simply will not go away. Rather, the impact on the company will be driven, in large part, from how aggressively the other side decides to pursue the litigation or how vigorously they choose to defend the litigation.

Even when litigation is managed well, it can be very expensive. When managed poorly, litigation will drain a corporation's bottom line. To avoid this risk, contractors should designate an in-house representative as the day-to-day manager of the litigation.

Irrespective of whether a company is a plaintiff or a defendant, they should, as a general rule, push to get the matter resolved at the outset of the litigation. Bad facts do not get better with time and witnesses' memories do not improve the further removed they are from an event. In the government contracts arena, however, what will likely determine the ultimate success or failure of a parties' case is its documents. Consequently, the first thing a contractor needs to do when litigation appears imminent is to identify and collect its relevant documents.

After this initial step, contractors should establish realistic expectations, as well as the final desired outcome of the litigation. Discussions regarding these goals should involve both legal and business people within the company. In addition, the company should revisit these goals at a minimum of every three (3) to six (6) months to make any adjustments necessary. Some of the objectives may include: a monetary settlement, some sort of business capture relationship, or enjoining a competitor from using data to pursue additional contracts.

As part of the process, the company should also require their outside counsel to provide them with a budget for the litigation. This budget should cover every aspect of the litigation: document production; written discovery; depositions; pre-trial motions; settlement discussions; and trial. As part of the budget process, contractors should ask for the names of the members of the litigation team as well as their hourly rates. Further, at the outset of the litigation, contractors should attempt to negotiate an agreement with the lawyers to obtain a discount on the attorney's rates or an agreement that the rates will be frozen throughout the litigation. The budget should be updated every three (3) to six (6) months and counsel should provide a periodic comparison of its fees to budget.

In addition, since litigation costs are generally unallowable, contractors must takes steps to segregate and separately account for these costs.[2] Furthermore, the Contracting Officer will generally withhold payment of such costs.[3] As a result, contractors should consider approaching the Contracting Officer regarding conditional payment of these costs. To obtain conditional payment of these litigation costs, the contractor will have to establish that payment is in the best interest of the Government and provide adequate assurance, as well as an agreement by the contractor, that all costs will be repaid, plus interest, if the Government ultimately deems them unallowable.[4]

In the government contracts arena, litigation may last several years before a case is resolved. For this type of litigation, companies should consider regular meetings or conference calls with their lawyers to discuss progress and key developments likely to effect outcome. At least once every six (6) months, companies should meet with their outside counsel to review the key pieces of evidence to date and assess how this data impacts the likelihood of prevailing in the dispute.

Given the cost of formal litigation, it is always prudent to consider whether less formal alternative processes are available which might expedite a favorable outcome. These alternatives include various forms of "Alternate Dispute Resolution," or "ADR," that can be tailored to the requirements and circumstances of a particular case. For example, it may be desirable to employ an independent legal or technical expert to receive a summary of each party's case and render a neutral evaluation of the likely outcome, from which the parties can fashion a settlement. Use of such a "third party neutral" may be successful where the contractor and the government have very different views and are unable to agree on key facts or legal issues. Another alternative involves structured mediation, in which a respected third party serves to facilitate communication between the contractor and the government in order to assist the parties in assessing the strengths and weaknesses of their cases to arrive at an acceptable settlement. Mediation can be particularly effective where the parties have a relatively good working relationship, but are having difficulty agreeing on the financial aspects of a case. There are many other forms of ADR that a contractor should discuss with counsel with a view towards reducing the financial and opportunity costs of formal litigation.

Once some companies become embroiled in litigation, they simply stop communicating with the opposing side. This is a mistake. If anything, it becomes even more important for the contractor to maintain an open line of communication with the government program and contract personnel involved in a claim. As noted above, the contractor is generally required to continue to perform the contract while a dispute is being resolved and failing to maintain open communication can impair contract performance and lead to even more acrimony. Moreover, communication with the govern-

---

[2]FAR 31.205-47(g).
[3]FAR 31.205-47(g).
[4]FAR 31.205-47(g).

ment should reassure the other side that you are simply looking for a principled, business resolution of the dispute and assure the other side that you want to maintain a business relationship with a valued customer. In addition, maintained communications may serve to remove some of the emotion from the dispute and lead to a more meaningful dialogue between the parties. Prior to making these calls, the business people should consider discussing their conversations with counsel so that they do not inadvertently make a statement that the other side then attempts to portray as an admission. Contractors generally should also never use phrases during these calls that begin with the statement "my attorney told me," as this may result in a loss of attorney-client privilege with respect to such information (and, in any event, is unlikely to impress the government official with whom the contractor is speaking).

Finally, never forget that the government contracts arena is a very small community. Today's enemy is very frequently tomorrow's (if not today's) team member. As a result, throughout this process, contractors and their counsel must take the long view of business relationships. Counsel should be firm, but fair. Counsel should rarely engage in "scorched earth" tactics that damage your business relationships and contractors should be wary and raise any concerns with counsel if this seems to be occurring. Tactics such as deposing the CEO or the Secretary of the Army or contacting the Secretary of Defense or other senior officials that may have minimal or no involvement in a dispute regarding your litigation should only be pursued after very careful consideration. Pursuing such a strategy in a case, while it might assist in short-term gains, may result in the overall destruction of the business relationship.

§ 9:5   Settlement considerations

As mentioned previously, a contractor must always keep in mind, no matter what course a dispute with the government or its subcontractor may take, the subsequent administrative rights of the government. If litigation is due to a statutory or regulatory allegation, it is likely that the government will also have an administrative cause of action. One such cause of action, the exclusionary action, can have a far more onerous impact on a contractor than a fine, or even a criminal conviction.

There are generally two types of exclusionary actions available to the federal government: 1) discretionary actions, which includes both suspension, a temporary form of exclusion, and debarment, an exclusionary action for a fixed period of time, and 2) disqualification pursuant to a statute or executive order (hereinafter "statutory disqualification"). Typically, suspension and debarment actions exclude companies from entering into new contracts or new participation in federal loans, grants or other federal financial assistance programs. These actions normally do not affect existing contracts or current loan or grant participation. Suspension is normally used where there is adequate evidence, such as an indictment, to believe that a cause for debarment exists but the criminal proceeding is not final. Suspension lasts during the pendency of such proceeding, but generally does not exceed 12 months. Debarments are often based upon final adjudications, such as a convictions, plea agreements, or settlements, and are for a fixed period of time, typically three years.

Both suspension and debarment have a complex procedural process and a number of nuances understood by experienced counsel. Further, because these administrative actions frequently run on parallel tracks with the government's criminal and civil actions, it is imperative that a global strategy be developed among counsel so that the issues arising in each area may be dealt with in a coordinated matter, as findings and admissions in one action may adversely impact the contractor's position in one or more of the other parallel actions. Contractors must be mindful of the fact that the resolution or settlement of a fraud claim with the Department of Justice (which handles criminal and civil matters) does not control the resolution of the government's administrative actions, which are handled by other executive agencies that are not typically parties to plea and settlement agreements.

As one can imagine, the ramifications of suspension or debarment may be significant in that they effectively preclude the contractor from entering into new federal work. The extent of a suspension or debarment may also have repercussions outside of the federal marketplace as many states and private entities often inquire into a contractor's suspension/debarment status, and may withhold offers from contractors that have been suspended or debarred by the federal government, especially for violations implicating the contractor's integrity, such as fraud. Thus, special attention should be given to all public contracts when suspended or debarred, because further issues could arise if a contractor were to improperly certify to a suspension/debarment inquiry, such as criminal prosecution under 18 U.S.C. § 1001.

Indeed, a contractor could successfully resolve an alleged fraud claim with the Department of Justice only to find itself suspended or debarred from future government work. Moreover, under recent case law, it is possible that a contractor may successfully resolve a potential debarment with one government agency only to face a potential debarment or adverse responsibility determination with another agency based upon the same conduct. Thus, the implications of the suspension or debarment can far outweigh the costs associated with a one time civil penalty.

§ 9:6 Conclusion

Litigation is a risk faced by all government contractors and involves many nuances and challenges that are not faced in the purely commercial setting. While litigation cannot always be avoided, the costs and disruption associated with litigation can be mitigated and managed. Considering litigation risk in the course of day-to-day operations and contract performance, in the form of the policies and other measures discussed above, can greatly enhance a contractor's chances of success at a manageable cost. Of course, the foregoing is intended to assist contractors in identifying and managing risks and is not intended as legal advice, which should only be provided by a lawyer you trust based upon a discussion of all of the facts and circumstances.

In the last chapter of this book, we provide a simple yet proven highly effective tool which can be used by government contractors to evaluate opportunities and risks prior to making a bid/no-bid decision on a U.S. government contract, and/or by government agencies prior to contract award.

§ 9:7   Questions to consider

1. In the past 3 years, has your organization been involved in any litigation, either with government agencies or your organization's subcontractors?
2. Does your organization actively promote and use alternative dispute resolution techniques?
3. How effectively does your organization manage risk in contract changes?

Chapter 10

Managing Subcontract Defective Pricing Liability

By Steven M. Masiello and Phillip R. Seckman

§ 10:1   Introduction
§ 10:2   Government subcontract defective pricing claims
§ 10:3   Effect of recent decisions
§ 10:4   Practical subcontracting implications
§ 10:5   Guidelines

KeyCite[R]: Cases and other legal materials listed in KeyCite Scope can be researched through the KeyCite service on Westlaw[R]. Use KeyCite to check citations for form, parallel references, prior and later history, and comprehensive citator information, including citations to other decisions and secondary materials.

---

§ 10:1   Introduction

For years, the Truth in Negotiations Act (TINA) has been an effective tool for the Federal Government to battle against poor business practices in the contractor community. The Act—and the claims for defective pricing that it enables—were initially intended to serve the purpose of placing the Government on equal footing with its prime contractor during the course of a negotiated procurement. Indeed, the target of the earliest defective pricing provisions was the prevention of inequitable prime contractor windfalls due to contract performance "underruns" caused by intentionally or inadvertently inflated cost estimates and not by a contractor's efficient contract performance. If the contractor knew, based upon past costs or other information, that it could obtain materials, labor, or subcontract effort for a certain price but failed to disclose the data, then the contractor might be liable to the Government for a price reduction to its contract for supplying defective cost or pricing data. The original provisions thus operated to ensure that the Government could negotiate with its prime contractors on roughly equal terms and also advanced the policy protecting the public against contractor excess and inefficiency.

Over the years, however, the implementation and interpretation of TINA has produced results that appear to reach beyond this original intent. Recently, two cases, one arising in the agency boards of contract appeals and the other in the U.S. Court of Appeals for the Federal Circuit, have further muddied the waters of defective pricing liability under TINA, particularly in the context of the relationships between contractors, at any tier, under Government contracts. No longer is TINA merely a tool by which the Government ensures it has equal access to information to which the prime contractor is privy. Rather, based upon these recent cases, prime

151

contractors face potential liability under TINA for the defective cost or pricing data supplied by the subcontractors, at any tier, and even by prospective subcontractors, regardless of whether the prime contractor processed the disputed data or even knew or should have known the disputed data existed. Due to these developments, among others it is crucial for all contractors to be aware of the risks TINA poses during the negotiation of their contracts. In addition, contractors, at every tier of Government contracting, must remain vigilant concerning the terms and administration of their contracts to minimize the risk of loss due to a Government assertion of defective pricing.

This briefing paper explores the impact of defective pricing liability under TINA on the relationships among the Government and its prime contractors and subcontractors. Specifically, this paper discusses (1) the statutory and regulatory framework of TINA, its limits, and the impact of the Government claims due to subcontractor defective pricing on prime contractors and subcontractors, (2) the effect of recent decisional law on the liability of prime contractors and subcontractors for subcontract defective pricing and the weakening of the defense that subcontracting cost or pricing data were not reasonably available to a prime contractor, (3) the practical implications of recent decisional law upon contractors at every tier, and (4) potential courses of action for prime contractors and their subcontractors to aid in reducing exposure to risk if subcontract defective pricing liability arises as a result of a Government claim.

§ 10:2   Government subcontract defective pricing claims

To provide a context for the issues of prime contractor liability (and derivative subcontractor liability to the prime contractor) for Government claims of defective pricing relating to subcontractor cost or pricing data, this section of the paper identifies the elements of a Government claim for defective pricing and the important moments in time under TINA and its implementing regulations when it will be determined whether the prime contractor or the subcontractor submitted accurate, complete, and current cost or pricing data. This section then turns to the question whether there are limits on the expansion of the obligations imposed by TINA-related regulations. This discussion lays the foundation for the main topic the impact of Government claims for defective pricing due to defective subcontractor data on prime contractors and their subcontractors.

● Element of a Government Defective Pricing Claim

The Government bears the burden of proof on any claim for defective pricing. To carry that burden, the Government must prove three elements to prevail: (1) the disputed information in question is "cost or pricing data" as defined by TINA, (2) the prime contractor failed to disclose the information or failed to provide the data in a usable, understandable format during the parties' negotiations, and (3) the Government relied to its detriment on defective cost or pricing data and the non-disclosure of cost or pricing data had an effect on the negotiated price. With respect to the third element of the test, the Government is aided by a rebuttable presumption that the nondisclosure of cost or pricing data has the "natural and probable" consequence of improperly inflating the negotiated price."

● When Cost or Pricing Data Must be Submitted

For the elements of a claim for defective pricing to become relevant to any Government contract or subcontract, an obligation to submit cost or pricing data relating to a contract or modification to a contract must exist. Under TINA, offerors, contractors, and subcontractors must submit "cost or pricing data" in four distinct circumstances anticipated to result in awards of Government contracts or subcontracts above the relevant TINA threshold ("pricing actions"), unless such pricing actions are subject to an exception or waiver. Submission of cost or pricing data is not required when the price agreed upon is based on adequate competition or prices set by law or regulation, the procurement is for a commercial item, or the head of the procuring agency decides a waiver is justified.

First, TINA provides that an *"offeror for a prime contract. . . shall be required to submit cost or pricing data before the award of the contract."* Second, a *"contractor for a prime contract. . . shall be required to submit cost or pricing data before the pricing of a change or modification to the contract.* Third, an *"offeror for a subcontract (at any tier) of a contract. . .shall be required to submit cost or pricing data before the award of the subcontract* if the prime contractor and each higher-tier subcontractor have been required to make available cost or pricing data." Finally, the *"subcontractor. . . shall be required to submit cost or pricing data before the pricing of a change or modification to the subcontract."*

Importantly, offerors for prime contracts and contractors seeking to modify and existing prime contract must submit cost or pricing data to the pertinent Government Contracting Officer's designated representative. Offerors for subcontracts and subcontractors seeking to modify an existing subcontract are directed to submit cost or pricing data to their respective prime contractor or higher-tier subcontractor.

Upon the parties' agreement on price for each relevant pricing action TINA mandates that the relevant offeror, contractor or subcontractor certify that its cost or pricing data are "accurate, complete, and current." "Cost or pricing data" mean:

[A]ll facts that, as of the date of agreement on the price of a contract (or the price of a contract modification), or, . . .another date agreed upon between the parties, a prudent buyer or seller would reasonably expect to affect price negotiations significantly.

Such term does not include information that is judgmental, but does include the factual information from which a judgment was derived.

Failure to submit accurate, complete, and current cost or pricing data as of the date of price agreement for the relevant pricing action may result in liability for defective pricing. Defective pricing liability arises under certain "Price Reduction" clauses incorporated into Government prime contracts under the FAR and under equivalent clauses placed in subcontracts to which TINA applies. The clauses permit the Government, prime contractor, or higher-tier subcontractor buyer of supplies or services to reduce the price of the relevant contract or subcontract in a amount determined sufficient to eliminate any price inflation caused by the seller's submission of the inaccurate, incomplete, or noncurrent cost or pricing data as of the date of price agreement between the parties to the contract or subcontract. It is this delivery of inaccurate, incomplete, or noncurrent cost or pricing data that is referred to as "defective pricing."

• Regulatory Expansion of TINA Submission Requirements

The statutory language of TINA does not expressly require that prime contractors demand cost or pricing data from their subcontractors or prospective subcontractors as of the date upon which the Government and prime contractor agree on price for the prime contract (hereinafter "Government price agreement"). The statutory language of TINA requires only that subcontractors or proposed subcontractors submit cost or pricing data that are accurate, complete, and current as of the date of the subcontractors' agreement on price with their respective prime contractors or higher-tier subcontractors (hereinafter "subcontract price agreement"). The Act is silent concerning the requirement of a "Price Reduction" clause in ay subcontract, and there is no clear intent to grant the Government relief for any subcontractor defective pricing that may exist as of the date of the subcontract price agreement.

The implementation of TINA in the Federal Acquisition Regulation, however, appears to expand the literal reach of the plain statutory language, at least with respect to the Government's rights to accurate, complete, and current subcontract cost or pricing data. For instance, the statutory language of TINA specifically provides that any prime contract must contain a "Price Reduction" clause permitting the Government to reduce the prime contract price for any contractor defective pricing that may have occurred as of the date of Government price agreement for the prime contract. This requirement of TINA is implemented in the FAR 52.215-10 "Price Reduction for Defective Cost or Pricing Data" clause in a manner that is susceptible to the broad interpretation that any subcontractors or prospective subcontractors are also required to submit cost or pricing data to the Government as of the date of the Government price agreement. The clause states:

(a) If any price, including profit or fee, negotiated in connection with this contract, or any cost reimbursable under this contract, was increased by any significant amount because

    1) *The Contractor or a subcontractor furnished cost or pricing data that were not complete, accurate, and current as certified in its Certificate of Current Cost or Pricing Data;*

    2) A subcontractor or prospective subcontractor furnished the Contractor cost or pricing data that were not complete, accurate, and current as certified in the Contractor's Certificate of Current Cost or Pricing Data; or

    3) Any of these parties furnished data of any description that were not accurate, the price or cost shall be reduced accordingly and the contract shall be modified to reflect the reduction. Moreover, FAR 52.215-10 would permit the Government to recover for defective pricing against a prime contractor relating to a prospective subcontractor's cost or pricing data, even if no subcontract relating to the cost or pricing data is ever consummated. In this circumstance, FAR 52.215-10 limits the Government's recovery from the prime contractor to the difference between the prospective subcontractor's cost estimate and the actual cost the prime contractor incurs for the pertinent subcontract effort to which the cost or pricing data relate.

In addition to the requirements of the "Price Reduction" clause, FAR 15.403-4 provides, in pertinent part:

(b) When cost or pricing data are required, the contracting officer shall require the contractor or prospective contractor to submit to the contracting officer (and to have any subcontractor or prospective subcontractor submit to the prime contractor or appropriate subcontractor tier) the following in support of any proposal:

1) The cost or pricing data.
2) A certificate of current cost or pricing data, in the format specified in 15.406-2, certifying that to the best of its knowledge and belief, the cost or pricing data were accurate, complete, and current as of the date of agreement on price or, if applicable, an earlier date agreed upon between the parities that is as close as practicable to the date of the agreement on price.

This regulation could be read, broadly, to require the prime contractor to "have any subcontractor or prospective subcontractor submit to the prime contractor" certified subcontractor cost or pricing data as of the date of the Government price agreement.

This requirement that subcontractor cost or pricing data be submitted as part of the prime contract's own data is similarly stated in several additional locations in FAR Part 15. All of these FAR provisions are susceptible to an interpretation that would unmistakably expand the obligations of contractors and subcontractors under TINA with respect to subcontract cost or pricing data. In some cases, where TINA is silent, these FAR provisions may be considered to serve as mere gap-fillers, such as clarifying that contractors and higher-tier subcontractors must conduct and include any analyses concerning the prices for subcontracts in their cost or pricing data supporting their proposals for a contract at any tier under a Government contract. In at least one respect, however, these FAR provisions may be read so broadly that the provisions exceed the scope of the statutory authority under TINA by requiring a contractor to "submit, or cause to be submitted" to the Government *certified* subcontract cost or pricing data *at the time of the Government price agreement for the prime contract.*

• Limits on Regulatory Authority

As noted above, TINA requires submissions of cost or pricing data under circumstances relating to four specific pricing actions. Prime contractor submission of certified subcontractor cost or pricing data to the Government as of the date of Government price agreement is *not* one of the specific circumstances set forth in TINA. Broad interpretation of the FAR requirements that a subcontractor or prospective subcontractor must submit certified cost or pricing data as of the date of Government price agreement to the prime contractor for transmittal to the Government, therefore, appears in consistent with the text of TINA.

Importantly, the inconsistency between such an interpretation of the FAR requirements and TINA may support an argument that the regulations implementing TINA, at least, in part, are an illegal ultra vires act by the FAR Council, to which Congress delegated the authority to implement TINA. The U.S. Supreme Court, in Chevron U.S.A., Inc. v. Natural Resources Defense Council, Inc., defined the limits on a regulatory body's authority to promulgate regulations pursuant to such a statutory delegation, stating:

If Congress has explicitly left a gap for the agency to fill, there is an express delegation of authority to the agency to elucidate a specific provision of the statute by regulation. Such legislative regulations are given controlling weight unless they are arbitrary, capricious, or *manifestly contrary* to the statute. Sometimes the legislative delegation to an agency on a particular question is implicit rather than explicit. In such a case, a court may not substitute its own construction of a statutory provision for a reasonable interpretation made by the administrator of an agency.

Under TINA, Congress clearly set forth the circumstances under which TINA shall apply, limiting the FAR Council's authority to implement rules relating to certain defined pricing actions and dates. These circumstances dictate when a contractor or subcontractor has a duty under TINA to submit cost or pricing data and to certify that such data are accurate, complete, and current.

If interpreted broadly, the regulations promulgated by the FAR Council, while long-standing and unchallenged, increase the number of circumstances under which such submission and certification is required under TINA. Moreover, TINA arguably, did not expressly leave gaps for the FAR Council to fill, and, therefore, the FAR Council lacked the express authority discussed in Chevron to add additional circumstances requiring submission of cost or pricing data that TINA does not require. Indeed, the Supreme Court stated that the agency's express authority is to "elucidate" a specific provision where there is an ambiguity. Since TINA set forth four specific circumstances for submission, there arguably was no ambiguity to clear up.

While it seems clear that a broad interpretation of the FAR Council's regulations implementing TINA would exceed the FAR Council's implicit authority under that statute, the success of such an argument in the boards or courts is uncertain. In other contexts, for example, it has been held that an agency has the implicit authority to create new requirements where the statute is unclear. In BellincCo, Inc., for example, the Armed Services Board of Contract Appeals held that a regulation imposing additional requirements on a contractor before contract award to qualify for a waiver to Miller Act bonding requirements was reasonable gap-filling by the agency, even where the statute set no such limits on entitlement. Though the statute in question did not limit the "availability of bond waivers to any particular time period," the board noted that other contractors were successful in obtaining waivers under the regulation, and, thus, the regulation did not unreasonably preclude participation in the waiver program as contemplated under the statute.

The board's decision in BellincCo provides support for the proposition that FAR Council, by creating new disclosure requirements for subcontract cost or pricing data, has not necessarily created regulations contrary to TINA. Because of the FAR Council merely added circumstances under which contractors and subcontractors would be required to submit certified cost or pricing data, such regulations arguably are not in direct conflict with any existing disclosure requirement and, therefore, are not unreasonable interpretations of TINA.

In any case, a question remains whether there is a line beyond which the FAR Council is not authorized to go in expanding the submission obligations of contractors and subcontractors under TINA. If a broad interpretation of the regulations implementing TINA to require additional submission obligations is not beyond the scope of the statute, then one wonders if any line exists. Indeed, if such a broad regulatory interpretation of TINA has not yet exceeded the implicit authority under Chevron, even further expansion of the number submissions a contractor or subcontractor must make of its cost or pricing data may occur. Such excessive expansion, however, undermines the premise that disclosure is meant to ensure the Government is on a "fair playing field" with its contractors during negotiations.

● **Impact of Government Subcontract Defective Pricing Claims**

Many Government defective pricing claims take advantage of the expansive interpretations of TINA's requirements afforded by the implementing FAR regulations regarding the nature and scope of submission and certification of subcontract cost or pricing data. Such Government claims often arise out of Defense Contract Audit Agency audits of prime contractor proposals submitted in connection with a pricing action leading to the award of a prime contract with the Government. The DCAA regularly concludes in such postaward audits that certain subcontractor information included in, or omitted from, a prime contractor's proposal (or otherwise directly submitted to the Government) resulted in defective pricing of the prime contract.

Upon the DCAA's recommendation, the Government commonly asserts that a price reduction is due under the prime contract pursuant to FAR 52.215-10 by virtue of defective subcontract cost or pricing data submitted to the Government by the prime contractor (or otherwise submitted). Essentially, therefore, the prime contractor must defend a defective pricing claim ostensibly caused by the subcontractor but directed by the Government against the prime contractor.

Recent developments in the context of such Government claims of subcontract defective pricing do not appear consistent with the policy and purpose underlying TINA. As a result of these developments, instead of setting the parties on equal footing in negotiations, unintended and inappropriate de facto strict liability may be imposed upon prime contractors to the Government for any subcontract savings experienced under prime contracts at the expense of the contractor community. Regardless of whether such an outcome is fair or consistent with the purpose of TINA, prime contractors and subcontractors must be aware of the inherent risks to their respective contracts and take informed action to reduce exposure to risk posed by Government claims for subcontract defective pricing.

§ 10:3 Effect of recent decisions

Recent case law has signaled that TINA's intended policy of placing the parties on equal footing may be coming to an end. In McDonnell Aircraft Co. and Aerojet Solid Prepulsion Co. v. White, the ASBCA and the Federal Circuit moved away from the equal footing policy in the context of the subcontractor relationship. The board and the Federal Circuit have sent a strong signal to the contractor community that a new policy prevails providing that the purpose of TINA is to make the prime contractor the Government's insurer against defective pricing by the subcontractor, regardless of whether the cost or pricing data are "reasonably available" to the prime contractor under TINA and the FAR. This section of the paper examines the erosion of the traditional approach under TINA to a prime contractor's liability for defective subcontractor cost or pricing data and the apparent replacement under recent decisions of the "reasonable availability" defense with a new strict liability standard.

• Traditional Decisional Law

A 1970 case illustrates the traditional case law approach to a prime contractor's liability to the Government for subcontractor defective pricing. In that case, Lockheed Aircraft Corp. v. United States. The prime contractor, Lockheed, and its subcontractor, Midwestern Instruments, Inc., concluded their subcontract negotiations and came to agreement on subcontract price *before* Lockheed and the Government entered into any price agreement. Lockheed had been awarded a letter contract with the Air Force for the production of a flight recording system for use in a B-52 aircraft. Lockheed negotiated the letter contract with the Air Force dated May 4, 1962. Later that year, on June 6, 1962, Lockheed definitized a subcontract with Midwestern for the production of a recorder for use as part of Lockheed's flight recording system. Later still, on April 15, 1963, the Air Force and Lockheed came to agreement on the prime contract by definitizing the price of their letter contract. Upon such price agreement with the Government., Lockheed certified its cost or pricing data that it had submitted in support of negotiations. During the course of an audit by the General Accounting Office, conducted in the fall of 1963, it came to light that the subcontractor had failed to disclose information showing lower actual material and labor costs for producing the recorders and labor costs for producing the recorders than had been disclosed to Lockheed at the time of the subcontract price agreement.

The Government subsequently brought an action for a downward price adjustment directly against Lockheed. Although the defect in the cost or pricing data was a problem within the subcontractor's data, Lockheed was found liable and made to bear the costs of a price reduction to its prime contract. The court stated that Lockheed was free to proceed against the subcontractor on the basis of the defective pricing terms in its subcontract.

The earlier cases such as Lockheed reached fair and reasonable results. Under TINA, subcontractors must certify their cost or pricing data as accurate, complete, and current as of the date of its agreement on the subcontract price. Under those circumstances, it is consistent with TINA to hold the prime contractor liable to the Government for any defective pricing that occurs in the negotiations of the subcontract because the prime contractor will have the ability to proceed against its subcontractor, assuming the subcontract contains a "Price Reduction" clause for defective pricing. Moreover, there are indications in Lockheed that the prime contractor was aware that the subcontractor had problems with its cost of pricing data before Lockheed's negotiations with the Government on a definitive prime contract. In fact, during the negotiations of the subcontract, Lockheed obtained two price reductions based upon its own analysis of the subcontractor's data. Thus, when a prime contractor is aware of a defect or is in receipt of defective certified subcontract cost or pricing data before its own agreement on price with the Government, holding the prime responsible is consistent with the purpose of TINA to place the Government on equal footing with its contractor.

• **"Reasonably Availability" Defense**

TINA's original intent to level the playing field between the Government and contractors is still echoed in recent decisional law. The ASBCA stated in a 2002 decision that the "purpose of TINA is to establish a level field for price negotiations by requiring a prospective contractor to furnish factual cost or pricing data significant to the price negotiations known to it so that the CO will have the same knowledge during negotiations." In addition, the DCAA *Contract Audit Manual* (DCAAM), which contains the Government's guidelines for defective pricing audits, states that the "objective in requiring cost or pricing data. . .is to enable the Government to perform cost or pricing analysis and ultimately enable the Government and the contractor to negotiate fair and reasonable contract prices." These statements reflect the policy of requiring contractors to disclose cost or pricing data that are reasonably available to ensure that the public fisc is protected from fraud, abuse, or contractor inefficiency. Indeed, there can be little objection to a policy of ensuring the Government is on equal footing with its contractors.

However, the policy of ensuring the parties are on equal footing has been stretched thin, likely to the point of disappearing, in the context of the relationships among the Government its prime contractors, and its subcontractors. The crucial change is in the inquiry whether cost or pricing data in the possession of subcontractors are "reasonably available" to the prime contractor at the time of the Government price agreement. The question whether cost or pricing data are reasonably available to the prime contractor on the date of the Government price agreement is inextricably tied to the notions of fairness that inspire the equal footing policy. Where cost or pricing data are not reasonably available to the prime contractor, it is not in advantaged position relative to the Government and, therefore, should not be found liable for defective pricing. Thus, the question when cost or pricing data are reasonably available to a prime contractor is a key determination.

Under the FAR, the CO, in making determination of whether and to what degree a price reduction is appropriate, must "consider the time by which the cost or pricing data became *reasonably available* to the contractor." The articulation of this inquiry under TINA and its modern implementing regulations in the FAR is substantially the same as it was under the pre-TINA regulations.

The inquiry whether cost or pricing data were reasonably available was interpreted by the board and courts in the past as a fact-intensive inquiry focusing on whether data were within the possession and control *of the relevant contractor* during price negotiations. A number of cases illustrate the use of a "knew or should have known" standard consistent with TINA's equal footing policy in determining whether cost or pricing data were reasonably available. The "knew or should have known" standard encourages contractors to avoid shoddy or negligent business practices.

In Conrac Corp., for example, the ASBCA was faced with the question whether information about the contractor's purchase history, that had been recorded on data cards, was reasonably available at the time of agreement on price with the Government. The board held that the contractor's data cards were reasonably available because there was evidence showing that the contractor had kept the purchase history cards on all of the component parts it purchased and that it knew, or should have known, that the data existed before the date of agreement on price. Thus, in this case, the important fact that helped determine whether data were reasonably available was that the contractor had a business practice of keeping data on all its parts, and, therefore, the contractor either knew the data existed or should have known the data existed.

In another case, Central Navigation & Trading Co., the board considered whether a contractor's invoices showing fuel and labor costs and the contractor's misapplication of exchange rates constituted cost or pricing data that were reasonably available at the time of the Government price agreement for the prime contract. The contractor here was faced with a very tight procurement schedule. Indeed, the contractor was allowed less than two days between the date it learned of the impending contract award and the date of certification of its cost or pricing data as accurate, complete, and current. The board, in discussing the reasonably availability inquiry, quoted its statement from an earlier decision that "the Government may not recover on its claim unless it can show, by a preponderance of the evidence, that more accurate, complete and current cost or pricing data were reasonably available to [the contractor] on the date of certification under the prevailing circumstances." Thus, the fact that time had compressed the contractor's bidding schedule so drastically and impinged on the contractor's ability to learn of the existence of any defective data played a significant role in guiding the board's decision concerning whether cost or pricing data were reasonably available. This case supports the notion that the "knew or should have known" standard used to determine reasonable availability of data had reasonable limits tied to the surrounding circumstances.

Indeed, in FMC Corp., the contractor argued that certain cost or pricing data had not been reasonably available when the data, in fact, existed before agreement on price with the Government, but had been beyond the knowledge of the contractor's negotiators. The board found a reasonable line between what the contractor knew or should have known by holding that the data within the contractor's organization on or before March 17, 1962 (the date of an internal memorandum calling the contractor's negotiator's attention to a price reduction), were reasonably available for use during negotiations, but that the data not within the "normal documentation channels" of the contractor's organization after that date were not reasonably available for negotiations." The board acknowledged the importance of the surrounding circumstances by essentially finding that the FMC negotiators were on equal footing with the Government with respect to data outside the company but should have known about the data that existed within the contractor's ordinary business operations before the date of the agreement on price."

• New "Strict Liability" Standard

As shown above, the determination whether cost or pricing data were reasonably available was once an inquiry anchored to good sense and a fair assessment of the facts concerning the knowledge of the prime contractor under the circumstances of the negotiations on the price of a Government prime contract. The policy today, however, is no longer to place the Government merely on equal footing with its prime contractor with respect to subcontract cost or pricing data but rather, to assign the Government's prime contractor under TINA "strictly liability" and, essentially, the burden of being the insurer against any price inflation experienced under subcontracts.

In McDonnell Aircraft, the prime contractor, McDonnell Aircraft Co. (McAir) argued that its subcontractor's price analysis of a second-tier subcontractor was not "reasonable available" at the time of the Government's price agreement. McAir negotiated with the Government for a contract relating to the F/A-18 aircraft and related items. The parties' contract was subject to TINA and contained the standard FAR clauses relating to price reductions for defective pricing. The parties initially entered into an advance agreement, leaving price to be separately determined at a later date. During the same time period, McAir received a proposal from a prospective subcontractor, Ford Aerospace and Communications Corporation. Ford's proposal included a quote from a second-tier prospective subcontractor, Ferranti Defense Systems Limited, for the supply of Forward Looking Infrared Radar arrays, a component of the F/A-18 aircraft's avionic systems.

The cost and pricing data from Ford, including the second-tier subcontract proposal of Ferranti were disclosed to the Government. However, during McAir's negotiations of price with the Government for the prime contract, Ford was conducting a preliminary pricing analysis of Ferranti's proposal. On June 24, 1988, McAir agreed to a price with the Government and certified its cost or pricing data as being accurate, complete, and current. Before McAir's certification of its cost or pricing data, it had made repeated requests of Ford for its cost or pricing data. Nevertheless, the existence of Ford's pricing analysis concerning Ferranti's second-tier subcontract proposal was not disclosed.

Approximately six months later, on January 16, 1989, Ford and McAir executed their subcontract. On August 2, 1989, Ford certified that its cost or pricing data were accurate, complete, and current as of the date of the execution of the subcontract. After the Government conducted on audit of McAir's prime contract, it concluded that defective pricing had occurred because the information concerning Ford's price analysis of Ferranti's second-tier subcontract cost proposal had not been disclosed by Ford to the Government.

McAir argued that a subcontractor, such as Ford, has an obligation to submit accurate, complete, and current cost or pricing data only upon the subcontractor price agreement. Moverover, McAir argued that Ford's nondisclosed data were not "reasonably available" to McAir. The ASBCA rejected both of McAir's arguments. First, the board found that while a subcontractor is obligated under TINA to certify only once, a prime contractor has an obligation to certify that its subcontractor's cost or pricing data are accurate, complete, and current on two occasions: once at the Government price agreement and again when the parties to the subcontract came to an agreement on price. As noted above, the board's statement about a prime contractor having a duty to certify on two occasions appears inconsistent with the plain language of TINA.

Second, the board found that the mere existence of Ford cost analysis at the time of agreement on price between McAir and Government made Ford's data "reasonably available" to McAir. Despite the prime's ignorance of its existence, and the fact that McAir had made repeated requests of Ford to update its cost or pricing data, the board determined these circumstances were not viable excuses for failing to discover the internal Ford cost analysis data.

Accordingly, in McDonnell Aircraft, the board wanders well away from the purported "equal footing" policy of TINA. Rather than requiring a prime contractor to disclose data for the purpose of placing the Government and the prime contractor on equal footing during negotiations, the prime contractor becomes the Government's insurer with respect to all proposed subcontract costs.

It appears that once freed from the policy of TINA, the boards and courts can significantly shift the traditional balance of risk for defective pricing under TINA in contracting with the Government. For example, the Aerojet, the Federal Circuit affirmed the board's decision that the contractor, Aeroject, committed defective pricing because it failed to disclose that it had received recent bids from prospective subcontractors that had been placed in a locked bid box and that remained unopened until after the Government price agreement and were not included in the bid the contractor had used to support its proposal to the Government. The Federal Circuit explained that Aerojet's knowledge of the mere existence of more recent bids had given it an unfair advantage over the Government, which was counter to the policy of TINA. The court did not accept Aerojet's argument that the Government and Aerojet were in the same negotiating position because Aerojet's negotiators were equally unaware of the existence or impact of the lockbox bids. The court said, "Cost or pricing data simply is not any less cost or pricing data because it has been selectively disseminated or not actually used."

The Federal Circuit's view is odd in light of its statement, not more than a handful of paragraphs earlier, that a "primary objective of TINA is to place Government and private contractors in roughly equal positions during contract negotiations." In this dissent, Judge Bryson pointed out this oddity, arguing that the majority's decision is Aerojet was disingenuous and wrong.

In any case, both McDonnell Aircraft and Aerojet indicate that even where the prime contractor acts with due diligence in attempting to ensure the Government is placed on equal footing with the prime contractor, the prime can nonetheless be held liable for defective pricing. In McDonnell Aircraft, the prime contractor was held liable solely because the data existed as of the Government price agreement, despite its repeated requests to Ford for all its cost or pricing data and its undisputed lack of knowledge of the existence of a flaw in Ford's cost or pricing data. McAir's diligence and sound business practice was discarded as insufficient to show that it did not know nor should it have known that other cost or pricing data existed. In Aerojet, the prime contractor was held liable despite its negotiator's reasonable lack of knowledge concerning the contents of the bids in its locked bid box at the time of the Government price agreement. These cases show that today the purpose of TINA is to make the prime contractor the Government's insurer, regardless of whether the cost or pricing data are actually "reasonably available" or whether the Government is disadvantaged in negotiations with its prime contractors.

§ 10:4 Practical subcontracting implications

As a result of these recent decisions under TINA, there are practical concerns for all Government prime contractors and subcontractors seeking to manage their respective defective pricing liability. While the recent decisions are difficult to reconcile with the ostensible purpose of TINA, the board in McDonnell Aircraft did suggest a course of action that prime contractors can take to protect themselves. The board stated that a "prime contractor. . .may insert a defective pricing clause into its subcontracts and proceed against its subcontractors pursuant to that clause if the Government reduces the prime contract price based on the subcontractor defective cost or pricing data.

Beyond the board's advice in McDonnell Aircraft, TINA and its implementing regulations provide little guidance on the practical impact of the seemingly strict liability imposed on prime contractors for subcontract defective pricing on the contractual relationships of prime contractors and subcontractors. Presumably, when the board in McDonnell Aircraft advised that prime contractors should manage their subcontract defective pricing liability by inserting a defective pricing clause into its subcontracts and proceeding against its subcontractors pursuant to that clause, the board was suggesting that the mere "flow down" of the standard FAR 52.215-10 "Price Reduction for Defective Cost or Pricing Data" clause is sufficient protection for prime contractors (and higher-tier subcontractors) buying subcontract supplies and services against loss resulting from any subcontract defective pricing claims brought by the Government. Because of the extraordinarily broad scope of the prime contractor's strict liability to the Government, however, the board's advice appears to miss the mark. For this reason, among others, Government contractors and subcontractors should review their subcontracting policies and procedures to ensure the mitigation of the impact of subcontract defective pricing liability.

• Limits On Flow Down of FAR 52.215-10

The typical flow down of the FAR 52.215-10 "Price Reduction" clause into subcontracts involves the modification of the terms of the clause to include the replacement of the names of the parties to the subcontract in place of the terms "Government" and "contractor" and the insertion of the term "subcontract" in place of "contract." Under the typical flow-down methodology, the terms of FAR 52.215-10 will not create a subcontractor obligation to submit accurate, complete, and current cost or pricing data before the subcontractor's agreement with the prime contractor (or higher-tier subcontractor), precluding any subcontractor obligation for what might occur before that date. Instead, subcontractors are obligated *only* to certify their cost or pricing data as accurate, complete, and current *as of the date of their subcontract price agreement* with their customer.

Accordingly, recovery for a prime contractor (or higher-tier subcontractor) under FAR 52.215-10 is limited to defective pricing existing *as of the date of the subcontract price agreement*. When a prime contractor (or higher-tier subcontractor) is faced with liability for subcontract defective pricing pursuant to a Government claim, this limitation of the typical flow-down "Price Reduction" clause, FAR 52.215-10, may present significant obstructions to recovery from the responsible subcontractor for any loss sustained as a result of the claim.

For example, a prime contractor (or higher-tier subcontractor) could be held liable for defective pricing for failure to "update" a subcontractor's cost or pricing data for developments that occur before the date of price agreement with their respective customers. Nevertheless, the prime contractor (or higher-tier subcontractor) could be denied relief under its subcontract for liability associated with such a claim because FAR 52.215-10 does not clearly impose upon subcontractors a duty to "up-date" their certified cost or pricing data *after* the date of the subcontract price agreement. Under such circumstances, the prime contractor (or higher-tier subcontractor) could also have problems establishing that it *relied* upon the allegedly defective data or that such disputed data had any *impact* on the subcontract price, since the disputed data are potentially irrelevant to the subcontracting parties' negotiation of the subcontract price.

Alternatively, since no subcontract duty exists to submit certified cost or pricing data before subcontract price agreement, the prime contractor (or higher-tier subcontractor) may be unable to prove that during its later negotiations with its customer it *relied* upon certain defective subcontract data, because the defective condition existed only at the date of the earlier Government price agreement. Finally, where no subcontract is ever consummated, it is impossible for a prime contractor (or higher-tier subcontractor) to recover under FAR 52.215-10 or any subcontract clause, of any kind, for subcontract defective pricing liability.

● **Subcontractor Submission of Cost or Pricing Data**

Practical problems also exist with the submission of subcontract cost or pricing data. Subcontractors often refuse to provide cost or pricing data directly to their prime contractors (or higher-tier subcontractors) due to concerns that such disclosure would reveal too much about the subcontractors' cost structure and undermine their competitive position. In addition, subcontractors routinely deny prime contractors (or higher-tier subcontractors) any audit rights. Without audit rights, prime contractors (or higher-tier subcontractors) are unable to inspect subcontractors' cost records supporting their proposals to determine the sufficiency of the subcontractor's cost or pricing data. Thus, prime contractors (or higher-tier subcontractors) often must rely entirely upon the Government's audit of their subcontractors' proposals and supporting cost or pricing data.

No specific guidance in statutory, regulatory, or decisional law exists to resolve this matter. The DCAAM, however, provides that the DCAA may "assist" the prime contractor (or higher-tier subcontractor) in evaluating proposals and accompanying cost or pricing data submitted by a subcontractor directly to DCAA, but only if the DCAA's assistance is requested by the Government CO and such assistance is in the interests of the Government. The DCAAM does not appear to stipulate the manner of submission of the subcontractor's data or that an audit of such submission would take the place of the submission by the prime contractor (or higher-tier subcontractor) of the subcontractor's cost or pricing data to the Government negotiation team. Regrettably, the lack of sufficient guidance with respect to the submission and audit of subcontractor cost or pricing data leaves all Government contractors, at every tier, exposed to unpredictable defective pricing liability.

For instance, the direct submission of a lower-tier subcontractor's cost or pricing data to the DCAA does not necessarily protect a prime contractor (or higher-tier subcontractor) from defective pricing liability for failure to disclose subcontractor cost or pricing data to the Government. In fact, the decisional law in this area casts some doubt concerning whether a subcontractor's direct submission to the DCAA of its cost or pricing data even could serve to satisfy the duty of a prime contractor (or higher-tier subcontractor) to disclose under TINA. To the extent the relevant DCAA auditor is not part of the Government's negotiation team, therefore, direct submission to the DCAA may be insufficient. Moreover, the direct submission of cost or pricing data to the DCAA means that the prime contractor (or higher-tier subcontractor) never receives the subcontractor data. Technically, therefore, such direct submission also would not discharge the subcontractor's duty to disclose cost or pricing data under the typical flow-down "Price Reduction" clause, FAR 52-215-10, because that provision requires disclosure to the prime contractor (or higher-tier subcontractor).

Assuming the direct submission is deemed to discharge the relevant parties' duty to disclose, the ability of the prime contractor (or higher-tier subcontractor) to recover for any defective pricing liability may be impaired as a result. Unless modified substantially, the terms of any flow-down version of FAR 52-215-10 would still require that the prime contractor (or higher-tier subcontractor) prove that (a) defective data were submitted by the subcontractor, (b) reliance occurred as of the date of the relevant subcontract agreement, and (c) the defective data affected the price of the subcontract. Since the prime contractor (or higher-tier subcontractor) never receives the cost or pricing data if such data were submitted directly to the Government, it may be difficult to establish any of these elements. This is a particularly significant problem for the prime contractor (or higher-tier subcontractor) if the Government's audit findings concerning the subject matter of subcontractor's allegedly defective cost or pricing data are not shared.

To reduce these uncertainties with respect to the submission obligations under TINA, prime contractors (or higher-tier subcontractors) may wish to enter into an agreement, before any award of any Government contract, that requires all subcontractors to submit cost or pricing data directly to the Government in lieu of submitting such data to the prime contractor or their respective higher-tier subcontractor. Moreover, such agreement should state that direct submission to the Government satisfies the subcontractors' duty to disclose under its subcontract and that the subcontractor consents to the Government's audit of its cost or pricing data and dissemination of the Government's audit findings to the prime contractor (or higher-tier subcontractor). Furthermore, the agreement should specify that all parties agree that the prime contractor (or higher-tier subcontractor) is deemed to have relied upon the subcontract data submitted directly to the Government and that such reliance affects the subcontract price—whether or not the contractor ever receives the data or any associated audit reports.

All Government contractors should consider including the relevant

Government CO as a party to this agreement concerning the direct submission of subcontractor cost or pricing data. In the absence of any law, regulatory guidance, or decisional law on the subject, inclusion of the CO in such agreements is appropriate to ensure a Government commitment to the performance of a preaward audit of the subcontractors' cost or pricing data and provision of the nonconfidential results of such an audit to the prime contractor (or higher-tier subcontractor). In addition, involvement of the CO is highly desirable to ensure that any disclosure made to the DCAA (or some other Government designee) of subcontract data will serve as "adequate disclosure" to the Government by the prime contractor for purposes of TINA.

• Indemnification: Prime Contractor's Perspective

Clearly, a prime contractor (or higher-tier subcontractor) is at risk that it will be held responsible for any liability arising out of its subcontractors' submittals of cost or pricing data. It is also clear that such risk is not effectively mitigated under FAR 52.215-10, the typical subcontract flowdown "Price Reduction" clause. Thus, a prime contractor (or higher-tier subcontractor) may wish to seek indemnification from its subcontractors and prospective subcontractors for subcontract defective pricing liability.

To effectively protect its interests, a prime contractor (or higher-tier subcontractor) should attempt to include in its subcontracts a defective pricing indemnity term requiring its subcontractors to indemnify it for any loss incurred as a result of any defective pricing relating to the subcontractor's cost or pricing data. The term should make it clear that the prime contractor (or higher-tier subcontractor) is entitled to indemnity for *any and all* loss, including the impact of the asserted defective pricing, and for any additional costs that are directly associated with the inclusion of the subcontractor's inflated costs as part of the prime contractor (or higher-tier subcontractor) proposal, such as indirect costs, profit, associated legal expenses, penalties, or interest assessed on the claim.

In addition, the subcontract indemnity term should be included in the subcontract *and* as part of the terms that the subcontractor must agree to *at the time it submits its proposal* before even the negotiation of any actual subcontract. While the enforceability of such a "pre-subcontract agreement" is not assured under various state laws that would govern such an agreement, its absence invites the subcontractor to disavow any liability for its submission of defective cost or pricing data where it fails to enter into any subcontract. The subcontractor's ability to disavow liability under such circumstances could leave the prime contractor (or higher-tier subcontractor) to absorb the loss resulting from a Government defective pricing claim relating to the subcontractor's data if the prime contractor agrees on price with the Government for the prime contract before agreeing on a subcontract price.

Moreover, the subcontract indemnity term should obligate the subcontractor to provide the prime contractor (or higher-tier subcontractor) with relief from any loss at the time that the prime contractor (or higher-tier subcontractor) experiences any actual loss arising out of a Government claim for subcontract defective pricing. This obligation ensures that the prime contractor (or higher-tier subcontractor) is made whole upon the enforcement of any price reduction to the relevant prime contract (or higher-tier subcontract), not after resolution of any legal action appealing the defective pricing claim, which often occurs years after the actual loss is sustained.

Furthermore, any subcontract indemnity term should obligate the subcontractor whenever possible to dispute a Government claim of subcontract defective pricing directly with the Government. That is, in the case of a first-tier subcontractor, the indemnity term should require such subcontractor to litigate the Government's claim at its own expense under the sponsorship of the prime contractor. The final decision of the litigation process would serve as the final adjudication of the prime contractor's entitlement to indemnification under the subcontract indemnity term. If the subcontractor is at the second-tier or below, the term should require such subcontractor to defend the higher-tier subcontractor against any liability in any relevant forum.

• Indemnification: Subcontractor's Perspective

Indemnity for subcontractor defective pricing claims is an onerous subcontract term, particularly considering subcontractors' relative lack of control over the negotiation of the prime contract (or higher-tier subcontract) price. A subcontractor, therefore, should resist providing indemnity for any loss resulting from subcontract defective pricing, to the extent possible.

A subcontractor's best defense against indemnity, or rather, any defective pricing liability is to establish that one of the *exemptions* to TINA applies to its subcontract. If an exemption applies the subcontractor is not obligated to submit cost or pricing data, and, thus, indemnity is entirely irrelevant. The most common exemption from TINA relates to the commercial nature of supplies or services subject to the subcontract. If the subcontract is for the acquisition of commercial items, it is exempt from any of the requirements of TINA.

If TINA's requirements and indemnity for subcontract defective pricing cannot be avoided, subcontractors should attempt to *limit* the indemnification to only defective pricing liability arising out of the subcontractors' submittal of cost or pricing data as of the date of the subcontract price agreement—i.e., liability consistent with FAR 52.215-10. As noted above, such an indemnity agreement would leave the prime contractor exposed to various risks without ability to recover against the subcontractor. Nevertheless, it is not necessarily appropriate for the subcontractor to insure the prime contractor against every risk. Indeed, in some circumstances it may be unreasonable for subcontractors (and particularly lower-tier subcontractors) to be held responsible for the accuracy, completeness, and currency of their cost or pricing data, if they are not provided an opportunity by the prime contractor (or higher-tier subcontractor) to "sweep" their organizations for the most current information at the time of each agreement on price for the relevant higher-tier subcontracts or prime contract.

To further limit indemnity liability, subcontractors may attempt to secure an agreement that the prime contractor (or higher-tier subcontractor) will not seek a price reduction to the subcontract for defective pricing, unless the *Government* first seeks a reduction for such subcontract defective pricing under a claim against the prime contract. This agreement narrows the potential claims that may be brought against the subcontractor to claims initiated by the Government, eliminating the possibility of a claim initiated by the prime contractor for a price reduction not affecting the prime contract price. In the case of a second-tier subcontract or below, the subcontractor should revise this limitation to provide that the relevant higher-tier subcontractor may not seek indemnity, unless faced with liability arising out of a Government claim that is levied on the higher-tier subcontractor through its higher-tier subcontract.

If indemnity is provided, the subcontractor should demand that the prime contractor (or higher-tier subcontractor) notify the subcontractor within a reasonable time before any agreement on price under any higher-tier subcontract or the prime contract. As noted above, the absence of such a term leaves the subcontractor helpless to control the sufficiency of its submitted cost or pricing data at the critical points at which a claim of subcontract defective pricing may arise. Presumably, if the subcontractor is given proper prior notice of the various price agreements, it can update its proposal submission to reflect the most accurate, complete, and current information and, thus, mitigate the likelihood of liability.

With respect to notice requirements, the subcontractor should also demand immediate notice of any defective pricing claim. Further, upon notice of a claim, the subcontractor should require the right to take control over the defense of the prime contractor (or higher-tier subcontractor) against the claim. Finally, the subcontractor should ensure that it is liable to the prime contractor (or higher-tier subcontractor) for a price reduction to its relevant subcontract, not a cash payment, unless compelled by the circumstances of the subcontract performance to reimburse the prime contractor (or higher-tier subcontractor) for full payment made under the relevant subcontract. Such a subcontract price reduction (or reimbursement of overpayments) would occur no earlier than the date on which a price reduction occurs on the relevant prime contract (or higher-tier subcontract).

§ 10:5 Guidelines

The *Guidelines* are designed to assist you in understanding the steps contractors at every tier may take to reduce the possibility of potential subcontract defective pricing liability. They are not, however, a substitute for professional representation in any specific situation.

1. Review your subcontracting policies and procedures to ensure they properly mitigate the impact of subcontract defective pricing liability.
2. Be aware that mere flow-down of the standard FAR "Price Reduction" clause may provide insufficient protection to a prime contractor or higher-tier subcontractor.
3. In the case where submission of the subcontractors' cost or pricing data conflicts with its confidentiality policies, bear in mind that direct submission to the DCAA or other Government officials may not be sufficient to fulfill TINA disclosure obligations. The subcontractor can request that the prime contractor agree with the Government to allow for direct submission of subcontractor cost or pricing data to the Government.
4. If you are a prime contractor (or higher-tier subcontractor), you

should attempt to include in your subcontracts a defective pricing indemnity term. The indemnity term should require the subcontractor to indemnify the prime contractor for any loss incurred as a result of any defective pricing relating to the subcontractor's cost or pricing data. The indemnity term should also require that the subcontractor agree to provide the prime contractor (or higher-tier subcontractor) indemnity at the time it submits its proposal.

5. On the other hand, if you are a subcontractor, you should resist, to the extent possible, any agreement whatsoever to provide indemnity for defective pricing liability to the prime contractor (or higher-tier subcontractor).

6. If you are a subcontractor, remember that you should always seek to determine whether the relevant subcontract fits within a TINA exemption.

7. If the prime contractor (or higher-tier subcontractors) demands more protection from you as a subcontractor, ask that the FAR "Price Reduction" clause be merely flowed down. The FAR "Price Reduction" clause creates a limited liability to the subcontractor for defective pricing.

8. If an indemnity provision in your subcontract is unavoidable, you should attempt to limit the coverage of the indemnity to only those claims for defective pricing brought by the Government.

9. If you are a subcontractor, you should only agree to remit payment under the indemnity term if/when the prime contractor (or higher-tier subcontractor) has been subject to a price reduction for defective pricing caused by defective subcontractor cost or pricing data.

10. Consult an attorney with TINA experience to ensure your contracting procedures properly mitigate the risks of TINA liability. The investment you make before defective pricing liability arises will help you avoid claims for defective pricing.

Chapter 11

Earned Value Management Systems (EVMS)

KeyCiteᴿ: Cases and other legal materials listed in KeyCite Scope can be researched through the KeyCite service on Westlawᴿ. Use KeyCite to check citations for form, parallel references, prior and later history, and comprehensive citator information, including citations to other decisions and secondary materials.

---

§ 11:1   Introduction

This chapter provides information pertaining to project planning, scheduling, and the Earned Value Management System (EVMS) required by the U.S. Department of Defense (DOD) Instruction 5000.2 and the Defense Acquisition Guidebook. It should be useful to project managers, program managers, technical representatives, project control managers, contract managers, subcontract managers, and others involved in project management.

§ 11:2   Earned Value Management (EVM)

Earned value management (EVM) is now a hot topic in the U.S. Department of Defense (DOD) and defense industry for a couple of reasons. First, the Office of Management and Budget (OMB) has added the requirement for EVM to the *Federal Acquisition Regulation*. Second, the Department of Defense (DOD) has recently made some relatively significant changes to its policy on this key project management process that has been used in the defense acquisition process for more than 35 years.

EVM is a widely accepted industry best practice for project management, which is used across the DOD, federal government, and the commercial sector. A common operational definition of EVM is "the use of an integrated management system that coordinates work scope, schedule, and cost goals and objectively measures progress toward these goals." The term EVM replaces the old term used since the 1960's Cost/Schedule Control Systems Criteria (C/SCSC).

On March 7, 2005, the defense acquisition executive signed a memorandum approving revisions to the department's EVM policy. The policy has been modified to provide consistency in application across DOD programs and to better manage the programs through improvements in DOD and industry practices.

§ 11:3   New application thresholds for EVM

EVM compliance is required on cost or incentive contracts, subcontracts, intra-government work agreements, and other agreements valued at or greater than $20 million dollars. An EVM system that has been formally validated and accepted by the cognizant contracting officer is required on cost or incentive contracts, subcontracts, intra-government work agreements, and other agreements valued at or greater than $50 million.

§ 11:4   Contract implementation of EVM

The changes to DOD's EVM policy are required to be implemented on applicable contracts that are awarded based on solicitations or requests for proposal valued at or greater than $20 million issued on or after April 6, 2005, using Defense Federal Acquisition Regulation Supplement (DFARS) clauses 252.242-7005 and 252.252-7006.

The revised policy has been incorporated into DOD Instruction 5000.2 and the Defense Acquisition Guidebook. The changes have been incorporated into the EVMIG—the principal reference for detailed implementation guidance, which is available on the Defense Contract Management Agency (DCMA) Web site at http://guidebook.dcma.mil/79/guidebook_process.htm.

§ 11:5   Understanding the Earned Value Management System (EVMS)

To understand how an Earned Value Management System (EVMS) works you must become familiar with the ten basic project management building blocks of: (1) organizing, (2) authorizing, (3) scheduling, (4) budgeting, (5) cost accumulation, (6) performance measurement, (7) variance analysis, (8) changes management, (9) internal audit, (10) performance formulae, analysis, DoD reviews, and reports.

1) ORGANIZING WORK

Organizing the work is the initial task of project management. The operations organization is made up of those individuals responsible for the various tasks required by the contract Statement of Work (SOW), or Performance Work Statement (PWS).

Work Breakdown Structure (WBS)

The WBS provides the framework for the organization of the contract effort. It is an indentured listing of all of the products (e.g. hardware, software, services, and data) to be furnished by Lucent. It is used as the basis for all contract planning, scheduling, and budgeting; cost accumulation; and performance reporting throughout the entire period of project performance.

Integrated Project Team (IPT)

The Integrated Project Team structure reflects the organization required to support the project. The project manager is responsible to ensure the cost, schedule, and technical management of the project. The Project Manager draws upon the functional groups to accomplish the work through the assignment of responsibility to appropriate managers.

Responsibility Assignment Matrix (RAM)

The RAM ties the work that is required by the WBS elements to the organization responsible for accomplishing the assigned tasks. The intersection of the WBS with the integrated project team structure identifies the control account. The RAM includes the organization and the individual responsible for the work, which is then tracked to a control account.

2) AUTHORIZING WORK

All work within a project should be described and authorized through the contractor's work authorization system. Work authorization ensures that performing organizations are specifically informed regarding their work scope, schedule for performance, budget, and charge number(s) for the work assigned to them.

Work authorization is formal process that can consist of various levels. Each level of authorization is agreed upon by the parties involved so that there is no question as to what is required.

The document involved in work authorization should be maintained in a current status throughout the lifecycle of the contract as revisions take place.

Customer Authorization

Customer authorization is comprised of:

- Basic contract
- Contract change notices
- Engineering change notices

Internal Authorization

Internal Authorization is comprised of these steps:

- Upon receipt of a contract (or change notice), the Contracts Management Team provides the Project Manager authorization to perform the contract work in the form of a Project Authorization Notice (PAN) or equivalent document.
- The Project Manager prepares a document authorizing the assigned functional manager to perform work. This authorization is a contract between the functional manager and the Project Manager.

The diagram below Figure 11-1, shows the typical contractor work authorization flow.

Figure 11-1 Work Authorization Documentation Flow

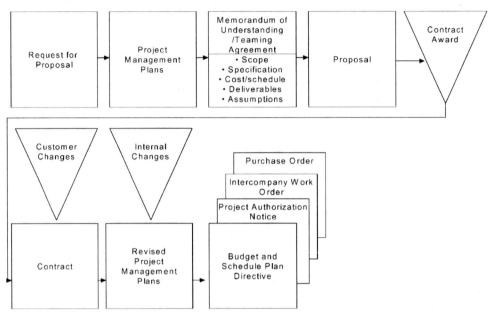

3) SCHEDULING WORK

The subjects of scheduling and budgeting are interrelated and iterative. In order to develop a time-phased budget plan, the schedule must be prepared first.

Scheduling is the process of integrating activities and resources into a meaningful arrangement, depicting the timing of the critical activities that will satisfy the customer's requirements.

Project Scheduling

Project scheduling is a logical time-phasing of the activities that are necessary to accomplish the entire project scope. It is the most important tool for cost and schedule:

- Planning
- Tracking
- Analysis of variances
- Reporting of project performance

Each activity in the network is characterized by scope, logical relationships, duration, and resources.

Figure 11-2, shows the steps required to build a project schedule.

Figure 11-2 Building Project Schedule

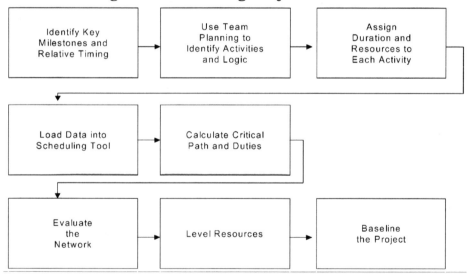

Scheduling Definitions

- Milestone—An event of particular significance that has no duration.
- Activity—Something that occurs over time; work that must be accomplished, also referred to as a "task."
- Sequential—Activities that are performed in sequence or right after each other.
- Concurrent/Parallel—Two or more activities that are performed at the same time or that overlap.

Scheduling Terms

- Finish-to-Start: The predecessor activity must be completed before the successor activity can begin.

- Start-to-Start: The predecessor activity must begin before the successor activity can begin.

- Finish-to-Finish: The predecessor activity must end before the successor activity can end.

- Lag—Any schedule time delay between two tasks. Lags can be positive or negative.
- Critical Path—Longest continuous sequence of tasks through the network, given the underlying relationships that will affect the project end date.
- Float—Difference between the time available (when tasks can start/finish) and the time necessary (when tasks must start/finish).

Schedule Outputs

There are three basic scheduling outputs:

- Network diagram
- Gantt chart
- Resource histogram

Once the project schedule is complete, the cost/schedule performance baseline is established. Figure 11-3 shows the steps required to establish the baseline and track and analyze performance on the project.

Figure 11-3 Steps to Build a Project Baseline

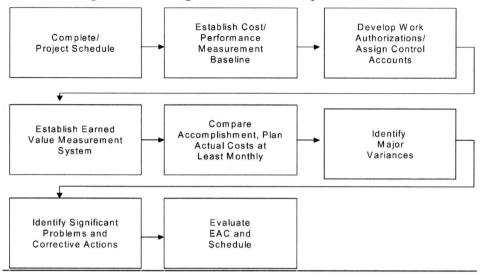

Figure 11-4 A Typical Performance Measurement System

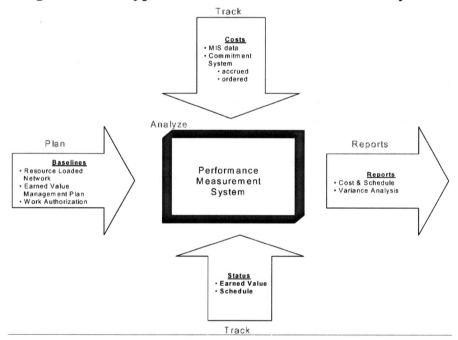

4) BUDGETING WORK

Budgeting is the process of distributing budgets to individual work segments. The following top-down illustration (see Figure 11-5) gives the overview of the relationships.

Figure 11-5

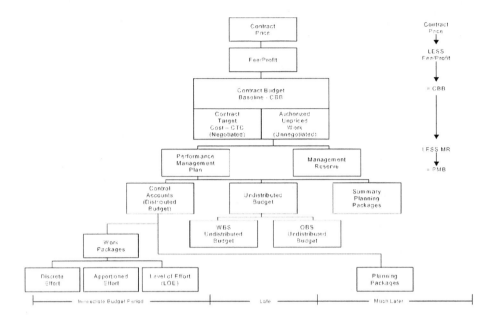

Total Allocated Budget (TAB)

The TAB is the sum of all budgets allocated to the contract. It is the same as the Contract Budget Base (CBB) unless an Over Target Baseline (OTB) has been established. (See *Changes* for an explanation of OTB).

Contract Budget Base (CBB)

The CBB is the sum of the Contract Target Cost (CTC) plus the estimated cost of any authorized unpriced (not yet negotiated) work. It is made up of the Performance Measurement Baseline and management reserve.

Performance Measurement Baseline (PMB)

The PMB is the time-phased budget plan against which contract performance is measured. It is composed of the budgets assigned to Control Accounts and Undistributed Budget. It equals the TAB minus management reserve.

Management Reserve (MR)

This is a budget amount that is set aside to provide for unforeseen, within-contract scope requirements.

Control Account (CA)

The control account is the focal point for planning, monitoring, and controlling project work as it represents the work within a single WBS element, and is the responsibility of a single organizational unit.

Virtually all aspects of the Performance Management System come together at the control account level, including budgets, schedules, work assignments, cost collection, progress assessment, problem identification, corrective actions, and Estimate at Completion (EAC) development. Day-to-day management is performed at the control account level.

The level selected for the establishment of a control account must be carefully considered to ensure that work is properly defined into manageable units with responsibilities clearly delineated.

Undistributed Budget (UB)

This is the budget that is applicable to a specific contract effort, but that has not yet been distributed to the WBS elements. Undistributed budget is intended to serve only as a temporary holding account until the budget is properly distributed.

Summary Planning Packages

Summary planning packages are used to plan time-phased budgets for far-term work that cannot practically be planned in full detail.

Work Packages

A work package is a detailed job that is established by the functional manager for accomplishing work within a control account.

A work package has these characteristics:

- Represents units of work (activities or tasks) at the levels where the work is performed.
- Is clearly distinct from all other work packages, and is the responsibility of a single organizational element.
- Has scheduled start and completion dates (with interim milestones, if applicable) that are representatives of physical task accomplishment.
- Has a budget or assigned value expressed in terms of dollars, labor hours, or other measurable units.
- Has a duration that is relatively short, unless it is subdivided by discrete milestones to permit objective measurement of work performed.
- Has a schedule that is integrated with all other activities occurring on the project.
- Has a unique Earned Value technique, either discrete, apportioned effort, or Level of Effort (LOE).

Planning Package

If a control account cannot be subdivided into fully detailed work packages, the far-term effort is identified in larger planning packages for budgeting and scheduling purposes. The budget for the planning package is identified according to the work for which it is intended, is time-phased, and should have controls that prevent its use in the performance of other work. Eventually, all work in planning packages will be planned to the appropriate level of detail in work packages.

5) COST ACCUMULATION

Cost accumulation is the process of recording and assembling the actual costs for a project. The lowest level of accumulation is the work package, although many large projects accumulate costs at the control account level. These actual costs plus accruals are called Actual Cost of Work Performed (ACWP).

Direct Cost Elements

Within the control account or a work package (depending upon the level of cost accumulation), there are direct cost elements.

Direct cost elements are:

Direct Labor
Other Direct Costs (ODCs)
Material
Subcontracts

- **Direct Labor**

  Timekeeping/cost collection for labor costs uses a labor distribution/accumulation system. The MIS reports biweekly expenditure data based on labor charges against control accounts or work packages.

- **Other Direct Costs** ODCs include charges such as: Travel and Per Diem Service Centers Purchased Services

- **Material/Subcontracts**

Indirect Cost Elements

Indirect cost elements consist of:

Overhead (OH) and Fringe
General and Administration (G&A)
Within each indirect cost element there are multiple sub-elements.

- **Overhead (OH) and Fringe**

  Overhead and fringe costs are accumulated in pools for biweekly distribution to projects. Overhead and fringe are allocated to each charge number in each organization based on the individual Lucent overhead and fringe rates.

- **General and Administrative (G&A)** These indirect costs are also accumulated in pools for biweekly distribution to project charge numbers.

6) PERFORMANCE MEASUREMENT

Performance measurement for the functional managers, project control managers, and others consist of evaluating work packages status calculated at the work package level. A comparison of the planned value (Budgeted Cost for Work Scheduled (BCWS) to Earned Value (Budgeted Cost for Work Performed (BCWP)) is made to obtain the schedule variance, and a comparison of the BCWP to the Actual Costs (ACWP) is made to obtain the cost variance. Performance measurement provides a basis for management decisions by the project manager, Lucent management and, in some cases, the customer.

Performance Measurement

- **Performance measurement provides:**
  - (1) Work progress status.
  - (2) Relationship of planned cost and actual cost to actual accomplishment
  - (3) Valid, timely, auditable data
  - (4) Basis for the EAC
- **Elements required to measure project progress and status are:**
  - A. Work package schedule status.
  - B. BCWS or the planned expenditure.
  - C. BCWP or Earned Value

    D. ACWP or MIS costs and accruals.

- **Control account/work packages:**
  - A. Measurable work and related event status form the basis for determining progress for BCWP calculations.
  - B. BCWP measurements at summary WBS levels result from accumulating BCWP upward through the control account from the work package levels.
    - (1) Within each control account, the inclusion of LOE is kept to a minimum to prevent distortion of the total BCWP.
    - (2) Calculation methods used for measuring work package performance are:
      - a. Short work packages (2 months or less) may use the measured effort or formula method, e.g., 0–100%, where a status can be applied each month.
      - b. Longer work packages (over 2 months) should have milestones assigned. The milestones are then statused monthly for the lifecycle of the work package.
      - c. In manufacturing, work packages may use the earned standards or equivalent units method to measure performance based on the manufacturing work measurement system output.
      - d. Effort that can be measured in direct proportion to other discrete work may be measured as apportioned effort work packages. Apportioned effort is used primarily in manufacturing.
      - e. Sustained efforts are planned using the LOE Earned Value method. The Earned Value for LOE work packages is equal to the time-phased plan (BCWS).
    - (3) The measurement method used depends on an analysis of the work to be performed in the work package. Whichever method is selected for planning (BCWS) must also be used for determining progress (BCWP).
- **Estimated to Complete (ETC) Preparation.**
  To develop an ETC, the CAM must consider and analyze.
  - A. Cumulative ACWP/ordered commitments.
  - B. Schedule status.
  - C. BCWP to date.
  - D. Remaining control account scope of work.
  - E. Previous ETC.
  - F. Historical data.
  - G. Required resources by type.
  - H. Projected cost and schedule efficiency.
  - I. Future actions.
  - J. Approved contract changes.
- **The functional managers or Control Account Managers (CAM) prepares the ETC as required by the Project Manager.**
- **EAC Preparation**. The ETC is then summarized to all necessary reporting levels, added to the ACWP and commitments, and reported to Corporate management and the customer, as appropriate.

- **A bottoms-up EAC should be prepared quarterly for all contracts at Lucent.**

The EAC is the estimated cost at the end of the project. It is composed of the cost of what has been accomplished and the estimated cost of the remaining work. This graph illustrates the two primary components of the EAC.

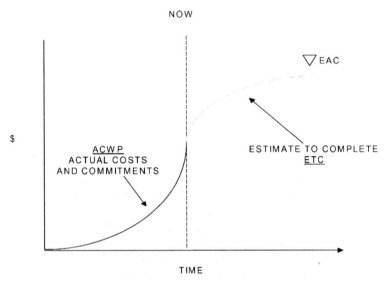

The following diagram shows the components of the EAC.

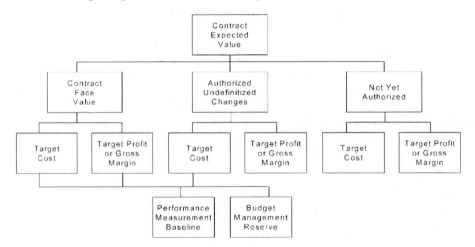

Revenues at Completion

Revenues at completion are the total revenues anticipated on the contract at the completion of the project. Revenues at completion are composed of the EAC and the EAC profit.

EAC Profit

EAC profit is the profit expected to be achieved at the completion of the project.

Estimate at Completion (EAC)

EAC is the cost of work performed to date plus the estimated cost of all remaining work on the project. The EAC is made up of four components: ACWP, open commitments, ETC, and hard reserves.

Actual Cost of Work Performed (ACWP)

ACWP is the cost of work performed to date plus accruals.

Accurals

Accurals are costs for goods or services received by Lucent for which we have yet to pay the bill.

Ordered Commitments

Ordered commitments are costs for goods or services on order where the work has not yet been performed.

Estimate to Complete (ETC)

ETC is the estimated cost of the remaining work on the project.

Hard Reserves

Hard reserves are reserves associated with the EAC and are to cover the potential cost of risks to be mitigated on the project. The hard reserves are equal to the sum of the mitigation costs plus the sum of the residual risk remaining.

7) VARIANCE ANALYSIS

If performance measurement produces schedule or cost variances in excess of pre-established thresholds, the cause must be determined. The functional managers or CAM is responsible for the analysis of the control account and understanding trends that indicate potential future problems.

Variance Calculations

There are three types of variances: schedule variances, cost variances, and Variances of Completion (VACs). They are calculated as follows:

$$SV = BCWP—BCWS$$

$$CV = BCWP—ACWP$$

$$VAC = BAC—EAC$$

Variance Thresholds

Variance analysis is required when one or more of the variances exceeds the threshold established for the project. Variance thresholds are defined by a percentage or a dollar amount, or a combination of the two. The latter method is usually more appropriate since it eliminates very small variances from the analysis requirement. The thresholds are generally established by the Sector, but may be provided by the customer.

Variance Analysis Operation

- The Variance Analysis Reports (VARs) provide current period, cumulative, and at-completion data. CAMs provide VARs for control accounts that have a schedule variance, cost variance, or VAC that exceeds the established thresholds.
- The CAM completes the VAR by providing a description of the cause of the variance, its imp0act on the control account and other elements of the project, the corrective action to be taken, and any follow-up on previous actions taken.
- The VAR is submitted through the appropriate project channels for approval.
- The Project Manager uses the control account VARs to report project status to upper management.
- The Project Manager has a continuing responsibility for monitoring corrective actions.
- Periodic, formal project reviews, scheduling meetings, and staff meetings serve as forums for variance trend analysis and corrective action monitoring.

8) CHANGES

When an authorized change is received, all affected work authorization, budget planning, and scheduling documents should be updated in a timely manner to reflect the change.

Revision Types

- **Internal Replanning**. This is the replanning that is undertaken within the scope, schedule and budget constraints of the current contract. It is often associated with the use of management reserve.
- **External Replanning**. These are contract changes directed and authorized by the customer.
- **Over Target Replanning**. This is replanning that results in the planning of a new PMB that is above the CBB. It results in a plan to overrun the contract value.

Replanning Rules

Four replanning rules are:

- Retroactive changes to BCWS, BCWP, or ACWP already incurred are strictly prohibited, except to correct accounting errors.
- Closed work packages or control accounts will not be reopened.
- Work scope will not be transferred from one control account to another without the associated budget transfer.
- Work packages that are open (in process) will not be replanned.

9) INTERNAL AUDIT/VERIFICATION

The functional manager or CAMs are the most significant contributors to the successful operation of the Earned Value Management System and to the successful completion of any subsequent audits or customer reviews, if appropriate. Day-to-day management of the project takes place at the control account level. If each control account is not managed competently, project performance will suffer. Because Lucent places emphasis on cost schedule and technical performance, the functional managers must be proficient in all areas of control account management. Audits are performed periodically to ensure that the management system is fully operational.

In addition to auditing the internal system, there is a responsibility to periodically audit our subcontractors to ensure that we receive reliable schedule and performance measurement data.

10) PERFORMANCE FORMULAE, ANALYSIS, DoD Reviews, & Reports

Legend

This legend is applicable to the formulae and charts that follow:

BCWS Budgeted Cost for Work Scheduled
BCWP Budgeted Cost for Work Performed
ACWP Actual Cost of Work Performed
BAC Budget at Completion
ETC Estimate to Complete
EAC Estimate at Completion

Cost Variance

$$CV = BCWP - ACWP$$

Cost Variance %

$$CV\% = \frac{CV}{BCWP} \times 100$$

Cost Performance Index

$$CPI = \frac{BCWP}{ACWP}$$

To Complete Performance Index

$$TCPI = \frac{BAC - BCWPcum}{EAC - ACWPcum}$$

Schedule Variance

$$SV = BCWP - BCWS$$

Schedule Variance %

$$SV\% = \frac{SV}{BCWS} \times 100$$

Schedule Performance Index

$$SPI = \frac{BCWP}{BCWS}$$

Schedule Variance in Months

$$SV\ months = \frac{SV\ cum}{BCWP\ current\ period}$$

Percent Spent

$$\% \text{ Spent} = \frac{\text{ACWPcum}}{\text{BAC}^*} \times 100$$

Percent Complete

$$\% \text{ Complete} = \frac{\text{BCWPcum}}{\text{BAC}^*}$$

*EAC, PMB, CBB, or TAB may also be used.

Statistical Examples

Independent EAC
The basic formulae are:

$$\text{EAC1} = \text{ACWPcum} + (\text{BAC—BCWP cum})$$

$$\text{EAC2} = \frac{\text{BAC}}{\text{CPIe}}$$

$$\text{EAC3} = [(\text{BAC—BCWP})/(\text{CPI} \times \text{SPI})] + \text{ACWP}$$

Variance at Completion %

$$\text{VAC}\% = \frac{\text{VAC} \times 100}{\text{BAC}}$$

Budget/Earned Rate

$$\text{B/E Rate} = \frac{\text{BCWP dollars}}{\text{BCWP hours}}$$

Actual Rate

$$\text{Actual Rate} = \frac{\text{ACWP dollars}}{\text{ACWP hours}}$$

Rate Variance

$$\text{Rate Variance} = (\text{B/E Rate—Actual Rate}) \times \text{Actual Hours}$$

To-Go-Rate

$$\text{To-Go Rate} = \frac{\text{ETC dollars}}{\text{ETC hours}}$$

Efficiency Variance

$$\text{Efficiency Variance} = (\text{BCWP hours—ACWP hours}) \times \text{B/E Rate}$$

Price Variance

$$\text{PV} = (\text{Planned/Earned Price—Actual Price}) \times \text{Actual Quantity}$$

Usage Variance

$$\text{UV} = (\text{Planned/Earned Quantity—Actual Quantity}) \times \text{Earned Price}$$

Cost and schedule performance data are often displayed graphically to give the analyst and the manager a picture of the trends. The two most common displays are shown here. These graphs can be used for a control account, an organization, a WBS element, or the entire project.

Figure 11-6
Cumulative BCWS, BCWP and ACWP

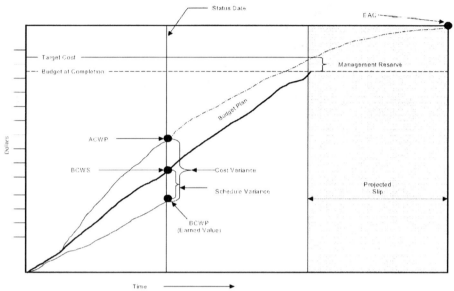

Figure 11-7 CPI and SPI

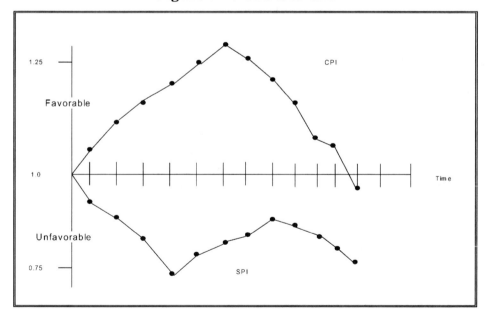

§11:6 DoD Performance Reviews & Reports

Integrated Baseline Reviews (IBRs)

An IBR is a joint assessment of the Performance Measurement Baseline

(PMB) conducted by the government program manager and the contractor. The IBR is not a one-time event. It is a process, and the plan should be continually evaluated as changes to the baseline are made (modifications, restructuring, etc.). IBRs should be used as necessary throughout the life of a project to facilitate and maintain mutual understanding.

- The scope of the PMB consistent with authorizing documents;
- Management control processes;
- Risks in the PMB associated with cost, schedules, and resources; and
- Corrective actions where necessary.

IBRs should be scheduled as early as practicable and the timing of the IBRs should take into consideration the contract period of performance. The process should be initiated not later than 180 calendar days (6 months) after: (1) contract award, (2) the exercise of significant contract options, and (3) the incorporation of major modifications.

IBRs are also performed at the discretion of the program manager or within a reasonable time after the occurrence of major events in the life of a program. These events may be completion of the preliminary design review, completion of the critical design review, a significant shift in the content and/or time phasing of the PMB, or when a major milestone such as the start of the production option of a development contract is reached. Continuous assessment of the PMB will identify when a new IBR should be conducted.

In accordance with USD (AT&L) policy memorandum dated March 7, 2005, program managers are required to conduct IBRs on all cost or incentive contracts that require the implementation of EVM (contracts valued at or greater than $20 million). However, conducting the IBR is not dependent on the contractor's Earned Value Management System (EVMS) being formally validated as complying with the EVMS guidelines in ANSI/EIA-748. Subcontractors, intra-government work agreements, and other agreements should also require IBRs as applicable. The scope of the IBRs should be tailored to the nature of the work effort.

Contract Performance Management Reporting

The Contract Performance Report (CPR) and the Integrated Master Schedule (IMS) apply to all contracts that meet the EVM applicability requirements in USD (AT&L) policy memorandum dated March 7, 2005. On contracts valued at or greater than $20 million but less than $50 million, it is recommended that CPR and IMS reporting be tailored. See the DoD Earned Value Management Implementation Guide for additional guidance on tailoring reporting.

A common Work Breakdown Structure (WBS) that follows the DoD Work Breakdown Structure Handbook (MIL-HDBK-881A) is required for the Contractor Performance Report (CPR), Integrated Master Schedule (IMS), and Contractor Cost Data Report (CCDR). Except for high-cost or high-risk elements, the required level of reporting detail should not normally exceed level three of the contract WBS.

Contract Performance Report (CPR)

The CPR provides contract cost and schedule performance data that is used to identify problems early in the contract and forecast future contract performance. The CPR should be the primary means of documenting the ongoing communication between the contractor and the program manager to report cost and schedule trends to date and to permit assessment of their effect on future performance.

The program manager should obtain a CPR (DD Form 2734) on all cost or incentive contracts, subcontracts, intra-government work agreements, and other agreements valued at or greater than $20 million. The CPR is not typically required for cost or incentive contracts valued at less than $20 million, contracts less than 12 months in duration, or Firm-Fixed Price contracts regardless of dollar value. The DoD Earned Value Management Implementation Guide (EVMIG) discusses some circumstances where the CPR may be appropriate for contracts in these categories.

Data Item Description (DID) DI-MGMT-81466A should be used to obtain the CPR. The contracting officer and contractor should negotiate reporting provisions in the contract, including frequency and selection of formats, level of detail, submission dates, variance thresholds and analysis, and the contract WBS to be used. The program manager should tailor the CPR to the minimum data necessary for effective management control, particularly on contracts valued at less than $50 million. See the DoD EVMIG for additional guidance on tailoring CPR reporting.

In exceptional cases, the contractor may determine that the performance measurement budget or existing contract schedule cannot be achieved and no longer represents a reasonable basis for management control. With government approval, the contractor may implement an Over Target Baseline or Over Target Schedule. For cost-reimbursement contracts, the contract budget base excludes changes for cost growth increases, other than for authorized changes to the contract scope.

Integrated Master Schedule (IMS)

The IMS is a time-based schedule containing the networked, detailed tasks necessary to ensure successful program/control execution. The IMS is traceable to the integrated master plan, the contract work breakdown structure, and the statement of work. The IMS is used to verify attainability of contract objectives, to evaluate progress toward meeting program objectives, and to integrate the program schedule activities with all related components.

The program manager should obtain an IMS on all cost or incentive contracts, subcontracts, intra-government work agreements, and other agreements valued at or greater than $20 million. The IMS is applicable to development, major modification, and low rate initial production efforts; it is not typically applied to full rate production efforts. It is also not normally required for contracts valued at less than $20 million, contracts less than 12 months in duration, or Firm-Fixed Price contracts regardless of dollar value. The DoD Earned Value Management Implementation Guide (EVMIG) discusses some circumstances where the IMS may be appropriate for contracts in these categories.

Contract Funds Status Report (CFSR)

The CFSR supplies funding data about defense contracts to program managers for:

- Updating and forecasting contract funds requirements;
- Planning and decision making on funding changes in contracts;
- Developing funds requirements and budget estimates in support of approved programs;
- Determining funds in excess of contract needs and available for deobligation;
- Obtaining rough estimates of termination costs; and
- Determining if sufficient funds are available by fiscal year to execute the contract.

The program manager should obtain a CFSR (DD Form 1586) on contracts over 6 months in duration. The CFSR has no specific application thresholds; however, the program manager should carefully evaluate application to contracts valued at less than $1.5 million (in then-year dollars).

DID DI-MGMT-81468 should be used to obtain the CFSR. The contracting officer and contractor should negotiate reporting provisions in the contract, including level of detail and reporting frequency. The program manager should require only the minimum data necessary for effective management control. The CFSR should not be applied to Firm-Fixed Price contracts unless unusual circumstances dictate specific funding visibility.

Contractor Cost Data Reporting (CCDR)

CCDR is the primary means that the Department of Defense uses to collect data on the costs incurred by DoD contractors in performing DoD programs (Acquisition Category ID and IC). DoD Instruction 5000.2 makes CCDR mandatory. This data enables reasonable program cost estimates and satisfies other analytical requirements. The Chair, Cost Analysis Improvement Group (CAIG), ensures consistent and appropriate CCDR application throughout the Department of Defense by defining the format for submission of CCDRs and CCDR system policies, and by monitoring implementation.

CCDR coverage extends from Milestone B or equivalent to the completion of production in accordance with procedures described in this section. Unless waived by the Chair, CAIG, CCDR reporting is required on all major contracts and subcontracts that support Acquisition Category ID and IC programs, regardless of contract type, when the contracts are valued at more than $50 million (FY2002 constant dollars). CCDR reporting is not required for contracts below $7 million. The CCDR requirements on high-risk or high-technical-interest contracts priced between $7 and $50 million is left to the discretion of the Cost Working-Level Integrated Product Team.

Exclusions. CCDR reporting is not required for procurement of commercial systems, or for non-commercial systems bought under competitively awarded, firm fixed-price contracts, as long as competitive conditions continue to exist.

Software Resources Data Report (SRDR)

SRDR is a recent initiative with a primary purpose to improve the ability of the Department of Defense to estimate the costs of software intensive programs. DoD Instruction 5000.2 requires that data be collected from software development efforts-with a projected value greater than $25 million (FY2002 dollars) contained within major automated information systems (Acquisition Category IA) and major defense acquisition programs (Acquisition Category IC and Acquisition Category ID).

Data collected from applicable projects describe the type and size of the software development, and the schedule and labor resources needed for the development. There are three specific data items to be provided.

- Initial Government Report (DD Form 2630-1), records the government program manager's estimate-at-completion for the project. This report is due 180 days prior to contract award, and is forwarded as part of the Cost Analysis Requirements Description.
- The Initial Developer Report (DD Form 2630-2), records the initial estimates by the developer (i.e., contractor or government central design activity). This report is due 60 days after contract award.
- The Final Developer Report (DD Form 2630-3), is used to report actual experience. This items is due within 60 days after final deliver.

For particularly small or large software developments, the program manager may choose to shorten or lengthen the submission deadlines, accordingly. Also, for projects with multiple releases, the program manager may elect to combine the SRDR reporting of incremental releases within a single contract, and provide SRDR data items for the overall project.

Further information is available in an on-line SRDR Manual. This manual provides additional background and technical details about the data collection. In particular, the manual contains information about the process by which each project defines, collects, and submits the data. The manual also contains sample data items, and provides suggested language to include in a request for proposal for this reporting requirement.

§ 11:7 Summary

This chapter provides a wealth of information to explain the ten building blocks of Earned Value Management Systems (EVMS). Specifically, this chapter serves as a guide to understand how government contractors should develop EVMS and prepare for EVMS compliance reviews, conducted by the Defense Contract Management Agency (DCMA). Increasingly, U.S. Federal Government agencies are following the U.S. Department of Defense's lead via requiring government contractors to implement effective EVMS on their critical government contracts and projects.

§ 11:8 Questions to consider

1. Does your organization have an effective EVMS?
2. Have you received education and training on EVMS?
3. Has you organization's EVMS been reviewed and validated by DCMA? If so, when?

§ 11:9 EVMS Acronyms

ACWP   Actual Cost of Work Performed
AE   Apportioned Effort

BAC	Budget At Completion
BCWP	Budgeted Cost for Work Performed
BCWS	Budgeted Cost for Work Scheduled
CA	Control Account
CAM	Cost Account Manager
CBB	Contract Budget Base
CPI	Cost Performance Index
CV	Cost Variance
CTC	Contract Target Cost
CP	Critical Path
EAC	Estimate at Completion (same as LRE)
EVMS	Earned Value Management System
IWO	Intercompany Work Order
G&A	General and Administrative
IPT	Integrated Project Team
LOE	Level of Effort
LRE	Latest Revised Estimate (same as EAC)
MIS	Management Information System
MOU	Memorandum of Understanding
MR	Management Reserve
OBS	Organizational Breakdown Structure
ODCs	Other Direct Costs
OH	Overhead
OTB	Over Target Baseline
PAN	Project Authorization Notice
PM	Project Manager
PMB	Performance Measurement Baseline
PP	Planning Package
QRAM	Quantitative Risk Analysis Matrix
RAM	Responsibility Assignment Matrix
RLN	Resource Loaded Network
SOW	Statement of Work
SPI	Schedule Performance Index
SV	Schedule Variance
TAB	Total Allocated Budget
UB	Undistributed Budget
VAC	Variance at Completion
VAR	Variance Analysis Report
WBS	Work Breakdown Structure
WP	Work Package

Chapter 12

Terminating Subcontractors: Challenges & Best Practices

By: Gregory A. Garrett and Tom Reid, Esq,

> **KeyCite®:** Cases and other legal materials listed in KeyCite Scope can be researched through the KeyCite service on Westlaw®. Use KeyCite to check citations for form, parallel references, prior and later history, and comprehensive citator information, including citations to other decisions and secondary materials.

§ 12:1   Introduction

As a prelude to understanding how to deal with a subcontractor, it is important to understand that government contract law and commercial contract law are two very different bodies of law. While there are similarities, there are also many significant differences. The Federal Common Law as embodied in longstanding judicial precedents and as further reflected in both federal statutes and regulations, including the Federal Acquisition Regulation (FAR) and the various agency supplements, controls the creation, administration, and interpretation of federal prime contracts. Since this is a matter dealing with a sovereign, the sovereign gets to make the rules. Numerous public policies come into play including such things as the Christian Doctrine, which requires that certain clauses are automatically read into a government contract whether or not it is actually contained in the contract. Such things do not generally appear in commercial contracts.

Commercial contracts are governed by the laws of the various states, commonly embodied in the Uniform Commercial Code (UCC) as adopted by that state. There have been many versions of the UCC since it was first introduced, and the states have great latitude in what provisions they enact and changes they might make to that body of law. So while the bulk of the UCC might be considered "uniform" among the states, it is important to refer to the specific version of the state law governing the contract to be sure the proper law is applied. Of critical importance here, however, is that the body of law governing your prime contract is significantly different from the body of law that governs your subcontracts, including the forums where disputes under those agreements would be heard. While some of this can be addressed through the use of various flow-down provisions from your prime contract, that is not always the case, and too many prime contractors are less than meticulous in their subcontracting processes thus introducing great risk to their performance and profitability. This becomes extremely clear when a termination is the issue.

The federal government reserves to itself the right to terminate a contract for its convenience. The policy underlying this right is that once a good or service is no longer required, the government should not be compelled to complete the contract at public expense. It should be permitted to effectively cancel the contract and by the terms of the clauses it uses, limit the damages the contractor will be entitled to receive. In commercial arenas, such an action is considered a breach of contract and entitles the non-breaching party to more significant damages for the other party's breach. Immediately you can see that a prime contractor that does not manage its subcontracts appropriately can get squeezed between the two competing legal systems.

So the questions become, what are the best practices that prime contractors should use to be prepared for dealing with the termination of its subcontracts, and what are they required to do in serving the their own best interests, as well as the interests of their subcontractors and the government customer.

§ 12:2 Including the right clause

Under the UCC the parties can agree to most anything they choose. If they are silent regarding certain matters, the UCC will fill in the blanks and find that a contract exists with these included provisions. The right of the parties to agree otherwise permits the parties to include items that would not be automatically filled in by the UCC. Thus the use of government flow-down provisions in subcontracts is completely legal and proper. The use of mandatory flowdowns is one way that the government ensures that its prime contract award will be effectively performed. Typically a prime contractor wants to ensure that it has included a termination clause in its subcontracts, and most often it should be a variation of the clause that appears in your prime contract.

Be careful though. Recall that FAR includes a series of clauses for different situations and contract types. If, for example, you are awarded a cost-type prime contract then that clause will appear in your prime. Your subcontracts, however, may be either cost-type or fixed price. Thus you may want to include in your subcontracts a clause similar to the fixed price termination clauses, rather than the cost-type clause that appears in your prime. In other words, you do not want to flow the prime contract clause down directly and simply change "government" to say "prime contractor" and "contractor" to mean "subcontractor" throughout, although this is exactly what some contractors do.

For starters this is poor contract drafting practice, but more importantly the prime clause implements the contracts disputes act giving the prime contractor the right to appeal contracting officer final decisions. The subcontractors, with no privity of contract with the government, have no such right. The flowdown clause should be tailored to the circumstances and while the prime contract clause is a good starting point, unconsidered inclusion verbatim is not good contract management.

The Termination clause is not a mandatory flowdown, so some might argue that it is unnecessary in a subcontract, but this is flawed thinking. For starters, when your customer has the right to terminate your contract for convenience and you do NOT reserve an appropriate right to yourself as against your subcontractors, any attempted termination will be viewed by the law as a breach that gives your subcontractor the right to be made whole. This usually includes anticipatory profits, or the profit they would have made if the contract had gone to normal completion. By agreeing with your subcontractors up front that their recovery will be limited, as yours will be, to work actually completed and accepted you minimize the cost to the government and avoid protracted litigation over your "breach."

The government will look carefully at your practices in this regard when conducting a Contractor Purchasing System Review (CPSR). To minimize its costs, the government expects you to include a termination clause in your subcontracts. If you fail to do so on a regular basis it will be a finding in their review. If you fail to do so in a particular termination, the Contracting Officer (CO) will look to see if you made a good faith effort to get one included. Since subcontracts are mutual agreements, there may be situations where a subcontractor will simply refuse to include such a clause. Your choice becomes whether to award the contract anyway for legitimate business reasons, or to seek a different subcontractor. This level of attention is expected by the government. Your failure to include the clause, thus increasing the costs to the government in a termination, can affect the settlement negotiations and the level of fee you may be entitled to for completed work.

There have been occasions where prime contractors have abused the use of the termination clause. By including this unilateral right, the prime can terminate for almost any reason it chooses, including as punishment to the subcontractor, a desire to take over the scope assigned to the subcontractor, or to extort more or different performance from the subcontractor. These are all inappropriate reasons to exercise the right of termination. As a defense, subcontractors will often ask that the clause be modified to include language that limits the right of the prime to terminate to those situations where the government has terminated that portion of the work covered by the subcontract. This is a fair compromise and affords the subcontractor a little more protection in an environment where they may have less bargaining power than the prime contractor.

§ 12:3 Putting a termination into effect

When you receive the government's notice of termination one of the immediate instructions is to notify all subcontractors of the termination (effectively terminating their subcontract if the right has been properly reserved) and to place no more orders. This may also include withholding funding any subcontract that is incrementally funded. Similar to the notice you receive from the government, you should have prepared a draft termination notice to give to your subcontractors. Do not delay in providing this notice since the continued accruing of costs against the government prime contract may be deemed unreasonable and ultimately disallowed. This can result in your obligation to pay the subcontractor with no commensurate right to be reimbursed by the government.

All of the same instructions received from the government — to stop all work, to place no further lower-tier subcontracts, to inventory property, to inform as to funding, et cetera, will apply to the subcontractor. Make clear that this is a definitive action and the subcontractor must comply with this instruction, citing the appropriate clause. Record in your files the date, time, and manner of notice given to the subcontractor and ask that they confirm receipt. This will demonstrate your compliance with the CO direction. The clause that you have flowed down should have shorter response times than those provided by the government to give you an opportunity to get the requisite data, the termination settlement claim, from all of your subcontractors so that they can be rolled up to your claim to the government. So rather than 120 days for property inventories, you might require 90. Make clear to the subcontractor that these dates are important and any delay will have consequences.

There will be subcontractors within your team who will have no concept of a government termination. Their entire business experience will have been based on commercial standards where such things don't happen. This may be particularly troubling if the subcontractor will lose a significant proportion of its total business due to this action. They may have ramped up production, or hired additional staff to meet your requirements and are now faced with a significant business disruption. You will ask them for a settlement proposal, and this entire process might be completely foreign to them. They may have no knowledge of government cost accounting rules or practices. In fact their entire accounting system may be completely inadequate to provide you the cost proposal that you are now requesting.

You can and should so several things as soon as possible to assist your subcontractors. Easing their concerns, to the degree you can, and giving them access to tools they may need will encourage prompt response from your subcontractors and avoid delays in getting your own proposal pulled together. Provide them a briefing of the termination settlement process. Inform them that while the contract has ended, they will be paid for the reasonable costs of putting the settlement proposal together. Assist them in retaining competent help to do so. These are reasonable costs in a termination. Caution them that all work MUST stop on this project and that continuing costs will not be covered. If they are providing a commercial item, or other item that they can use, let them know the process that will permit them to convert these items to their own use. Give them prompt instructions concerning property disposal and the preservation of all work in process (WIP). In a nutshell, they will need to do everything that you are doing internally to effect the termination. The difference is that you understand the process and requirements far better than they do. Many of them will need significant hand-holding, yet you also must make sure that your dealings with them are at arm's-length. This can be a delicate balance, but it is necessary.

How you treat your subcontractors in this process is one factor that CO's will consider in determining your fee for the completed work. Your termination settlement effort is always at cost with no fee, but there is latitude on the fee you earn on the underlying terminated contract. Abuse of subcontractors serves no one's interests. This can be very disruptive and occasionally catastrophic to small businesses. Deal with them professionally but with appropriate sensitivities to their situation. It's good business and simply the right thing to do.

§ 12:4 The termination settlement process

The process must begin with a settlement proposal. Your notice to the subcontractor should ask for one. If the underlying subcontract is cost-type, then you have made a prior determination that the subcontractor's accounting system can accommodate government cost accounting. Preparing a proposal from such a system is relatively easy if proper charge numbers and cost accounting disciplines have been used. The proposal should be prepared on the inventory basis and the reasonableness of the proposal should be relatively straightforward. The lower in the subcontracting tiers you go, however, the more likely you are to encounter fixed price subcontracts with subcontractors who use a very unsophisticated accounting system. The determination to award them a fixed price contract may have rested solely on the fact that their accounting system cannot perform government cost accounting. And yet what is the first thing you ask them for? — a proposal based on their costs expended to the date of termination.

This may be a situation where a total cost proposal is appropriate, but you must remain cognizant of the pitfalls such a proposal entails. The simple theory behind a total cost proposal is: I spent this much money, so you owe me that amount. What this ignores is whether the original proposal had any real basis for the numbers, whether the work proceeded effectively and efficiently, whether the contractor experienced excessive or unnecessary spoilage or waste, and whether the contractor included any costs that would typically be considered unallowable on a government contract. Unfortunately this may be the only alternative when a proper cost proposal cannot be generated. This is why permission from the CO is required before such a proposal is accepted by the government. Depending on instructions from your CO, you may need to obtain their approval for such a proposal even from the subcontractor. This is again a situation where an outside resource may be beneficial to both the subcontractor and the prime. Experts experienced in such costing matters can be well worth their cost to both the subcontractor and, ultimately, the government.

Many subcontractors are going to be inexperienced or otherwise lack sophistication necessary to prepare such a proposal. While you can provide certain levels of guidance and even training, keep in mind the need to maintain arm's-length dealings. While the proposal needs to be generated promptly, it must also be accurate. Speed can introduce errors that take longer to identify and correct than if care had been taken in the initial proposal. Your timelines in reporting to the government and submitting your settlement proposal are relatively firm. Further both you and the subcontractor may begin to experience cash flow impacts during this process. Everyone is better served by getting proposals in promptly and then negotiating a settlement as soon as practicable. Delay causes many problems such as fading memories, lost records, and we have even seen the disappearance of the subcontractor. Failing to deal with subcontractors effectively can also encourage litigation. It is important to have the right response team available to assist in getting the subcontractor proposals in timely and negotiated promptly.

You may also need to request from the government an assist audit where the subcontractor's costs are proprietary, such as when you are teaming with a company that sometimes is your prime, sometimes is your subcontractor, and always is your competitor. These audits can greatly delay settlement and as a result should be identified and requested as soon as possible. Otherwise you will need to conduct a proper audit of the subcontractor's proposal. This is where you need to properly balance whatever assistance you provide to the subcontractor with your need to maintain the arm's-length dealings. If your company is large enough, different teams of people might be engaged to keep a firewall between these two functions.

If the subcontractor is particularly recalcitrant and you are unable to negotiate a settlement with them you have several options all of which must be considered in consultation with your CO. Litigation may be the only option in some cases, but certainly not a preferred approach. You must alert the CO if litigation is initiated against you during this process, and you must have specific CO permission to initiate litigation. Failure to do so can result in unallowable costs. You also have the option, with CO consent, to omit that subcontractor from your proposal and transfer the responsibility for settlement to the government. This is a rare situation, but recognized in the regulations as an option. We have personally seen this occur when certain long-term environmental issues would have inappropriately delayed settlement of all other issues under the contract and when extensive property records needed to be reviewed and audited in the midst of a plant closing that was continuing beyond the termination of the prime contract.

§ 12:5   Conclusion

Rarely are government programs managed exclusively with the internal resources of a prime contractor. Inevitably there will be subcontractors and often there will be many subcontractors with many tiers of subcontractors below them. In a termination all of these business arrangements must be concluded and closed out. Quick action on the part of the prime contract manager, prompt sharing of as much information and expertise as possible, and appropriate use of outside resources will greatly facilitate the preparation of the prime contractor's settlement proposal. Cash flow issues will arise and will need to be addressed. Early identification of government property, and constant communication among all of the parties, will facilitate contract close-out.

The body of law that governs a government contract is different from the body of law that governs your subcontracts. A failure to recognize those differences and deal with them effectively can result in costs being incurred that you will not be able to recover from the government under your prime contract. It takes careful administration of both the prime and the subcontracts, with close attention to detail in both cases, to make this process as painless as possible.

§ 12:6   Best practices in managing subcontract terminations

1. Understand the differences between federal common law and applicable state Uniform Commercial Code principles.
2. Use the correct termination clause, but properly modified for the specific relationship between the prime and the subcontractor.
3. Don't overreach with your subcontractors in the use of a termination clause.
4. Provide training for your subcontractors *before* it is needed.
5. Be reasonable in settlements.
6. Assure that you have the requisite authority from your CO before settling subcontract claims.
7. Be conscious of your subcontractors' cash flow needs; negotiate settlements promptly.

APPENDICES

APPENDIX A

References

Agrawal, Raj. *Overcoming Software Estimation Challenges*. McLean, VA.: MITRE, May, 22, 2007

Albert, Neil F. *Cost Estimating: The Starting Point of Earned Value Management*. McLean, VA.: MCR LLC, June 2005.

Albert, Neil F. *Developing a Work Breakdown Structure*. McLean, VA.: MCR LLC, June 16, 2005.

Anderson, Mark, and David Nelson. *Developing an Averaged Estimate at Completion (EAC) Utilizing Program Performance Factors and Maturity*. Arlington, VA.: Tecolote Research Inc., June 14-17, 2005.

Atkinson, William, *"Beyond the Basics"* PM Network Magazine, May 2003 (Project Management Institute)

Badgerow, Dana B., Gregory A. Garrett, Dominic F. DiClementi, and Barbara M. Weaver, *Managing Contracts for Peak Performance* (Vienna, Va.: National Contract Management Association, 1990).

Barkley, Bruce T., and Saylor, James H., *"Customer Driven Project Management: A New Paradigm in Total Quality Implementation,"* (New York: McGraw-Hill, 1993).

Black, Hollis M. *Impact of Cost Risk Analysis on Business Decisions*. Huntsville, Ala.: Boeing, June 14-17, 2005.

Bonaldo, Guy, *Interview with Business 2.0 Magazine*, Business Intelligence, February 2003.

Bossidy, Larry and Charan, Ram, *Confronting Realty: Doing What Matters to Get Things Right,* (New York: Crown Business, 2004).

Bruce, David L., Norby, Marlys, and Ramos, Victor, *Guide to the Contract Management Body of Knowledge (CMBOK)* 1st Edition (Vienna, VA: National Contract Management Association, 2002).

Christensen, David S., and Carl Templin. *An Analysis of Management Reserve Budget on Defense Acquisition Contracts*. Cedar City: Southern Utah University, 2000.

Cleland, David I., *Project Management: Strategic Design and Implementation*. (New York: McGraw-Hill, 1994).

Cleland, David I., and King, William R., *Project Management Handbook, Second Edition* (New York: Van Nostrand Reinhold, 1988).

Coleman, Richard L., Shishu S. Gupta, and Jessica R. Summerville. *Two Timely Short Topics: Independence and Cost Realism*. Chantilly, VA.: Northrop Grumman, The Analytical Sciences Corporation, and Intelligence Community Cost Analysis Improvement Group, June 16, 2005.

Coleman, Richard L., and Jessica R. Summerville. *Advanced Cost Risk*. Chantilly, VA.: Northrop Grumman, The Analytical Sciences Corporation, June 16, 2005.

Coleman, Richard L., and Jessica R. Summerville. *Basic Cost Risk*. Chantilly, VA.: Northrop Grumman, The Analytical Sciences Corporation, June 15, 2005.

Collins, Jim, *"Good to Great: Why Some Companies Make the Leap...and Others Don't,"* (New York: Harper Collins, 2001).

Coulson-Thomas, Colin, *Creating the Global Company*, (New York: McGraw-Hill, 1992).

Covey, Stephen R., *The Seven Habits of Highly Effective People* (New York: Simon and Schuster, Inc., 1989).

DAU (Defense Acquisition University). *Cost Estimating Methodologies.* Fort Belvoir, VA.: April, 2005.

Fisher, Roger, Elizabeth Kopelman, and Andrea K. Schneider, *Beyond Machiavelli: Tools for Coping with Conflict* (Cambridge: Harvard University Press, 1994).

Fleming, Quentin W. *Earned Value Management (EVM) Light...But Adequate for All Projects.* Tustin, Calif.: Primavera Systems, Inc., November 2006.

Fleming, Quentin W., and Joel M. Koppelman. *"The Earned Value Body of Knowledge."* Presented at the 30th Annual Project Management Institute Symposium, Philadelphia, PA, October 10-16, 1999.

Flett, Frank. *Organizing and Planning the Estimate.* McLean, VA.: MCR LLC, June 12-14-2005.

Galorath, Daniel D. *Software Estimation Handbook.* El Segundo, Calif.: Galorath Inc., n.d.

GAO. *Cost Assessment Guide, GAO-07-11345P.* Washington, DC.: July 2007.

Garrett, Gregory A., *Achieving Customer Loyalty*, Contract Management Magazine, August 2002, (National Contract Management Association).

Garrett, Gregory A., *Performance-Based Acquisition: Pathways to Excellence,* (McLean, VA, NCMA 2005)

Garrett, Gregory A., *World-Class Contracting* (Chicago, CCH Incorporated, Fourth Edition, 2007).

Garrett, Gregory A., *Managing Complex Outsourced Projects,* (Chicago, CCH Incorporated, 2004).

Garrett, Gregory A., *Contract Negotiations: Skills, Tools, & Best Practices,* (Chicago: CCH Incorporated, 2005).

Garrett, Gregory A. and Bunnik, Ed, *"Creating a World-Class PM Organization,"* PM Network Magazine, September 2000 (Project Management Institute).

Garrett, Gregory A., and Kipke, Reginald J., *The Capture Management Life-Cycle: Winning More Business,* (Chicago: CCH Incorporated, 2003).

Garrett, Gregory A. and Rendon, Rene G., *Contract Management Organizational Assessment Tools,* (McLean, VA, NCMA, 2005).

Garrett, Gregory A. and Rendon, Rene G., *U.S. Military Program Management: Lessons Learned and Best Practices.* (McLean, VA., Management Concepts, 2007).

Gates, Bill, *Business @ The Speed of Thought: Using a Digital Nervous System* (New York: Warner Books USA, 1999).

Harris, Phillip R., and Robert T. Moran, *Managing Cultural Differences* (Houston: Gulf Publishing Company, 1996).

Hassan H. and Blackwell R., *Global Marketing,*(New York: Harcourt Brace Publishing, 1994).

Horton, Sharon, *"Creating and Using Supplier Scorecards,"* Contract Management Magazine, McLean, VA, NCMA, September 2004, pgs. 22-25.

Johnson, Jim, and others. "Collaboration: Development and Management—Collaborating on Project Success." *Software Magazine,* Sponsored Supplement, February-March 2001.

Kantin, Bob, *Sales Proposals Kit for Dummies* (New York: Hungry Minds, 2001).

Kerzner, Harold, *In Search of Excellence in Project Management,*(New York: Van Nostrand Reinhold, 1998).

Kirk, Dorthy, "Managing Expectations,"*PM Network Magazine,* August 2000 (Project Management Institute).

Kratzert, Keith. *Earned Value Management (EVM): The Federal Aviation Administration (FAA) Program Manager's Flight Plan.* Washington, D.C.: Federal Aviation Administration, January 2006.

Kumley, Alissa, and others. *Integrating Risk Management and Earned Value Management: A Statistical Analysis of Survey Results.* N.p.: June 14-17, 2005.

Lewis, James P., *Mastering Project Management: Applying Advanced Concepts of Systems Thinking, Control and Evalution, Resource Allocation* (New York: McGraw-Hill, 1998).

Liker, Jeffrey K. and Choi, Thomas Y., "*Building Deep Supplier Relationships,*" Harvard Business Review, Boston, MA December 2004, pgs. 104-113.

McFarlane, Eileen Luhta, *Developing International Proposals in a Virtual Environment,* Journal of the Association of Proposal Management, Spring 2000 (Association of Proposal Management Professionals).

Monroe, Kent B., *Pricing: Making Profitable Decisions,* 2d ed. (New York: McGraw-Hill Publishing Company, 1990).

Moran, J. and Riesenberger M., *The Global Challenge,* (New York: McGraw-Hill, 1994).

The National Contract Management Association, *The Desktop Guide to Basic Contracting Terms,* 4th ed. (Vienna, Virginia, 1994).

O'Connell, Brian, *B2B.com: Cashing-in on the Business-to-Business E-commerce Bonanza* (Holbrook, Massachusetts: Adams Media Corp., 2000).

Ohmae, Kenichi, *The Borderless World: Power and Strategy in the Interlinked Economy* (New York: Harper Collins Pubs., Inc., 1991).

Patterson, Shirley, "*Supply Base Optimization and Integrated Supply Chain Management,*" Contract Management Magazine, McLean, VA, NCMA, January 2005, pgs. 24-35.

Project Management Institute Standards Committee, *A Guide to the Project Management Body of Knowledge* (Upper Darby, Pa.: Project Management Institute, 2001).

RAND Corp. *Impossible Certainty: Cost Risk Analysis for Air Force Systems.* Arlington, VA.: 2006

SCEA (Society of Cost Estimating and Analysis). *Cost Programmed Review of Fundamentals (CostPROF): Basic Data Analysis Principles—What to Do Once You Get the Data.* Vienna, VA.: 2003.

Tichy, Noel, "*The Leadership Engine,*" (New York: Harper Business Press, 1997)

Webster's Dictionary, The New Lexicon of the English Language (New York: Lexicon Publications, Inc., 1989).

Zubrow, Dave. *Earned Value Management (EVM): Basic Concepts.* Pittsburgh, PA.: Carnegie Mellon Software Engineering Institute, 2002.

Zubrow, Dave. *Implementing Earned Value Management (EVM) to Manage Program Risk.* Pittsburg, PA.: Carnegie Mellon Software Engineering Institute, 2002.

APPENDIX B
Glossary of Key Terms

acceptance (1) The taking and receiving of anything in good part, and as if it were a tacit agreement to a preceding act, which might have been defeated or avoided if such acceptance had not been made. (2) Agreement to the terms offered in a contract. An acceptance must be communicated, and (in common law) it must be the mirror image of the offer.

acquisition cost The money invested up front to bring in new customers

acquisition plan A plan for an acquisition that serves as the basis for initiating the individual contracting actions necessary to acquire a system or support a program.

acquisition strategy The conceptual framework for conducting systems acquisition. It encompasses the broad concepts and objectives that direct and control the overall development, production, and deployment of a system.

act of God An inevitable, accidental, or extraordinary event that cannot be foreseen and guarded against, such as lightning, tornadoes, or earthquakes.

actual authority The power that the principal intentionally confers on the agent or allows the agent to believe he or she possesses.

actual damages See compensatory damages.

affidavit A written and signed statement sworn to under oath.

agency A relationship that exists when there is a delegation of authority to perform all acts connected within a particular trade, business, or company. It gives authority to the agent to act in all matters relating to the business of the principal.

agent An employee (usually a contract manager) empowered to bind his or her organization legally in contract negotiations.

allowable cost A cost that is reasonable, allocable, and within accepted standards, or otherwise conforms to generally accepted accounting principles, specific limitations or exclusions, or agreed-on terms between contractual parties.

alternative dispute resolution Any procedure that is used, in lieu of litigation, to resolve issues in controversy, including but not limited to, settlement negotiations, conciliation, facilitation, mediation, fact finding, mini-trials and arbitration.

amortization Process of spreading the cost of an intangible asset over the expected useful life of the asset.

apparent authority The power that the principal permits the perceived agent to exercise, although not actually granted.

as is A contract phrase referring to the condition of property to be sold or leased; generally pertains to a disclaimer of liability; property sold in as-is condition is generally not guaranteed.

assign To convey or transfer to another, as to assign property, rights, or interests to another.

assignment The transfer of property by an assignor to an assignee.

audits The systematic examination of records and documents and/or the securing of other evidence by confirmation, physical inspection, or otherwise, for one or more of the following purposes: determining the propriety or legality of proposed or completed transactions; ascertaining whether all transactions have been recorded and are reflected accurately in accounts; determining the existence of recorded assets and inclusiveness of recorded liabilities; determining the accuracy of financial or statistical statements or reports and the fairness of the facts they represent; determining the degree of compliance with established policies and procedures in terms of financial transactions and business management; and appraising an account system and making recommendations concerning it.

base profit The money a company is paid by a customer, which exceeds the company's cost.

best value The best trade-off between competing factors for a particular purchase requirement. The key to successful best-value contracting is consideration of life-cycle costs, including the use of quantitative as well as qualitative techniques to measure price and technical performance trade-offs between various proposals. The best-value concept applies to acquisitions in which price or price-related factors are not the primary determinant of who receives the contract award.

bid An offer in response to an invitation for bids (IFB).

bid development All of the work activities required to design and price the product and service solution and accurately articulate this in a proposal for a customer.

bid phase The period of time a seller of goods and/or services uses to develop a bid/proposal, conduct internal bid reviews, and obtain stakeholder approval to submit a bid/proposal.

bilateral contract A contract formed if an offer states that acceptance requires only for the accepting party to promise to perform. In contrast, a unilateral contract is formed if an offer requires actual performance for acceptance.

bond A written instrument executed by a seller and a second party (the surety or sureties) to ensure fulfillment of the principal's obligations to a third party (the obligee or buyer), identified in the bond. If the principal's obligations are not met, the bond ensures payment, to the extent stipulated, of any loss sustained by the obligee.

breach of contract (1) The failure, without legal excuse, to perform any promise that forms the whole or part of a contract. (2) The ending of a contract that occurs when one or both of the parties fail to keep their promises; this could lead to arbitration or litigation.

buyer The party contracting for goods and/or services with one or more sellers.

cancellation The withdrawal of the requirement to purchase goods and/or services by the buyer.

capture management The art and science of winning more business

capture management life cycle The art and science of winning more business throughout the entire business cycle

capture project plan A document or game plan of who needs to do what, when, where, how often and how much to win business.

change in scope An amendment to approved program requirements or specifications after negotiation of a basic contract. It may result in an increase or decrease.

change order/purchase order amendment A written order directing the seller to make changes according to the provisions of the contract documents.

claim A demand by one party to contract for something from another party, usually but not necessarily for more money or more time. Claims are usually based on an argument that the party making the demand is entitled to an adjustment by virtue of the contract terms or some violation of those terms by the other party. The word does not imply any disagreement between the parties, although claims often lead to disagreements. This book uses the term dispute to refer to disagreements that have become intractable.

clause A statement of one of the rights and/or obligations of the parties to a contract. A contract consists of a series of clauses.

collaboration software Automated tools that allow for the real-time exchange of visual information using personal computers.

collateral benefit The degree to which pursuit of an opportunity will improve the existing skill level or develop new skills which will positively affect other or future business opportunities.

compensable delay A delay for which the buyer is contractually responsible that excuses the seller's failure to perform and is compensable.

compensatory damages Damages that will compensate the injured party for the loss sustained and nothing more. They are awarded by the court as the measure of actual loss, and not as punishment for outrageous conduct or to deter future transgressions. Compensatory damages are often referred to as "actual damages." See also incidental and punitive damages.

competitive intelligence Information on competitors or competitive teams which is specific to an opportunity.

competitive negotiation A method of contracting involving a request for proposals that states the buyer's requirements and criteria for evaluation; submission of timely proposals by a maximum number of offerors; discussions with those offerors found to be within the competitive range; and award of a contract to the one offeror whose offer, price, and other consideration factors are most advantageous to the buyer.

condition precedent A condition that activates a term in a contract.

condition subsequent A condition that suspends a term in a contract.

conflict of interest Term used in connection with public officials and fiduciaries and their relationships to matters of private interest or gain to them. Ethical problems connected therewith are covered by statutes in most jurisdictions and by federal statutes on the federal level. A conflict of interest arises when an employee's personal or financial interest conflicts or appears to conflict with his or her official responsibility.

consideration (1) The thing of value (amount of money or acts to be done or not done) that must change hands between the parties to a contract.

(2) The inducement to a contract — the cause, motive, price, or impelling influence that induces a contracting party to enter into a contract.

contract negotiation Is the process of unifying different positions into a unanimous joint decision, regarding the buying and selling of products and/or services.

contract negotiation process A three phased approach composed of planning, negotiating, and documenting a contractual agreement between two or more parties to buy or sell products and/or services.

constructive change An oral or written act or omission by an authorized or unauthorized agent that is of such a nature that it is construed to have the same effect as a written change order.

contingency The quality of being contingent or casual; an event that may but does not have to occur; a possibility.

contingent contract A contract that provides for the possibility of its termination when a specified occurrence takes place or does not take place.

contra proferentem A legal phrase used in connection with the construction of written documents to the effect that an ambiguous provision is construed most strongly against the person who selected the language.

contract (1) A relationship between two parties, such as a buyer and seller, that is defined by an agreement about their respective rights and responsibilities. (2) A document that describes such an agreement.

contract administration The process of ensuring compliance with contractual terms and conditions during contract performance up to contract closeout or termination.

contract closeout The process of verifying that all administrative matters are concluded on a contract that is otherwise physically complete — in other words, the seller has delivered the required supplies or performed the required services, and the buyer has inspected and accepted the supplies or services.

contract fulfillment The joint Buyer/Seller actions taken to successfully perform and administer a contractual agreement and met or exceed all contract obligations, including effective changes management and timely contract closeout.

contract interpretation The entire process of determining what the parties agreed to in their bargain. The basic objective of contract interpretation is to determine the intent of the parties. Rules calling for interpretation of the documents against the drafter, and imposing a duty to seek clarification on the drafter, allocate risks of contractual ambiguities by resolving disputes in favor of the party least responsible for the ambiguity.

contract management The art and science of managing a contractual agreement(s) throughout the contracting process.

contract type A specific pricing arrangement used for the performance of work under the contract.

contractor The seller or provider of goods and/or services.

controversy A litigated question. A civil action or suit may not be instigated unless it is based on a "justifiable" dispute. This term is important in that judicial power of the courts extends only to cases and "controversies."

copyright A royalty-free, nonexclusive, and irrevocable license to reproduce, translate, publish, use, and dispose of written or recorded material, and to authorize others to do so.

cost The amount of money expended in acquiring a product or obtaining a service, or the total of acquisition costs plus all expenses related to operating and maintaining an item once acquired.

cost of good sold (COGS) Direct costs of producing finished goods for sale.

cost accounting standards Federal standards designed to provide consistency and coherency in defense and other government contract accounting.

cost-plus-award fee (CPAF) contract A type of cost-reimbursement contract with special incentive fee provisions used to motivate excellent contract performance in such areas as quality, timeliness, ingenuity, and cost-effectiveness.

cost-plus-fixed fee (CPFF) contract A type of cost-reimbursement contract that provides for the payment of a fixed fee to the contractor. It does not vary with actual costs, but may be adjusted if there are any changes in the work or services to be performed under the contract.

cost-plus-incentive fee (CPIF) contract A type of cost-reimbursement contract with provision for a fee that is adjusted by a formula in accordance with the relationship between total allowable costs and target costs.

cost-plus-a-percentage-of-cost (CPPC) contract A type of cost-reimbursement contract that provides for a reimbursement of the allowable cost of services performed plus an agreed-on percentage of the estimated cost as profit.

cost-reimbursement (CR) contract A type of contract that usually includes an estimate of project cost, a provision for reimbursing the seller's expenses, and a provision for paying a fee as profit. CR contracts are often used when there is high uncertainty about costs. They normally also include a limitation on the buyer's cost liability.

cost-sharing contract A cost-reimbursement contract in which the seller receives no fee and is reimbursed only for an agreed-on portion of its allowable costs.

cost contract The simplest type of cost-reimbursement contract. Governments commonly use this type when contracting with universities and nonprofit organizations for research projects. The contract provides for reimbursing contractually allowable costs, with no allowance given for profit.

cost proposal The instrument required of an offeror for the submission or identification of cost or pricing data by which an offeror submits to the buyer a summary of estimated (or incurred) costs, suitable for detailed review and analysis.

counteroffer An offer made in response to an original offer that changes the terms of the original.

customer revenue growth The increased revenues achieved by keeping a customer for an extended period of time.

customer support costs Costs expended by a company to provide information and advice concerning purchases.

default termination The termination of a contract, under the standard default clause, because of a buyer's or seller's failure to perform any of the terms of the contract.

defect The absence of something necessary for completeness or perfection. A deficiency in something essential to the proper use of a thing. Some structural weakness in a part or component that is responsible for damage.

defect, latent A defect that existed at the time of acceptance but would not have been discovered by a reasonable inspection.

defect, patent A defect that can be discovered without undue effort. If the defect was actually known to the buyer at the time of acceptance, it is patent, even though it otherwise might not have been discoverable by a reasonable inspection.

definite-quantity contract A contractual instrument that provides for a definite quantity of supplies or services to be delivered at some later, unspecified date.

delay, excusable A contractual provision designed to protect the seller from sanctions for late performance. To the extent that it has been excusably delayed, the seller is protected from default termination or liquidated damages. Examples of excusable delay are acts of God, acts of the government, fire, flood, quarantines, strikes, epidemics, unusually severe weather, and embargoes. See also forbearance and force majeure clause.

depreciation Amount of expense charged against earnings by a company to write off the cost of a plant or machine over its useful live, giving consideration to wear and tear, obsolescence, and salvage value.

design specification (1) A document (including drawings) setting forth the required characteristics of a particular component, part, subsystem, system, or construction item. (2) A purchase description that establishes precise measurements, tolerances, materials, in-process and finished product tests, quality control, inspection requirements, and other specific details of the deliverable.

direct cost The costs specifically identifiable with a contract requirement, including but not restricted to costs of material and/or labor directly incorporated into an end item.

direct labor All work that is obviously related and specifically and conveniently traceable to specific products.

direct material Items, including raw material, purchased parts, and subcontracted items, directly incorporated into an end item, which are identifiable to a contract requirement.

discount rate Interest rate used in calculating present value.

discounted cash flow (DCF) Combined present value of cash flow and tangible assets minus present value of liabilities.

discounts, allowances and returns Price discounts, returned merchandise.

dispute A disagreement not settled by mutual consent that could be decided by litigation or arbitration. Also see claim.

e-business Technology-enabled business that focuses on seamless integration between each business, the company, and its supply partners.

EBITDA Earnings Before Interest, Taxes, Depreciation and Amortization, but after all product/service, sales and overhead (SG&A) costs are accounted for. Sometimes referred to as Operating Profit.

EBITDARM Acronym for Earnings Before Interest, Taxes, Depreciation, Amortization. Rent and Management fees.

e-commerce A subset of e-business, Internet-based electronic transactions.

electronic data interchange (EDI) Private networks used for simple data transactions, which are typically batch- processed.

elements of a contract The items that must be present in a contract if the contract is to be binding, including an offer, acceptance (agreement), consideration, execution by competent parties, and legality of purpose.

enterprise resource planning (ERP) An electronic framework for integrating all organizational functions, evolved from Manufacturing Resource Planning (MRP).

entire contract A contract that is considered entire on both sides and cannot be made severable.

e-procurement Technology-enabled buying and selling of goods and services.

estimate at completion (EAC) The actual direct costs, plus indirect costs allocable to the contract, plus the estimate of costs (direct or indirect) for authorized work remaining.

estoppel A rule of law that bars, prevents, and precludes a party from alleging or denying certain facts because of a previous allegation or denial or because of its previous conduct or admission.

ethics Of or relating to moral action, conduct, motive, or character (such as ethical emotion). Also, treating of moral feelings, duties, or conduct; containing precepts of morality; moral. Professionally right or befitting; conforming to professional standards of conduct.

e-tool An electronic device, program, system, or software application used to facilitate business.

exculpatory clause The contract language designed to shift responsibility to the other party. A "no damages for delay" clause would be an example of one used by buyers.

excusable delay See delay, excusable.

executed contract A contract that is formed and performed at the same time. If performed in part, it is partially executed and partially executory.

executed contract (document) A written document, signed by both parties and mailed or otherwise furnished to each party, that expresses the requirements, terms, and conditions to be met by both parties in the performance of the contract.

executory contract A contract that has not yet been fully performed.

express Something put in writing, for example, "express authority."

fair and reasonable A subjective evaluation of what each party deems as equitable consideration in areas such as terms and conditions, cost or price, assured quality, timeliness of contract performance, and/or any other areas subject to negotiation.

Federal Acquisition Regulation (FAR) The government-wide procurement regulation mandated by Congress and issued by the Department of

Defense, the General Services Administration, and the National Aeronautics and Space Administration. Effective April 1, 1984, the FAR supersedes both the Defense Acquisition Regulation (DAR) and the Federal Procurement Regulation (FPR). All federal agencies are authorized to issue regulations implementing the FAR.

fee An agreed-to amount of reimbursement beyond the initial estimate of costs. The term "fee" is used when discussing cost-reimbursement contracts, whereas the term "profit" is used in relation to fixed-price contracts.

firm-fixed-price (FFP) contract The simplest and most common business pricing arrangement. The seller agrees to supply a quantity of goods or to provide a service for a specified price.

fixed cost Operating expenses that are incurred to provide facilities and organization that are kept in readiness to do business without regard to actual volumes of production and sales. Examples of fixed costs consist of rent, property tax, and interest expense.

fixed price A form of pricing that includes a ceiling beyond which the buyer bears no responsibility for payment.

fixed-price incentive (FPI) contract A type of contract that provides for adjusting profit and establishing the final contract price using a formula based on the relationship of total final negotiated cost to total target cost. The final price is subject to a price ceiling, negotiated at the outset.

fixed-price redeterminable (FPR) contract A type of fixed-price contract that contains provisions for subsequently negotiated adjustment, in whole or in part, of the initially negotiated base price.

fixed-price with economic price adjustment A fixed-price contract that permits an element of cost to fluctuate to reflect current market prices.

forbearance An intentional failure of a party to enforce a contract requirement, usually done for an act of immediate or future consideration from the other party. Sometimes forbearance is referred to as a nonwaiver or as a one-time waiver, but not as a relinquishment of rights.

force majeure clause Major or irresistible force. Such a contract clause protects the parties in the event that a part of the contract cannot be performed due to causes outside the control of the parties and could not be avoided by exercise of due care. Excusable conditions for nonperformance, such as strikes and acts of God (e.g., typhoons) are contained in this clause.

fraud An intentional perversion of truth to induce another in reliance upon it to part with something of value belonging to him or her or to surrender a legal right. A false representation of a matter of fact, whether by words or conduct, by false or misleading allegations, or by concealment of that which should have been disclosed, that deceives and is intended to deceive another so that he or she shall act upon it to his or her legal injury. Anything calculated to deceive.

free on board (FOB) A term used in conjunction with a physical point to determine (a) the responsibility and basis for payment of freight charges and (b) unless otherwise agreed, the point at which title for goods passes to the buyer or consignee. FOB origin — The seller places the goods on the conveyance by which they are to be transported. Cost of shipping and risk of loss are borne by the buyer. FOB destination — The seller delivers the goods on the seller's conveyance at destination. Cost of shipping and risk of loss are borne by the seller.

functional specification A purchase description that describes the deliverable in terms of performance characteristics and intended use, including those characteristics that at minimum are necessary to satisfy the intended use.

general and administrative (G&A) (1) The indirect expenses related to the overall business. Expenses for a company's general and executive offices, executive compensation, staff services, and other miscellaneous support purposes. (2) Any indirect management, financial, or other expense that (a) is not assignable to a program's direct overhead charges for engineering, manufacturing, material, and so on, but (b) is routinely incurred by or allotted to a business unit, and (c) is for the general management and administration of the business as a whole.

general accepted accounting principles (GAAP) A term encompassing conventions, rules, and procedures of accounting that are "generally accepted" and have "substantial authoritative support." The GAAP have been developed by agreement on the basis of experience, reason, custom, usage, and to a certain extent, practical necessity, rather than being derived from a formal set of theories.

General Agreement on Tariffs and Trade (GATT) A multi-national trade agreement, signed in 1947 by 23 nations.

gross profit margin Net Sales minus Cost of Goods Sold. Also called Gross Margin, Gross Profit or Gross Loss

gross profit margin % or ratio Gross Profit Margin $ divided by Net Sales.

gross sales Total revenues at invoice value before any discounts or allowances.

horizontal exchange A marketplace that deals with goods and services that are not specific to one industry.

imply To indirectly convey meaning or intent; to leave the determination of meaning up to the receiver of the communication based on circumstances, general language used, or conduct of those involved.

incidental damages Any commercially reasonable charges, expenses, or commissions incurred in stopping delivery; in the transportation, care and custody of goods after the buyer's breach; or in connection with the return or resale of the goods or otherwise resulting from the breach.

indefinite-delivery/indefinite-quantity (IDIQ) contract A type of contract in which the exact date of delivery or the exact quantity, or a combination of both, is not specified at the time the contract is executed; provisions are placed in the contract to later stipulate these elements of the contract.

indemnification clause A contract clause by which one party engages to secure another against an anticipated loss resulting from an act or forbearance on the part of one of the parties or of some third person.

indemnify To make good; to compensate; to reimburse a person in case of an anticipated loss.

indirect cost Any cost not directly identifiable with a specific cost objective but subject to two or more cost objectives.

indirect labor All work that is not specifically associated with or cannot be practically traced to specific units of output.

intellectual property The kind of property that results from the fruits of mental labor.

internet The World Wide Web.

interactive chat A feature provided by automated tools that allow for users to establish a voice connection between one or more parties and exchange text or graphics via a virtual bulletin board.

intranet An organization specific internal secure network.

joint contract A contract in which the parties bind themselves both individually and as a unit.

liquidated damages A contract provision providing for the assessment of damages on the seller for its failure to comply with certain performance or delivery requirements of the contract; used when the time of delivery or performance is of such importance that the buyer may reasonably expect to suffer damages if the delivery or performance is delinquent.

mailbox rule The idea that the acceptance of an offer is effective when deposited in the mail if the envelope is properly addressed.

marketing Activities that direct the flow of goods and services from the producer to the consumers.

market intelligence Information on your competitors or competitive teams operating in the marketplace or industry.

market research The process used to collect and analyze information about an entire market to help determine the most suitable approach to acquiring, distributing, and supporting supplies and services.

memorandum of agreement (MOA)/memorandum of understanding (MOU) The documentation of a mutually agreed-to statement of facts, intentions, procedures, and parameters for future actions and matters of coordination. A "memorandum of understanding" may express mutual understanding of an issue without implying commitments by parties to the understanding.

method of procurement The process used for soliciting offers, evaluating offers, and awarding a contract.

modifications Any written alterations in the specification, delivery point, rate of delivery, contract period, price, quantity, or other provision of an existing contract, accomplished in accordance with a contract clause; may be unilateral or bilateral.

monopoly A market structure in which the entire market for a good or service is supplied by a single seller or firm.

monopsony A market structure in which a single buyer purchases a good or service.

NCMA CMBOK Definitive descriptions of the elements making up the body of professional knowledge that applies to contract management.

negotiation A process between buyers and sellers seeking to reach mutual agreement on a matter of common concern through fact-finding, bargaining, and persuasion.

net marketplace Two-sided exchange where buyers and sellers negotiate prices, usually with a bid-and-ask system, and where prices move both up and down.

net present value (NPV) The lifetime customer revenue stream discounted by the investment costs and operations costs.

net sales Gross sales minus discounts, allowances and returns.

North America Free Trade Agreement (NAFTA) A trilateral trade and investment agreement, between Canada, Mexico, and the United States ratified on January 1, 1994.

novation agreement A legal instrument executed by (a) the contractor (transferor), (b) the successor in interest (transferee), and (c) the buyer by which, among other things, the transferor guarantees performance of the contract, the transferee assumes all obligations under the contract, and the buyer recognizes the transfer of the contract and related assets.

offer (1) The manifestation of willingness to enter into a bargain, so made as to justify another person in understanding that his or her assent to that bargain is invited and will conclude it. (2) An unequivocal and intentionally communicated statement of proposed terms made to another party. An offer is presumed revocable unless it specifically states that it is irrevocable. An offer once made will be open for a reasonable period of time and is binding on the offeror unless revoked by the offeror before the other party's acceptance.

oligopoly A market dominated by a few sellers.

operating expenses SG&A plus depreciation and amortization.

opportunity A potential or actual favorable event

opportunity engagement The degree to which your company or your competitors were involved in establishing the customer's requirements.

opportunity profile A stage of the Capture Management Life Cycle, during which a seller evaluates and describes the opportunity in terms of what it means to your customer, what it means to your company, and what will be required to succeed.

option A unilateral right in a contract by which, for a specified time, the buyer may elect to purchase additional quantities of the supplies or services called for in the contract, or may elect to extend the period of performance of the contract.

order of precedence A solicitation provision that establishes priorities so that contradictions within the solicitation can be resolved.

Organizational Breakdown Structure (OBS) A organized structure which represents how individual team members are grouped to complete assigned work tasks.

outsourcing A contractual process of obtaining another party to provide goods and/or services that were previously done internal to an organization.

overhead An accounting cost category that typically includes general indirect expenses that are necessary to operate a business but are not directly assignable to a specific good or service produced. Examples include building rent, utilities, salaries of corporate officers, janitorial services, office supplies, and furniture.

overtime The time worked by a seller's employee in excess of the employee's normal workweek.

parol evidence Oral or verbal evidence; in contract law, the evidence drawn from sources exterior to the written instrument.

parol evidence rule A rule that seeks to preserve the integrity of written agreements by refusing to permit contracting parties to attempt to alter a written contract with evidence of any contradictory prior or contemporaneous oral agreement (parol to the contract).

payments The amount payable under the contract supporting data required to be submitted with invoices, and other payment terms such as time for payment and retention.

payment bond A bond that secures the appropriate payment of subcontracts for their completed and acceptable goods and/or services.

Performance-based contract (PBC) A documented business arrangement, in which the buyer and seller agree to use: a Performance work statement, performance-based metrics, and a quality assurance plant o ensure contract requirements are met or exceeded.

performance bond A bond that secures the performance and fulfillment of all the undertakings, covenants, terms, conditions, and agreements contained in the contract.

performance specification A purchase description that describes the deliverable in terms of de¬sired operational characteristics. Performance specifications tend to be more restrictive than functional specifications, in that they limit alternatives that the buyer will consider and define separate performance standards for each such alternative.

Performance Work Statement (PWS) A statement of work expressed in terms of desired performance results, often including specific measurable objectives.

post-bid phase The period of time after a seller submits a bid/proposal to a buyer through source selection, negotiations, contract formation, contract fulfillment, contract closeout, and follow-on opportunity management.

pre-bid phase The period of time a seller of goods and/or services uses to identify business opportunities prior to the release of a customer solicitation.

pricing arrangement An agreed-to basis between contractual parties for the payment of amounts for specified performance; usually expressed in terms of a specific cost-reimbursement or fixed-price arrangement.

prime/prime contractor The principal seller performing under the contract.

private exchange A marketplace hosted by a single company inside a company's firewall and used for procurement from among a group of preauthorized sellers.

privity of contract The legal relationship that exists between the parties to a contract that allows either party to (a) enforce contractual rights against the other party and (b) seek remedy directly from the other party.

procurement The complete action or process of acquiring or obtaining goods or services using any of several authorized means.

procurement planning The process of identifying which business needs can be best met by procuring products or services outside the organization.

profit The net proceeds from selling a product or service when costs are subtracted from revenues. May be positive (profit) or negative (loss).

program management Planning and execution of multiple projects that are related to one another.

progress payments An interim payment for delivered work in accordance with contract terms; generally tied to meeting specified performance milestones.

project management Planning and ensuring the quality, on-time delivery, and cost of a specific set of related activities with a definite beginning and end.

promotion Publicizing the attributes of the product/service through media and personal contacts and presentations, e.g., technical articles/presentations, new releases, advertising, and sales calls.

proposal Normally, a written offer by a seller describing its offering terms. Proposals may be issued in response to a specific request or may be made unilaterally when a seller feels there may be an interest in its offer (which is also known as an unsolicited proposal).

proposal evaluation An assessment of both the proposal and the offeror's ability (as conveyed by the proposal) to successfully accomplish the prospective contract. An agency shall evaluate competitive proposals solely on the factors specified in the solicitation.

protest A written objection by an interested party to (a) a solicitation or other request by an agency for offers for a contract for the procurement of property or services, (b) the cancellation of the solicitation or other request, (c) an award or proposed award of the contract, or (d) a termination or cancellation of an award of the contract, if the written objection contains an allegation that the termination or cancellation is based in whole or in part on improprieties concerning the award of the contract.

punitive damages Those damages awarded to the plaintiff over and above what will barely compensate for his or her loss. Unlike compensatory damages, punitive damages are based on actively different public policy consideration, that of punishing the defendant or of setting an example for similar wrongdoers.

purchasing The outright acquisition of items, mostly off-the-shelf or catalog, manufactured outside the buyer's premises.

quality assurance The planned and systematic actions necessary to provide adequate confidence that the performed service or supplied goods will serve satisfactorily for the intended and specified purpose.

quotation A statement of price, either written or oral, which may include, among other things, a description of the product or service; the terms of sale, delivery, or period of performance; and payment. Such statements are usually issued by sellers at the request of potential buyers.

reasonable cost A cost is reasonable if, in its nature and amount, it does not exceed that which would be incurred by a prudent person in the conduct of competitive business.

request for information (RFI) A formal invitation to submit general and/or specific information concerning the potential future purchase of goods and/or services.

request for proposals (RFP) A formal invitation that contains a scope of work and seeks a formal response (proposal), describing both methodology and compensation, to form the basis of a contract.

request for quotations (RFQ) A formal invitation to submit a price for goods and/or services as specified.

request for technical proposals (RFTP) Solicitation document used in two-step sealed bidding. Normally in letter form, it asks only for technical information; price and cost breakdowns are forbidden.

revenue value The monetary value of an opportunity.

risk Exposure or potential of an injury or loss

sealed-bid procedure A method of procurement involving the unrestricted solicitation of bids, an opening, and award of a contract to the lowest responsible bidder.

selling, general & administrative (SG&A) expenses Administrative costs of running business.

severable contract A contract divisible into separate parts. A default of one section does not invalidate the whole contract.

several A circumstance when more than two parties are involved with the contract.

single source One source among others in a competitive marketplace that, for justifiable reason, is found to be most worthy to receive a contract award.

small business concerns A small business is one that is independently owned and operated, and is not dominant in its field; a business concern that meets government size standards for its particular industry type.

socioeconomic programs Programs designed to benefit particular groups. They represent a multitude of program interests and objectives unrelated to procurement objectives. Some examples of these are preferences for small business and for American products, required sources for specific items, and minimum labor pay levels mandated for contractors.

solicitation A process through which a buyer requests, bids, quotes, tenders, or proposes orally, in writing, or electronically. Solicitations can take the following forms: request for proposals (RFP), request for quotations (RFQ), request for tenders, invitation to bid (ITB), invitation for bids, and invitation for negotiation.

solicitation planning The preparation of the documents needed to support a solicitation.

source selection The process by which the buyer evaluates offers, selects a seller, negotiates terms and conditions, and awards the contract.

Source Selection Advisory Council A group of people who are appointed by the Source Selection Authority (SSA). The Council is responsible for reviewing and approving the source selection plan (SSP) and the solicitation of competitive awards for major and certain less-than-major procurements. The Council also determines what proposals are in the competitive range and provides recommendations to the SSA for final selection.

source selection plan (SSP) The document that describes the selection criteria, the process, and the organization to be used in evaluating proposals for competitively awarded contracts.

specification A description of the technical requirements for a material, product, or service that includes the criteria for determining that the requirements have been met. There are generally three types of specifications used in contracting: performance, functional, and design.

stakeholders Individuals who control the resources in a company needed to pursue opportunities or deliver solutions to customers.

standard A document that establishes engineering and technical limitations and applications of items, materials, processes, methods, designs, and engineering practices. It includes any related criteria deemed essential to achieve the highest practical degree of uniformity in materials or products, or interchangeability of parts used in those products.

standards of conduct The ethical conduct of personnel involved in the acquisition of goods and services. Within the federal government, business shall be conducted in a manner above reproach and, except as authorized by law or regulation, with complete impartiality and without preferential treatment.

statement of work (SOW) That portion of a contract describing the actual work to be done by means of specifications or other minimum requirements, quantities, performance date, and a statement of the requisite quality.

statute of limitations The legislative enactment prescribing the periods within which legal actions may be brought upon certain claims or within which certain rights may be enforced.

stop work order A request for interim stoppage of work due to nonconformance, funding, or technical considerations.

subcontract A contract between a buyer and a seller in which a significant part of the supplies or services being obtained is for eventual use in a prime contract.

subcontractor A seller who enters into a contract with a prime contractor or a subcontractor of the prime contractor.

supplementary agreement A contract modification that is accomplished by the mutual action of parties.

technical factor A factor other than price used in evaluating offers for award. Examples include technical excellence, management capability, personnel qualifications, prior experience, past performance, and schedule compliance.

technical leveling The process of helping a seller bring its proposal up to the level of other proposals through successive rounds of discussion, such as by pointing out weaknesses resulting from the seller's lack of diligence, competence, or inventiveness in preparing the proposal.

technical/management proposal That part of the offer that describes the seller's approach to meeting the buyer's requirement.

technical transfusion The disclosure of technical information pertaining to a proposal that re-suits in improvement of a competing proposal. This practice is not allowed in federal government contracting.

term A part of a contract that addresses a specific subject.

termination An action taken pursuant to a contract clause in which the buyer unilaterally ends all or part of the work.

terms and conditions (Ts and Cs) All clauses in a contract, including time of delivery, packing and shipping, applicable standard clauses, and special provisions.

unallowable cost Any cost that, under the provisions of any pertinent law, regulation, or contract, cannot be included in prices, cost-reimbursements, or settlements under a government contract to which it is allocable.

uncompensated overtime The work that exempt employees perform above and beyond 40 hours per week. Also known as competitive time, deflated hourly rates, direct allocation of salary costs, discounted hourly rates, extended work week, full-time accounting, and green time.

Uniform Commercial Code (UCC) A U.S. model law developed to standardize commercial contracting law among the states. It has been adopted by 49 states (and in significant portions by Louisiana). The UCC comprises articles that deal with specific commercial subject matters, including sales and letters of credit.

unilateral See bilateral contract.

unsolicited proposal A research or development proposal that is made by a prospective contractor without prior formal or informal solicitation from a purchasing activity.

variable costs Costs associated with production that change directly with the amount of production, e.g., the direct material or labor required to complete the build or manufacturing of a product.

variance The difference between projected and actual performance, especially relating to costs.

vertical exchange A marketplace that is specific to a single industry.

waiver The voluntary and unilateral relinquishment a person of a right that he or she has. See also forbearance.

warranty A promise or affirmation given by a seller to a buyer regarding the nature, usefulness, or condition of the goods or services furnished under a contract. Generally, a warranty's purpose is to delineate the rights and obligations for defective goods and services and to foster quality performance.

warranty, express A written statement arising out of a sale to the consumer of a consumer good, pursuant to which the manufacturer, distributor, or retailer undertakes to preserve or maintain the utility or performance of the consumer good or provide compensation if there is a failure in utility or performance. It is not necessary to the creation of an express warranty that formal words such as "warrant" or "guarantee" be used, or that a specific intention to make a warranty be present.

warranty, implied A promise arising by operation of law that something that is sold shall be fit for the purpose for which the seller has reason to know that it is required. Types of implied warranties include implied warranty of merchantability, of title, and of wholesomeness.

warranty of fitness A warranty by the seller that goods sold are suitable for the special purpose of the buyer.

warranty of merchantability A warranty that goods are fit for the ordinary purposes for which such goods are used and conform to the promises or affirmations of fact made on the container or label.

warranty of title An express or implied (arising by operation of law) promise that the seller owns the item offered for sale and, therefore, is able to transfer a good title and that the goods, as delivered, are free from any security interest of which the buyer at the time of contracting has no knowledge.

web portals A public exchange in which a company or group of companies list products or services for sale or provide other transmission of business information.

win strategy A collection of messages or points designed to guide the customer's perception of you, your solution, and your competitors.

Work Breakdown Structure (WBS) A logical, organized, decomposition of the work tasks within a given project, typically uses a hierarchical numeric coding scheme.

World Trade Organization (WTO) A multi-national legal entity which serves as the champion of fair trade globally, established April 15, 1995.

APPENDIX C

Articles of the Uniform Commercial Code

THE BATTLE OF THE FORMS

The Problem

A buyer sends the seller his standard form offering to buy goods on the terms set forth in the form. The seller can either (a) reject the offer; (b) accept the offer by agreeing to all of the buyer's terms; (c) accept some of the buyer's terms and reject others (possibly substituting his own for those rejected); or (d) accept all the buyers terms but add some of his own. Often buyer and seller informally agree on a sale, and one then sends the other a confirming memo which covers all they agreed on but adds terms they never discussed. What are the consequences of these actions?

Standard Contract Mirror Image Rule

As we have already noted, normally there is no acceptance where the seller alters the terms of the buyer's offer. Rather the seller's action amounts to a counteroffer which must be accepted by the buyer before a contract results.[1]

The UCC's Effect

The UCC changes the standard rule by providing that "[a] definite and seasonable expression of acceptance or a written confirmation which is sent within a reasonable time operates as an acceptance even though it states terms additional to or different from those offered or agreed upon,

---

[1]Restatement (Second) of Contracts, § 59 (1981).

unless acceptance is expressly made conditional on assent to the additional or different terms."

What's in the Contract

As a result of the preceding UCC provision a contract may result, but are the additional terms (proposed by the offeree) part of that contract? The UCC states that "[t]he additional terms are to be construed as proposals for addition to the contract." Between merchants such terms become part of the contract unless: (a) the offer expressly limits acceptance to the terms of the offer; (b) they materially alter it; or (c) notification of objection to them has already been given or is given within a reasonable time after notice of them is received.

Effects of Conduct

Even if the documents passing between the buyer and seller do not result in the formation of a contract (through the standard offer-and-acceptance procedure), the Section states that: "Conduct by both parties which recognizes the existence of a contract is sufficient to establish a contract for sale... In such case the terms of the particular contract consist of those terms on which the writings of the parties agree, together with any supplementary terms incorporated under any other provisions of the [UCC]."[2]

Modifying the Contract

Contract modifications are covered by Section 2-209 of the UCC. The rules represent a sharp departure both from prior contract law, and from the present law as it applies to Federal Contracts.

Basically, Section 2-209 provides that an existing contract can be modified without consideration, but the modification must satisfy the "statute of frauds" provision if the contract as modified falls within those provisions.

However, if a signed contract states that it can only be modified by a signed writing, no other method of modification is permissible.

If an attempted modification does not satisfy the above requirements, it might still operate as a waiver; but a party who has granted a waiver relating to an unperformed portion of a contract may retract the waiver by giving reasonable notice to the other party of its intent to do so.

Note that, in any case, a modification must meet the "good faith" test of Section 1-203, and if it is coerced without a legitimate commercial reason, it is ineffective.[2]

---

[2]See Tunis Mfg. Corp., 386 N.Y.S.2d 911 (1976) (arbitration clause ineffective).

[2]Erie County Water Auth. V. Hen-Gar Constr. Corp., 473 F. Supp. 1310, 1313 (W.D.N.Y. 1979) (extortion of a modification without legitimate commercial reason is ineffective as a violation of the duty of good faith).

APPENDIX D

Contractor Team Arrangements

Subpart 9.6—Contractor Team Arrangements

9.601 Definition.

"Contractor team arrangement," as used in this subpart, means an arrangement in which—

(1) Two or more companies form a partnership or joint venture to act as a potential prime contractor; or

(2) A potential prime contractor agrees with one or more other companies to have them act as its subcontractors under a specified Government contract or acquisition program.

9.602 General.

(a) Contractor team arrangements may be desirable from both a Government and industry standpoint in order to enable the companies involved to—

(1) Complement each other's unique capabilities; and

(2) Offer the Government the best combination of performance, cost, and delivery for the system or product being acquired.

(b) Contractor team arrangements may be particularly appropriate in complex research and development acquisitions, but may be used in other appropriate acquisitions, including production.

(c) The companies involved normally form a contractor team arrangement before submitting an offer. However, they may enter into an arrangement later in the acquisition process, including after contract award.

9.603 Policy.

The Government will recognize the integrity and validity of contractor team arrangements; *provided*, the arrangements are identified and company relationships are fully disclosed in an offer or, for arrangements entered into after submission of an offer, before the arrangement becomes effective. The Government will not normally require or encourage the dissolution of contractor team arrangements.

9.604 Limitations.

Nothing in this subpart authorizes contractor team arrangements in violation of antitrust statutes or limits the Government's rights to—

(a) Require consent to subcontracts (see Subpart 44.2);

(b) Determine, on the basis of the stated contractor team arrangement, the responsibility of the prime contractor (see Subpart 9.1);

(c) Provide to the prime contractor data rights owned or controlled by the Government;

(d) Pursue its policies on competitive contracting, subcontracting, and component breakout after initial production or at any other time; and

(e) Hold the prime contractor fully responsible for contract performance, regardless of any team arrangement between the prime contractor and its subcontractors.

APPENDIX E

Subcontracting Policies and Procedures

PART 44—SUBCONTRACTING POLICIES AND PROCEDURES

44.000 Scope of part.

(a) This part prescribes policies and procedures for consent to subcontracts or advance notification of subcontracts. and for review. evaluation. and approval of contractors' purchasing systems.

(b) The consent and advance notification requirements of Subpart 44.2 are not applicable to prime contracts for commercial items acquired pursuant to Part 12.

Subpart 44.1—General

44.101 Definitions.

As used in this part—

"Approved purchasing system" means a contractor's purchasing system that has been reviewed and approved in accordance with this part.

"Contractor" means the total contractor organization or a separate entity of it. such as an affiliate. division. or plant. that performs its own purchasing.

"Contractor purchasing system review (CPSR)" means the complete evaluation of a contractor's purchasing of material and services. subcontracting. and subcontract management from development of the requirement through completion of subcontract performance.

"Subcontract" means any contract as defined in Subpart 2.1 entered into by a subcontractor to furnish supplies or services for performance of a prime contract or a subcontract. It includes but is not limited to purchase orders. and changes and modifications to purchase orders.

"Subcontractor" means any supplier. distributor. vendor. or firm that furnishes supplies or services to or for a prime contractor or another subcontractor.

Subpart 44.2—Consent to Subcontracts

44.201 Consent and advance notification requirements.

44.201-1 Consent requirements.

(a) If the contractor has an approved purchasing system, consent is required for subcontracts specifically identified by the contracting officer in the subcontracts clause of the contract. The contracting officer may require consent to subcontract if the contracting officer has determined that an individual consent action is required to protect the Government adequately because of the subcontract type, complexity, or value, or because the subcontract needs special surveillance. These can be subcontracts for critical systems, subsystems, components, or services. Subcontracts may be identified by subcontract number or by class of items (*e.g.*, subcontracts for engines on a prime contract for airframes).

(b) If the contractor does not have an approved purchasing system, consent to subcontract is required for cost-reimbursement, time-and-materials, labor-hour, or letter contracts, and also for unpriced actions (including unpriced modifications and unpriced delivery orders) under fixed-price contracts that exceed the simplified acquisition threshold, for—

(1) Cost-reimbursement, time-and-materials, or labor-hour subcontracts; and

(2) Fixed-price subcontracts that exceed—

(i) For the Department of Defense, the Coast Guard, and the National Aeronautics and Space Administration, the greater of the simplified acquisition threshold or 5 percent of the total estimated cost of the contract; or

(ii) For civilian agencies other than the Coast Guard and the National Aeronautics and Space Administration, either the simplified acquisition threshold or 5 percent of the total estimated cost of the contract.

(c) Consent may be required for subcontracts under prime contracts for architect-engineer services.

(d) The contracting officer's written authorization for the contractor to purchase from Government sources (see Part 51) constitutes consent.

44.201-2 Advance notification requirements.

Under cost-reimbursement contracts, the contractor is required by statute to notify the contracting officer as follows:

(a) For the Department of Defense, the Coast Guard, and the National Aeronautics and Space Administration, unless the contractor maintains an approved purchasing system, 10 U.S.C. 2306 requires notification before the award of any cost-plus-fixed-fee subcontract, or any fixed-price subcontract that exceeds the greater of the simplified acquisition threshold or 5 percent of the total estimated cost of the contract.

(b) For civilian agencies other than the Coast Guard and the National Aeronautics and Space Administration, even if the contractor has an approved purchasing system, 41 U.S.C. 254(b) requires notification before the award of any cost-plus-fixed-fee subcontract, or any fixed-price subcontract that exceeds either the simplified acquisition threshold or 5 percent of the total estimated cost of the contract.

44.202 Contracting officer's evaluation.

44.202-1 Responsibilities.

(a) The cognizant administrative contracting officer (ACO) is responsible for consent to subcontracts, except when the contracting officer retains the contract for administration or withholds the consent responsibility from delegation to the ACO. In such cases, the contract administration office should assist the contracting office in its evaluation as requested.

(b) The contracting officer responsible for consent shall review the contractor's notification and supporting data to ensure that the proposed subcontract is appropriate for the risks involved and consistent with current policy and sound business judgment.

(c) Designation of specific subcontractors during contract negotiations does not in itself satisfy the requirements for advance notification or consent pursuant to the clause at 52.244-2. However, if, in the opinion of the contracting officer, the advance notification or consent requirements were satisfied for certain subcontracts evaluated during negotiations, the contracting officer shall identify those subcontracts in paragraph (j) of the clause at 52.244-2.

44.202-2 Considerations.

(a) The contracting officer responsible for consent must, at a minimum, review the request and supporting data and consider the following:

(1) Is the decision to subcontract consistent with the contractor's approved make-or-buy program, if any (see 15.407-2)?

(2) Is the subcontract for special test equipment, equipment or real property that are available from Government sources?

(3) Is the selection of the particular supplies, equipment, or services technically justified?

(4) Has the contractor complied with the prime contract requirements regarding—

(i) Small business subcontracting, including, if applicable, its plan for subcontracting with small, veteran-owned, service-disabled veteran-owned, HUBZone, small disadvantaged and women-owned small business concerns (see Part 19); and

(ii) Purchase from nonprofit agencies designated by the Committee for Purchase From People Who Are Blind or

Severely Disabled (Javits-Wagner-O'Day Act (41 U.S.C. 48)) (see Part 8)?

(5) Was adequate price competition obtained or its absence properly justified?

(6) Did the contractor adequately assess and dispose of subcontractors' alternate proposals, if offered?

(7) Does the contractor have a sound basis for selecting and determining the responsibility of the particular subcontractor?

(8) Has the contractor performed adequate cost or price analysis or price comparisons and obtained accurate, complete, and current cost or pricing data, including any required certifications?

(9) Is the proposed subcontract type appropriate for the risks involved and consistent with current policy?

(10) Has adequate consideration been obtained for any proposed subcontract that will involve the use of Government-provided equipment and real property?

(11) Has the contractor adequately and reasonably translated prime contract technical requirements into subcontract requirements?

(12) Does the prime contractor comply with applicable cost accounting standards for awarding the subcontract?

(13) Is the proposed subcontractor in the Excluded Parties List System (see Subpart 9.4)?

(b) Particularly careful and thorough consideration under paragraph (a) of this section is necessary when—

(1) The prime contractor's purchasing system or performance is inadequate;

(2) Close working relationships or ownership affiliations between the prime and subcontractor may preclude free competition or result in higher prices;

(3) Subcontracts are proposed for award on a non-competitive basis, at prices that appear unreasonable, or at prices higher than those offered to the Government in comparable circumstances; or

(4) Subcontracts are proposed on a cost-reimbursement, time-and-materials, or labor-hour basis.

44.203 Consent limitations.

(a) The contracting officer's consent to a subcontract or approval of the contractor's purchasing system does not constitute a determination of the acceptability of the subcontract terms or price, or of the allowability of costs, unless the consent or approval specifies otherwise.

(b) Contracting officers shall not consent to—

(1) Cost-reimbursement subcontracts if the fee exceeds the fee limitations of 15.404-4(c)(4)(i);

(2) Subcontracts providing for payment on a cost-plus-a-percentage-of-cost basis;

(3) Subcontracts obligating the contracting officer to deal directly with the subcontractor;

(4) Subcontracts that make the results of arbitration, judicial determination, or voluntary settlement between the prime contractor and subcontractor binding on the Government; or

(5) Repetitive or unduly protracted use of cost-reimbursement, time-and-materials, or labor-hour subcontracts (contracting officers should follow the principles of 16.103(c)).

(c) Contracting officers should not refuse consent to a subcontract merely because it contains a clause giving the subcontractor the right of indirect appeal to an agency board of contract appeals if the subcontractor is affected by a dispute between the Government and the prime contractor. Indirect appeal means assertion by the subcontractor of the prime contractor's right to appeal or the prosecution of an appeal by the prime contractor on the subcontractor's behalf. The clause may also provide that the prime contractor and subcontractor shall be equally bound by the contracting officer's or board's decision. The clause may not attempt to obligate the contracting officer or the appeals board to decide questions that do not arise between the Government and the prime contractor or that are not cognizable under the clause at 52.233-1, Disputes.

44.204 Contract clauses.

(a)(1) The contracting officer shall insert the clause at 52.244-2, Subcontracts, in solicitations and contracts when contemplating—

(i) A cost-reimbursement contract;

(ii) A letter contract that exceeds the simplified acquisition threshold;

(iii) A fixed-price contract that exceeds the simplified acquisition threshold under which unpriced contract actions (including unpriced modifications or unpriced delivery orders) are anticipated;

(iv) A time-and-materials contract that exceeds the simplified acquisition threshold; or

(v) A labor-hour contract that exceeds the simplified acquisition threshold.

(2) If a cost-reimbursement contract is contemplated, for civilian agencies other than the Coast Guard and the National Aeronautics and Space Administration, the contracting officer shall use the clause with its Alternate I.

(3) Use of this clause is not required in—

(i) Fixed-price architect-engineer contracts; or

(ii) Contracts for mortuary services, refuse services, or shipment and storage of personal property, when an agency-prescribed clause on approval of subcontractors' facilities is required.

(b) The contracting officer may insert the clause at 52.244-4, Subcontractors and Outside Associates and Consultants (Architect-Engineer Services), in architect-engineer contracts.

(c) The contracting officer shall, when contracting by negotiation, insert the clause at 52.244-5, Competition in Subcontracting, in solicitations and contracts when the contract amount is expected to exceed the simplified acquisition threshold, unless—

(1) A firm-fixed-price contract, awarded on the basis of adequate price competition or whose prices are set by law or regulation, is contemplated; or

(2) A time-and-materials, labor-hour, or architect-engineer contract is contemplated.

Subpart 44.3—Contractors' Purchasing Systems Reviews

44.301 Objective.

The objective of a contractor purchasing system review (CPSR) is to evaluate the efficiency and effectiveness with which the contractor spends Government funds and complies with Government policy when subcontracting. The review provides the administrative contracting officer (ACO) a basis for granting, withholding, or withdrawing approval of the contractor's purchasing system.

44.302 Requirements.

(a) The ACO shall determine the need for a CPSR based on, but not limited to, the past performance of the contractor, and the volume, complexity and dollar value of subcontracts. If a contractor's sales to the Government (excluding competitively awarded firm-fixed-price and competitively awarded fixed-price with economic price adjustment contracts and sales of commercial items pursuant to Part 12) are expected to exceed $25 million during the next 12 months, perform a review to determine if a CPSR is needed. Sales include those represented by prime contracts, subcontracts under Government prime contracts, and modifications. Generally, a CPSR is not performed for a specific contract. The head of the agency responsible for contract administration may raise or lower the $25 million review level if it is considered to be in the Government's best interest.

(b) Once an initial determination has been made under paragraph (a) of this section, at least every three years the ACO shall determine whether a purchasing system review is necessary. If necessary, the cognizant contract administration office will conduct a purchasing system review.

44.303 Extent of review.

A CPSR requires an evaluation of the contractor's purchasing system. Unless segregation of subcontracts is impracticable, this evaluation shall not include subcontracts awarded by the contractor exclusively in support of Government contracts that are competitively awarded firm-fixed-price, competitively awarded fixed-price with economic price adjustment, or awarded for commercial items pursuant to Part 12. The considerations listed in 44.202-2 for consent evaluation of particular subcontracts also shall be used to evaluate the contractor's purchasing system, including the contractor's policies, procedures, and performance under that system. Special attention shall be given to—

(a) The degree of price competition obtained;

(b) Pricing policies and techniques, including methods of obtaining accurate, complete, and current cost or pricing data and certification as required;

(c) Methods of evaluating subcontractor responsibility, including the contractor's use of the Excluded Parties List

System (see 9.404) and, if the contractor has subcontracts with parties on the list, the documentation, systems, and procedures the contractor has established to protect the Government's interests (see 9.405-2);

(d) Treatment accorded affiliates and other concerns having close working arrangements with the contractor;

(e) Policies and procedures pertaining to small business concerns, including small disadvantaged, women-owned, veteran-owned, HUBZone, and service-disabled veteran-owned small business concerns;

(f) Planning, award, and postaward management of major subcontract programs;

(g) Compliance with Cost Accounting Standards in awarding subcontracts;

(h) Appropriateness of types of contracts used (see 16.103); and

(i) Management control systems, including internal audit procedures, to administer progress payments to subcontractors.

44.304 Surveillance.

(a) The ACO shall maintain a sufficient level of surveillance to ensure that the contractor is effectively managing its purchasing program.

(b) Surveillance shall be accomplished in accordance with a plan developed by the ACO with the assistance of subcontracting, audit, pricing, technical, or other specialists as necessary. The plan should cover pertinent phases of a contractor's purchasing system (preaward, postaward, performance, and contract completion) and pertinent operations that affect the contractor's purchasing and subcontracting. The plan should also provide for reviewing the effectiveness of the contractor's corrective actions taken as a result of previous Government recommendations. Duplicative reviews of the same areas by CPSR and other surveillance monitors should be avoided.

44.305 Granting, withholding, or withdrawing approval.

44.305-1 Responsibilities.

The cognizant ACO is responsible for granting, withholding, or withdrawing approval of a contractor's purchasing system. The ACO shall—

(a) Approve a purchasing system only after determining that the contractor's purchasing policies and practices are efficient and provide adequate protection of the Government's interests; and

(b) Promptly notify the contractor in writing of the granting, withholding, or withdrawal of approval.

44.305-2 Notification.

(a) The notification granting system approval shall include—

(1) Identification of the plant or plants covered by the approval;

(2) The effective date of approval; and

(3) A statement that system approval—

(i) Applies to all Federal Government contracts at that plant to the extent that cross-servicing arrangements exist;

(ii) Waives the contractual requirement for advance notification in fixed-price contracts, but not for cost-reimbursement contracts;

(iii) Waives the contractual requirement for consent to subcontracts in fixed-price contracts and for specified subcontracts in cost-reimbursement contracts but not for those subcontracts, if any, selected for special surveillance and identified in the contract Schedule; and

(iv) May be withdrawn at any time at the ACO's discretion.

(b) In exceptional circumstances, consent to certain subcontracts or classes of subcontracts may be required even though the contractor's purchasing system has been approved. The system approval notification shall identify the class or classes of subcontracts requiring consent. Reasons for selecting the subcontracts include the fact that a CPSR or continuing surveillance has revealed sufficient weaknesses in a particular area of subcontracting to warrant special attention by the ACO.

(c) When recommendations are made for improvement of an approved system, the contractor shall be requested to reply within 15 days with a position regarding the recommendations.

44.305-3 Withholding or withdrawing approval.

(a) The ACO shall withhold or withdraw approval of a contractor's purchasing system when there are major weaknesses or when the contractor is unable to provide sufficient information upon which to make an affirmative determination. The ACO may withdraw approval at any time on the basis of a determination that there has been a deterioration of the contractor's purchasing system or to protect the Government's interest. Approval shall be withheld or withdrawn when there is a recurring noncompliance with requirements, including but not limited to—

(1) Cost or pricing data (see 15.403);

(2) Implementation of cost accounting standards (see 48 CFR Chapter 99 (FAR Appendix, loose-leaf edition));

(3) Advance notification as required by the clauses prescribed in 44.204; or

(4) Small business subcontracting (see Subpart 19.7).

(b) When approval of the contractor's purchasing system is withheld or withdrawn, the ACO shall within 10 days after completing the in-plant review (1) inform the contractor in writing, (2) specify the deficiencies that must be corrected to qualify the system for approval, and (3) request the contractor to furnish within 15 days a plan for accomplishing the necessary actions. If the plan is accepted, the ACO shall make a follow-up review as soon as the contractor notifies the ACO that the deficiencies have been corrected.

44.306 Disclosure of approval status.

Upon request, the ACO may inform a contractor that the purchasing system of a proposed subcontractor has been approved or disapproved, but shall caution that the Government will not keep the contractor advised of any changes in the approval status. If the proposed subcontractor's purchasing system has not been reviewed, the contractor shall be so advised.

44.307 Reports.

The ACO shall distribute copies of CPSR reports; notifications granting, withholding, or withdrawing system approval; and Government recommendations for improvement of an approved system, including the contractor's response, to at least—

(a) The cognizant contract audit office;

(b) Activities prescribed by the cognizant agency; and

(c) The contractor (except that furnishing copies of the contractor's response is optional).

Subpart 44.4—Subcontracts for Commercial Items and Commercial Components

44.400 Scope of subpart.

This subpart prescribes the policies limiting the contract clauses a prime contractor may be required to apply to any subcontractors that are furnishing commercial items or commercial components in accordance with Section 8002(b)(2) (Public Law 103-355).

44.401 Applicability.

This subpart applies to all contracts and subcontracts. For the purpose of this subpart, the term "subcontract" has the same meaning as defined in Part 12.

44.402 Policy requirements.

(a) Contractors and subcontractors at all tiers shall, to the maximum extent practicable:

(1) Be required to incorporate commercial items or non-developmental items as components of items delivered to the Government; and

(2) Not be required to apply to any of its divisions, subsidiaries, affiliates, subcontractors or suppliers that are furnishing commercial items or commercial components any clause, except those—

(i) Required to implement provisions of law or executive orders applicable to subcontractors furnishing commercial items or commercial components; or

(ii) Determined to be consistent with customary commercial practice for the item being acquired.

(b) The clause at 52.244-6, Subcontracts for Commercial Items and Commercial Components, implements the policy in paragraph (a) of this section. Notwithstanding any other clause in the prime contract, only those clauses identified in the clause at 52.244-6 are required to be in subcontracts for commercial items or commercial components.

(c) Agencies may supplement the clause at 52.244-6 only as necessary to reflect agency unique statutes applicable to the acquisition of commercial items.

44.403 Contract clause.

The contracting officer shall insert the clause at 52.244-6, Subcontracts for Commercial Items, in solicitations and contracts other than those for commercial items.

*   *   *   *   *   *

52.244-1 [Reserved]

52.244-2 Subcontracts.

As prescribed in 44.204(a)(1), insert the following clause:

SUBCONTRACTS (JUNE 2007)

(a) *Definitions.* As used in this clause—

"Approved purchasing system" means a Contractor's purchasing system that has been reviewed and approved in accordance with Part 44 of the Federal Acquisition Regulation (FAR).

"Consent to subcontract" means the Contracting Officer's written consent for the Contractor to enter into a particular subcontract.

"Subcontract" means any contract, as defined in FAR Subpart 2.1, entered into by a subcontractor to furnish supplies or services for performance of the prime contract or a subcontract. It includes, but is not limited to, purchase orders, and changes and modifications to purchase orders.

(b) When this clause is included in a fixed-price type contract, consent to subcontract is required only on unpriced contract actions (including unpriced modifications or unpriced delivery orders), and only if required in accordance with paragraph (c) or (d) of this clause.

(c) If the Contractor does not have an approved purchasing system, consent to subcontract is required for any subcontract that—

(1) Is of the cost-reimbursement, time-and-materials, or labor-hour type; or

(2) Is fixed-price and exceeds—

(i) For a contract awarded by the Department of Defense, the Coast Guard, or the National Aeronautics and Space Administration, the greater of the simplified acquisition threshold or 5 percent of the total estimated cost of the contract; or

(ii) For a contract awarded by a civilian agency other than the Coast Guard and the National Aeronautics and Space Administration, either the simplified acquisition threshold or 5 percent of the total estimated cost of the contract.

(d) If the Contractor has an approved purchasing system, the Contractor nevertheless shall obtain the Contracting Officer's written consent before placing the following subcontracts:

_____

_____

(e)(1) The Contractor shall notify the Contracting Officer reasonably in advance of placing any subcontract or modification thereof for which consent is required under paragraph (b), (c), or (d) of this clause, including the following information:

(i) A description of the supplies or services to be subcontracted.

(ii) Identification of the type of subcontract to be used.

(iii) Identification of the proposed subcontractor.

(iv) The proposed subcontract price.

(v) The subcontractor's current, complete, and accurate cost or pricing data and Certificate of Current Cost or Pricing Data, if required by other contract provisions.

(vi) The subcontractor's Disclosure Statement or Certificate relating to Cost Accounting Standards when such data are required by other provisions of this contract.

(vii) A negotiation memorandum reflecting—

(A) The principal elements of the subcontract price negotiations;

(B) The most significant considerations controlling establishment of initial or revised prices;

(C) The reason cost or pricing data were or were not required;

(D) The extent, if any, to which the Contractor did not rely on the subcontractor's cost or pricing data in determining the price objective and in negotiating the final price;

(E) The extent to which it was recognized in the negotiation that the subcontractor's cost or pricing data were not accurate, complete, or current; the action taken by the Contractor and the subcontractor; and the effect of any such defective data on the total price negotiated;

(F) The reasons for any significant difference between the Contractor's price objective and the price negotiated; and

(G) A complete explanation of the incentive fee or profit plan when incentives are used. The explanation shall identify each critical performance element, management decisions used to quantify each incentive element, reasons for the incentives, and a summary of all trade-off possibilities considered.

(2) The Contractor is not required to notify the Contracting Officer in advance of entering into any subcontract for which consent is not required under paragraph (b), (c), or (d) of this clause.

(f) Unless the consent or approval specifically provides otherwise, neither consent by the Contracting Officer to any subcontract nor approval of the Contractor's purchasing system shall constitute a determination—

(1) Of the acceptability of any subcontract terms or conditions;

(2) Of the allowability of any cost under this contract; or

(3) To relieve the Contractor of any responsibility for performing this contract.

(g) No subcontract or modification thereof placed under this contract shall provide for payment on a cost-plus-a-percentage-of-cost basis, and any fee payable under cost-reimbursement type subcontracts shall not exceed the fee limitations in FAR 15.404-4(c)(4)(i).

(h) The Contractor shall give the Contracting Officer immediate written notice of any action or suit filed and prompt notice of any claim made against the Contractor by any subcontractor or vendor that, in the opinion of the Contractor, may result in litigation related in any way to this contract, with respect to which the Contractor may be entitled to reimbursement from the Government.

(i) The Government reserves the right to review the Contractor's purchasing system as set forth in FAR Subpart 44.3.

(j) Paragraphs (c) and (e) of this clause do not apply to the following subcontracts, which were evaluated during negotiations:

_____

_____

_____

(End of clause)

Alternate I (June 2007). As prescribed in 44.204(a)(2), substitute the following paragraph (e)(2) for paragraph (e)(2) of the basic clause:

(e)(2) If the Contractor has an approved purchasing system and consent is not required under paragraph (c), or (d) of this clause, the Contractor nevertheless shall notify the Contracting Officer reasonably in advance of entering into any (i) cost-plus-fixed-fee subcontract, or (ii) fixed-price subcontract that exceeds either the simplified acquisition threshold or 5 percent of the total estimated cost of this contract. The notification shall include the information required by paragraphs (e)(1)(i) through (e)(1)(iv) of this clause.

52.244-3 [Reserved]

52.244-4 Subcontractors and Outside Associates and Consultants (Architect-Engineer Services).

As prescribed in 44.204(b), insert the following clause:

SUBCONTRACTORS AND OUTSIDE ASSOCIATES AND CONSULTANTS (ARCHITECT-ENGINEER SERVICES) (AUG 1998)

Any subcontractors and outside associates or consultants required by the Contractor in connection with the services covered by the contract will be limited to individuals or firms that were specifically identified and agreed to during negotiations. The Contractor shall obtain the Contracting Officer's written consent before making any substitution for these subcontractors, associates, or consultants.

(End of clause)

52.244-5 Competition in Subcontracting.

As prescribed in 44.204(c), insert the following clause:

COMPETITION IN SUBCONTRACTING (DEC 1996)

(a) The Contractor shall select subcontractors (including suppliers) on a competitive basis to the maximum practical

extent consistent with the objectives and requirements of the contract.

(b) If the Contractor is an approved mentor under the Department of Defense Pilot Mentor-Protégé Program (Pub. L. 101-510, section 831 as amended), the Contractor may award subcontracts under this contract on a noncompetitive basis to its protégés.

(End of clause)

52.244-6 Subcontracts for Commercial Items.

As prescribed in 44.403, insert the following clause:

SUBCONTRACTS FOR COMMERCIAL ITEMS (AUG 2009)

(a) *Definitions.* As used in this clause—

"Commercial item" has the meaning contained in Federal Acquisition Regulation 2.101, Definitions.

"Subcontract" includes a transfer of commercial items between divisions, subsidiaries, or affiliates of the Contractor or subcontractor at any tier.

(b) To the maximum extent practicable, the Contractor shall incorporate, and require its subcontractors at all tiers to incorporate, commercial items or nondevelopmental items as components of items to be supplied under this contract.

(c)(1) The Contractor shall insert the following clauses in subcontracts for commercial items:

(i) 52.203-13, Contractor Code of Business Ethics and Conduct (DEC 2008) (Pub. L. 110-252, Title VI, Chapter 1 (41 U.S.C. 251 note)), if the subcontract exceeds $5,000,000 and has a performance period of more than 120 days. In altering this clause to identify the appropriate parties, all disclosures of violation of the civil False Claims Act or of Federal criminal law shall be directed to the agency Office of the Inspector General, with a copy to the Contracting Officer.

(ii) 52.203-15, Whistleblower Protections Under the American Recovery and Reinvestment Act of 2009 (Section 1553 of Pub. L. 111-5), if the subcontract is funded under the Recovery Act.

(iii) 52.219-8, Utilization of Small Business Concerns (MAY 2004) (15 U.S.C. 637(d)(2) and (3)), if the subcontract offers further subcontracting opportunities. If the subcontract (except subcontracts to small business concerns) exceeds $550,000 ($1,000,000 for construction of any public facility), the subcontractor must include 52.219-8 in lower tier subcontracts that offer subcontracting opportunities.

(iv) 52.222-26, Equal Opportunity (MAR 2007) (E.O. 11246).

(v) 52.222-35, Equal Opportunity for Special Disabled Veterans, Veterans of the Vietnam Era, and Other Eligible Veterans (SEPT 2006) (38 U.S.C. 4212(a));

(vi) 52.222-36, Affirmative Action for Workers with Disabilities (JUNE 1998) (29 U.S.C. 793).

(vii) 52.222-39, Notification of Employee Rights Concerning Payment of Union Dues or Fees (Dec 2004) (E.O.

13201), if flow down is required in accordance with paragraph (g) of FAR clause 52.222-39).

(viii) 52.222-50, Combating Trafficking in Persons (FEB 2009) (22 U.S.C. 7104(g)).

(ix) 52.247-64, Preference for Privately Owned U.S.-Flag Commercial Vessels (FEB 2006) (46 U.S.C. App. 1241 and 10 U.S.C. 2631), if flow down is required in accordance with paragraph (d) of FAR clause 52.247-64).

(2) While not required, the Contractor may flow down to subcontracts for commercial items a minimal number of additional clauses necessary to satisfy its contractual obligations.

(d) The Contractor shall include the terms of this clause, including this paragraph (d), in subcontracts awarded under this contract.

(End of clause)

APPENDIX F

Dollar Thresholds

DOLLAR THRESHOLD CHANGES IMPACTING SUBCONTRACTS

Effective 2011
Micro Purchase Threshold:
Remains $3,000

Simplified Acquisition Threshold:
From $100,000   To $150,000

Commercial Items Test Program:
Remains $550,000

Cost or Pricing Data Threshold:
From $650,000   To $700,000

Small Business Subcontracting Plan:
From $550,000   To $650,000

Award of Subcontract to Company Suspended or Debarred:
Remains $30,000

Disabled Viet Nam Vet Clauses:
From $100,000   To $150,000

Various other reporting requirements and administrative thresholds that apply to the Government contracting agency have been revised. The $150,000 SAT has been frequently changed to state the "simplified acquisition threshold."

COST ACCOUNTING STANDARDS (CAS) THRESHOLDS
FAR Part 30, Appendix B, Part 9903

Individual Contracts (Effective 2011)
From $650,000   To $700,000

CAS Board Actions
Separate Business Unit Applicability (Trigger Contract)
Remains $7,500,000

Modified CAS Coverage—See Trigger Contract
Standards 9904-401, 402, 405, 406
Clauses 52.230-3; 52.230-6

Full CAS Coverage—Clauses 52.230-2; 52.230-6
        Remains $50,000,000

Disclosure Statement Filing—Prime Contractor
        Remains $50,000,000

Disclosure Statement Filing—Company Segment
        From $550,000   To $700,000

Award of Subcontract to Company Suspended or Debarred:
        Remains $10,000,000

Disclosure Statement Filing—Educational Institution
        Remains $10,000,000

SOCIOECONOMIC PROGRAMS
SMALL BUSINESS SUBCONTRACTING (FAR PART 19)

It is the policy of the Government to provide maximum practicable opportunities in its acquisitions to small business concerns and to various socioeconomic small business concerns. These concerns must also have the maximum practicable opportunity to participate as SUBCONTRACTORS in the contracts awarded by any executive, agency, consistent with EFFICIENT contract performance. Under FAR Part 13, Simplified Acquisition Procedures, all prime contract awards between $3,000 and $150,000 are designated small business set asides.

◆ **NOTE** There is no provision for prime contractors to exclude a contractor from an award based on its business status or size unless the awardee is the lowest price offer or best value offeror.

Small business size determination

NAICS Code (SIC Code)

Number of employees—employees (common); Revised proposal is three-year rolling average

Annual Revenue (Three-year rolling average, wide variation)

Socioeconomic Programs

Small Business Concerns

Very Small Business Concerns (Pilot program cancelled in 2006)

Emerging Small Business Concerns

Geographic Distribution of Subcontracts (NASA)

Use of Rural Small Business (NASA)

Small Disadvantaged Business Concerns
Women Owned Small Business Concerns
Veteran Owned Small Business Concerns
Service Disabled Veteran Owned Small Business Concerns
HUBZone Small Business Concerns

Other preference programs FAR Part 26

Tribal Organizations
HBCU/MI

FAR 52.2 19-8 Utilization of Small Businesss Concerns

Required for all contracts ova the simplified acquisition threshold ($100,000)

FAR 52.2 19-9 Small Business Subcontracting Plan

Required in all subcontracts that exceed $500,000 ($650,000, June 2007) and are with large business concerns. Includes value of options. A small business sub contracting plan must be submitted. The plan must contain standard requirements for establishing goals, tracking subcontracting actuals by status of business concerns, and reporting subcontracting results to the prime or Government.

Small Business Liaison Officer

Establishing subcontracting goals

Tracking and Reporting

Individual Contract Plan

       SF 294 Subcontracting Report for Individual Contracts

          One for each contract with a subcontracting plan.

          Each six months, electronic submittal. (See NASA Variation)

       SF 295 Summary Subcontracting Report

          One for each executive agency.

          Each six months, electronic submittal.

Master Plan

Commercial Plan

Periodic audit of contractor performance by executive agency and/or SBA.

Government set asides fox small business and socioeconomic small business concerns.

Representations and certifications

CCR Verification by Prime Contractor for SDB and HUBZone

Other clauses in prime contract

Employment and Equal Opportunity programs (FAR Part 22)
Administered by Department of Labor

Service Contracts Act/Davis Bacon Act

EEO Clearance over $10M

Preferential Programs (FAR Part 8)

Federal Prison Industries (UNICOR)
NIB/MISH (JWOD) ABILJTY ONE
GSA Stock Programs
Federal Supply Schedules

APPENDIX G

EG & G, Inc. v. The Cube Corporation

Circuit Court of Virginia, Nineteenth Judicial Circuit.

EG & G, INC.

v.

THE CUBE CORPORATION,

No. 178996.

Dec. 23, 2002.

Dear Counsel:

*1 This case was heard by the Court on September 11, 12 and 16 2002.

FACTS

EG & G Technical Services, Inc. ("EG & G") is a large company with extensive experience in providing management, scientific, technical, engineering, and logistics services to the federal government and others. Approximately 90% of its business involves government contracts. In its 50-year plus history, EG & G has provided services to several federal agencies.[1]

The Cube Corporation ("Cube"), founded in 1994, is also engaged in the business of providing management, operations, and maintenance support services to agencies of the federal government as well as commercial customers. In 1999, Cube was classified as a small, minority-owned business. As a result of this status, Cube is eligible to bid on certain contracts that the federal government has set aside for competition by such businesses.[2]

In Deceber 1999, the National Aeronautics and Space Administration ("NASA"), and the U.S. Navy ("Navy") announced that several contracts, which were at the time being performed at the Wallops Institutional Flight Facility on Wallops Island, Virginia, were going to be combined into a single, consolidated contract. The resulting consolidated contract was to be called the Wallops Institutional Consolidated Contract ("WICC").

With respect to the WICC contract, NASA and the Navy announced their intent to issue a Request for Proposals ("RFP") for the procurement of operations and maintenance support services at NASA's flight facility on Wallops Island. The announcement described the WICC as a cost-plus incentive fee/award term contract, with an initial term of four years and

---

[1] EG & G's federal contracts have included those with the National Aeronautics and Space Administration (NASA), the U.S. Navy, the Department of Defense, the Department of Justice, the Department of Energy, and the U.S. Customs Service, among others.

[2] See generally 15 USC § 631 et seq. (2002).

the potential for an award of up to six additional years, depending on performance. The announcement also noted that the WICC procurement would be a small business set-aside.[3]

In 2000, when the initial proposals were due in response to the NASA RFP, Cube qualified as a small business eligible to compete for the prime contractor position under the WICC. Cube, however, lacked the necessary experience in certain areas that were to be included on the WICC.[4]

EG & G, on the other hand, did possess the requisite experience to provide the types of services that were required under the WICC. Although interested in participating in the WICC, EG & G as a large business was not eligible to bid on the WICC contract as a prime contractor.

Given their respective positions in terms of experience and eligibility to bid on the WICC, Cube and EG & G decided to join forces. In late 1999, in anticipation of submitting a proposal as prime contractor in response to the NASA RFP, Cube and EG & G met to discuss the idea of teaming together to bid on the WICC. Shortly thereafter, Cube and EG & G entered into a Subcontract Agreement (known between the parties and hereafter as the "Teaming Agreement").[5]

The Teaming Agreement expressed a two-part bargain. First, EG & G agreed to work with Cube to prepare a response to the anticipated RFP for the WICC. Specifically, the parties' intent was that Cube, as prime contractor, and EG & G, as subcontractor, would combine their expertise and resources to develop, edit, produce and deliver a compliant proposal in response to NASA's RFP.

*2 Second, in exchange for EG & G's efforts on the proposal, the Teaming Agreement stated, "If the contract is awarded to The Cube Corporation, EG & G will be performing certain functional areas as a subcontractor to The Cube... with the functions to be determined, once the RFP is released,"[6] and that EG & G would perform up to "49% of the contract dollar value."[7] The Teaming Agreement further noted that the parties would work together "on an exclusive basis."

With respect to compensation, Exhibit 1 to the Teaming Agreement stated that Cube would "[a]gree with EG & G Logistics at the time of proposal submission on a fully loaded fee structure,[8] to be used by both The Cube and EG & G Logistics." Exhibit 1 additionally provided that if the

---

[3]The effect of NASA's RFP being issued on a small set-aside basis was that only businesses qualified under applicable regulations as "small businesses" could submit proposals to NASA to be the prime contractor under the WICC.

[4]Areas in which Cube lacked experience included emergency services, environmental management, and telecommunications.

[5]Teaming Agreements between and among different companies are commonly used in connection with federal procurements of numerous and varied types of services. In addition to its Teaming Agreement with EG & G, Cube executed teaming agreements with five other companies for the purpose of preparing its proposal for the WICC.

[6]Article 2.2 of the Teaming Agreement describes the work that EG & G would perform as subcontractor.

[7]Because the WICC is a small business set-aside, the small business prime contractor, such as Cube here, must be responsible for at least 51% of the work.

[8]The elements of such a fee structure include general and administrative expenses ("G & A"), overhead, and profit. The term "G & A" refers to those management, financial, and other expenses incurred by a business for the general management and administration

WICC were awarded to Cube, the parties would "enter into a prime/subcontract agreement for the sole purpose of performing the contract requirements."

In the spring of 2000, NASA and the Navy issued a draft RFP for the WICC. The draft RFP contained a Statement of Work ("SOW") that outlined sixteen particular functions, called Work Breakdown Structures ("WBS") that the government sought to have performed at the NASA/Navy Wallops Institutional Flight Facility on Wallops Island, Virginia. The final RFP for the WICC was issued July 10, 2000.

As envisioned by Article 2.2 of the Teaming Agreement, Cube and EG & G divided up the SOWs according to each company's abilities and areas of expertise. The parties then worked together to prepare a proposal for the WICC (the "Initial Proposal").[9]

On August 28, 2000, Cube, as prime contractor, submitted the Initial Proposal[10] to the government. The proposal incorporated summary cost data for EG & G's portion of the work.[11] In addition, both Cube and EG & G submitted detailed cost proposals directly to NASA, under seal, in order to preserve the proprietary and confidential nature of certain costs, such as the specific G & A rates that each company was applying to the WICC.[12] Cube's Cost Proposal volume recognized that EG & G, in addition to recouping its costs, was to share in the fee (profit) award that Cube proposed to earn on the WICC.[13]

NASA reviewed Cube's Initial Proposal. Subsequently, NASA conducted discussions with Cube, informing Cube of the proposal's strengths and weaknesses. At the conclusion of the discussions, NASA requested that Cube submit a Final Proposal Revision ("FPR"). Cube, with EG & G's participation and support, prepared the FPR.[14] Cube submitted the FPR to NASA, in three volumes, on May 21, 2001.

---

of the business as a whole. Generally, a company's G & A rate is calculated by dividing its total allowable G & A expense pool by its total direct allowable contract costs. In the context of a government cost reimbursement contract, a contractor may recover its G & A expenses in addition to the direct costs incurred in performing a contract. Under such a contract, a contractor may elect to recover less than its actual G & A expense.

[9]In preparing their proposal, Cube and EG & G hired consultants, researched existing contracts and functions being performed at Wallops Island that were to be consolidated into the WICC, and examined staff levels and rates needed to perform the functions at the WICC.

[10]The Initial Proposal consisted of three volumes: A Technical Proposal (Vol.I), a Cost Proposal (Vol.II), and a Management Proposal (Vol.III).

[11]EG & G's cost data included EG & G's proposed fully-loaded labor rates (i.e., pay rates with G & A and overheard costs) for the categories that EG & G expected to furnish in performing designated functional areas (i.e., SOWs) under the WICC.

[12]EG & G and Cube, per agreement, did not disclose to each other their respective specific G & A rates, fringe rates or any overhead rates, which made up part of their fully loaded labor rates. This procedure for disclosing information was acknowledged in Cube's Cost Proposal volume.

[13]As agreed by the parties, only Cube's cost proposal included fee (profit), which if earned, would be shared by the parties. EG & G did not include in its own cost proposal any proposed fee.

[14]EG & G spent more than $70,000 in direct did and proposal ("B & P") costs for preparing the WICC proposal. In addition, EG & G spent significant time and effort on the WICC proposal that is not accounted for in the B & P numbers.

With the exception of certain edits and additions that were made in the FPR in response to NASA's comments, the Initial Proposal and the FPR contained much of the same information. As with the Initial Proposal, EG & G gave a summary of its estimated fully-loaded costs to Cube, while providing detailed cost information directly to NASA. Cube incorporated EG & G's summary data into its overall Cost Proposal for the WICC, which included a G & A rate cap of 3.9%.[15] As before, Cube prepared a proposal for calculating fee on the WICC, and noted that EG & G would share in the proposed fee award.[16]

*3 Throughout the written proposals[17] submitted to NASA, EG & G was described as Cube's "principal subcontractor," and a large part of the "Cube Team."[18] Moreover, EG & G's abilities and experience were touted throughout the proposals submitted to NASA, and EG & G was named as the company that would be responsible for several of the SOWs,[19] including the handling of the materials purchasing function.[20] By assigning this latter function to EG & G, the parties apportioned approximately 41% of the total proposed cost for Year 1 of the WICC to EG & G.[21] For subsequent years of the WICC, EG & G's proposed proportion of costs equaled approximately 43% of the total proposed cost.

Unbeknownst to EG & G, Cube in its final Cost Proposal offered to limit the G & A rates to 3.9% of the total contact costs. Although Cube's proposed cap on G & A rates arguably made its proposal more attractive to NASA and the Navy, such a cap was never discussed with EG & G prior to the

---

[15]As both parties would discover later, the 3.9% G & A rate cap offered by Cube was significantly less than the 8.77% rate proposed by EG & G in the FPR with respect to EG & G's *actual costs* on the WICC project.

[16]Prior to submission of the FPR, Cube and EG & G agreed that they would share any fee based on each parties' proportion of actual incurred costs compared to total contract costs. Testimony of Thomas Walter, September 11, 2002. EG & G was the only subcontractor on the WICC permitted to share fees with Cube.

[17]"Written proposals" refer to both the Initial Proposal and the FPR.

[18]Each page of both the Initial Proposal and the FPR contained the header, "The Cube Team." The company logos for Cube, EG & G, and another major subcontractor, Unisys, are shown at the bottom of each page of the proposal.

[19]The SOWs in which EG & G was responsible for included: SOW 7 (Chemical and Biological Laboratory Support Services); SOW 8 (Environmental Management Support Services); SOW 11 (Emergency Services); SOW 12 (Telecommunication and Engineering Support Services). SOW 13 (Information Resources Management Services); SOW 14 (Technical Services); SOW 15 (Logistics); and SOW 16 (Financial Resources Management Services).

[20]One change from the Initial Proposal to the FPR involved increasing EG & G's responsibilities to include the materials purchasing function for the WICC. This change addressed one of the concerns that NASA and the Navy raised with Cube upon review of the Initial Proposal. In its Initial Proposal, Cube had proposed to handle the purchasing function, but it lacked demonstrable qualifications sufficient to assure the government that Cube could perform the function. EG & G, on the other hand, possessed the requisite qualifications.

[21]The assignment of the purchasing function to EG & G afforded EG & G the opportunity to earn a fee on the WICC that was consistent with the parties' original intent in the Teaming Agreement, that EG & G would perform up to 49% of the WICC.

submission of the final Cost Proposal, nor did Cube suggest to EG & G that it adopt a cap on its G & A rates.[22]

On July 26, 2001, NASA and the Navy awarded the WICC to Cube, as a cost reimbursement, incentive fee, award fee/award term contract. This meant that under the prime contract, Cube and its subcontractors would be paid for their actual costs incurred in performing the contract based on the fully-loaded labor rates proposed and accepted by NASA. In addition to recovering its costs, Cube as the prime contractor could earn a fee, the amount of which was determined under the prime contract based on whether actual costs incurred by Cube were under, over, or at the target cost established for each contract year.

The phase-in period for the WICC took place during August 2001, after which the WICC was to have a base period of four years and six one-year option periods,[23] referred to as "Award Terms," in the contract. During the phase-in period, Cube began hiring employees to work on the WICC, as did EG & G and other subcontractors.

In mid-August 2001, Cube hired Robert Coffman to be the contract manager for the WICC. Mr. Coffman on behalf of Cube executed letter subcontracts[24] with Cube's subcontractors in order to establish interim terms for each subcontractor's performance under the WICC for a 90-day period. During this phase-in period, Cube intended to negotiate the details of a definitized subcontract agreement with its subcontractors.[25]

On or about August 27, 2001, Mr. Coffman sent a proposed letter subcontract ("Letter Subcontract") to the Vice President of Business Operations for EG & G's Installations and Logistics Division, Mr. Thomas Walter. The Letter Subcontract's period of performance was designated as September 1, 2001 through November 30, 2001, unless the parties mutually negotiated a definitized subcontract by November 30, 2001. The Letter Subcontract further stated that the period of performance for the definitized subcontract would be a period of one year starting on September 1, 2001, and that additional option periods would be provided "to the subcontractor on the same basis as provided to the contractor."[26]

*4 Mr. Walter reviewed the proposed Letter Subcontract, which stated that EG & G would perform SOWs 7, 8, 11, 12, 13, 14, 15, and 16 under

---

[22]Testimony of Thomas Walter, September 11, 2002.

[23]The WICC did not guarantee that the contract would extend for a full ten years. Rather, the WICC included a Section G.7 that set forth the criteria governing NASA's exercise of the six optional award terms. This section provided that Cube would be required to achieve specified technical performance and cost goals before it would be entitled to the award of the six option periods. If Cube failed to achieve the requisite technical performance rating and cost budget goal in years three or four of the base period, then neither Cube nor its subcontractors would be eligible to perform the WICC beyond the four-year base period.

[24]A letter subcontract is a temporary agreement that allows work on a government contract to begin while the parties (usually the Government and its prime contractor) are working out the details of a definitized contract.

[25]Mr. Coffman was also responsible for drafting the "definitized" subcontracts for the WICC. "Definitized" contracts refer to subcontracts that include comprehensive terms and provisions.

[26]Letter Subcontract of August 27, 2002, Def. Ex. 5.

the WICC,[27] and provided a budget of $1,500,000.00 for the 90-day period covered by the Letter Subcontract. On August 29, 2001, after editing the proposed Letter Subcontract to reflect the parties' agreement that EG & G's subcontract was to be coextensive with Cube's prime contract-the WICC-Mr. Walter executed the Letter Subcontract on behalf of EG & G and faxed the executed copy to Mr. Coffman at Cube. That same day, Mr. Coffman executed the Letter Subcontract on behalf of Cube and returned the fully executed signature page to Mr. Walter.

Performance on the WICC officially began on September 1, 2001. During the course of its performance, EG & G submitted regular invoices for its actual costs[28] to Cube. EG & G also submitted a monthly invoice for a fee equal to 4% of EG & G's total monthly costs.[29] With each submittal, Cube processed and paid EG & G's invoices for both cost and fee. Cube continued to do such, despite apparent cost increases that Cube was experiencing, and had been aware of, as early as August 2001.[30]

Although the original Letter Subcontract of August 29, 2001 was to last only 90 days, the parties did not finalize a Definitized Contract in that period of time. To allow EG & G's performance to continue while the parties negotiated the Definitized Contract, Cube extended the term of the original temporary Letter subcontract to EG & G several times over the course of ten months.[31]

---

[27]The Letter Subcontract refers to Statements of Work (SOW) and Work Breakdown Structures (WBS) and specifically refers to EG & G's responsibilities as WBSs. In addition to its "baseline" responsibilities within each SOW, each SOW for which EG & G is responsible occasionally requires EG & G to propose and perform work on an "Indefinite Delivery Indefinite Quantity" (IDIQ) basis within EG & G's SOWs.

[28]"Actual costs" include labor, overheard, fringe and G & A. Additionally, when EG & G performs IDIQ work (see note 27, *supra*), its costs for that work are reflected in its regular invoices to Cube. Fees earned on IDIQ work are also included in EG & G's regular fee invoices to Cube.

[29]Under the WICC, Cube can claim 4% of its costs from the fee pool that it proposed each month. At the end of each year, the total fee pool is calculated according to how Cube has performed against its target costs, and any additional amounts awarded to Cube and not claimed during the year are distributed to Cube. EG & G's portion of this annual fee directly relates to the proportion that its work in dollars bears to all baseline work performed on the WICC.

[30]According to Cube, NASA during the phase-in period "strongly encouraged" Cube (and its subcontractors) to hire incumbent personnel who had been providing services to NASA under the contracts that preceded the WICC. Many of predecessor incumbents were either employed in professional positions exempt from the minimum wage requirements imposed upon government contractors or were union members covered by collective bargaining agreements between predecessor contractors and the representative labor unions. Given these circumstances, Cube learned that their labor rates would be higher than those proposed in the FPR submitted to NASA in response to the RFP. Cube's concern over potential cost budget overruns would prove to be a major factor that influenced many of its future decisions with respect to its business relationship with EG & G.

[31]Between November 2001 and June 2002, Cube issued nine separate Letter Subcontract extensions to EG & G, which extended and basically-although not exactly-mirrored the terms of the initial Letter Subcontract.

In late January 2002, Cube and EG & G met to discuss the terms of a Definitized Subcontract.[32] The parties' discussions focused on Cube's desire to take over and perform the purchasing function under the WICC, a task that was currently being performed by EG & G. The parties discussed how the parties would split the fee pool when it was reconciled at the end of each contract year.

At the January 31, 2002 meeting, the parties reached an agreement on the purchasing function and the fee split, and memorialized such in a February 21, 2002 letter sent by Mr. Coffman at Cube to Mr. Walter at EG & G. EG & G agreed to transfer the purchasing function to Cube. In exchange, Cube agreed to guarantee a fee split of 41% to EG & G irrespective of costs.[33]

A few days after making this agreement, however, the Vice President of Contracts and Pricing for Cube, John Schultheis, called EG & G to rescind the agreement with respect to the fee split. Instead, Mr. Schultheis insisted that the fee be shared based on EG & G's proportion of actual costs compared to total contract costs, as per the parties' original understanding.[34] As a result of Cube's withdrawal of the agreement, the purchasing function was not transferred from EG & G to Cube.

On April 9, 2002, Mr. Coffman forwarded a new draft Definitized Subcontract to EG & G for review. In a cover-email, Mr. Coffman noted two new major points to be considered under the draft, namely a proposed cap on EG & G's allowable G & A rate[35] and a termination for convenience clause without limitation.[36]

*5 From that point on, the parties' negotiations revolved around the issues of a cap on EG & G's G & A rate and a termination for convenience clause in the Definitized Subcontract. In continuing correspondence from April through June 2002, EG & G contended that Cube's attempt to insert these terms in a Definitized Subcontract were contrary to the agreement that the parties had reached pursuant to their Teaming Agreement. Notwithstanding, Cube insisted that EG & G agree to cap its G & A rate

---

[32]Cube sent a first draft of the proposed Definitized Subcontract to EG & G on or about October 30, 2001.

[33]Testimony of Thomas Walter, September 11, 2002.

[34]See notes 16, 20, 21, 28, and 29, *supra.*

[35]EG & G in its confidential initial submission to NASA had proposed an 8.77% G & A rate-nearly twice as high as the 3.9% G & A rate cap proposed by Cube.

[36]Cube claims that this latter termination provision was also part of the first draft of the Definitized Subcontract submitted to EG & G in October 2001. The WICC included a termination clause from the Federal Acquisition Regulation ("FAR") (Def.Ex. 28), which governs federal procurement activities, at FAR Clause 52.249-6 (48 C.F.R. § 52.249-6 (2002)). The termination clause in the WICC provides that NASA may terminate the prime contract in the event of Cube's default of its contractual obligations, and it may terminate the prime contract at any time, in whole or in part, for NASA's "convenience" if it is determined that such termination is in the Government's interest. The October 2001 draft subcontract sent by Cube to EG & G incorporated by reference the same FAR clause 52.249-6, although the clause itself was not set out. By incorporating this clause in the first draft subcontract, Cube allegedly proposed to have the right to terminate the subcontract either for default or for convenience.

at 3.9% for all remaining years under the contract and accept a termination for convenience clause.[37]

In an effort to make concessions and move the negotiations of a Definitized Subcontract forward, EG & G offered to cap its G & A rates at 6.5% for Years 2 through 5 of the WICC; at 6.34% for Year 6; and at 6.32% for Years 7 through 10 of the contract, if awarded. EG & G also agreed to accept most of Cube's proposed form of termination provision, with the exception of the paragraph which would permit Cube to terminate EG & G based on another subcontractor's poor performance.[38]

Cube rejected EG & G's offers to compromise. On June 25, 2002, Cube sent EG & G a letter declaring that the parties had reached an "impasse" in their negotiations of a Definitized Subcontract. Cube notified EG & G that the Letter Subcontract of June 14, 2002 would be allowed to expire on June 30, 2002,[39] and gave EG & G only 5 or 6 days to remove more than 100 of its employees from Wallops Island.[40]

In response to these circumstances, on June 27, 2002 EG & G filed a Bill of Complaint seeking specific performance of the Teaming Agreement[41] and a permanent injunction enjoining Cube from terminating EG & G as a subcontractor on the WICC, together with a Motion for Preliminary Injunction. This Court issued a 90-day temporary injunction to preserve the status quo until the merits of EG & G's claims could be heard.

Over the course of three days, commencing on September 11, 2002, the merits of EG & G's claims were tried before this Court.

Specifically, EG & G asserts that specific performance is appropriate in this case, where all of the essential terms of the promised contract are established through mechanisms provided for in the Teaming Agreement. EG & G also claims that those essential terms are supported by substantial evidence, including the parties' Initial Proposal and FPR, the Letter Subcontracts, and the parties' performance under the WICC since September 1, 2001.

Additionally, EG & G claims that if Cube is allowed to terminate EG & G as a subcontractor on the WICC-a major government contract-such will cause EG & G irreparable harm, thereby making its request for permanent injunctive relief appropriate. Specifically, EG & G claims termination will cause irreparable harm to its business reputation and good will, particularly with its NASA and Navy Customers, and that it will lose both

---

[37]Cube cited anticipated cost overruns beginning in Year 2 of the WICC, and Cube's need to control costs under the contract, for its necessity to cap EG & G's G & A rate. See note 30, *supra.*

[38]See note 36, *supra.* After EG & G refused to incorporate the above-mentioned FAR provision by reference, instead offering a termination clause that would permit Cube to terminate EG & G for cause-namely, failures by EG & G to meet performance and budget targets-Cube responded with its own proposed termination clause which, in part, would allow Cube to terminate EG & G for "cause" based upon the failure of the entire "Cube Team" to meet performance and budget targets, even if EG & G were able to meet its individual targets.

[39]Cube insisted, however, that EG & G continue to perform its functions under the WICC through July 15, 2002, when Cube would assume responsibility for those areas.

[40]Testimony of Robert Coffman, September 12, 2002.

[41]Specifically, EG & G seeks to enforce the parties' Teaming Agreement by requiring specific performance of Cube's promise that EG & G will be a subcontractor on the WICC.

government contracting opportunities and certain commercialization opportunities.[42]

*6 In its defense, Cube alleges that the Teaming Agreement is not itself a subcontract between the parties setting forth the particulars of each party's performance of the WICC. Rather, Cube characterizes the Teaming Agreement as an unenforceable "agreement to agree."[43] Cube further contends that the agreements[44] the parties did make, and the parties' conduct over the past year, constitute nothing more than evidence that Cube and EG & G "intended to be bound under a subcontract only if the formal subcontract[45] was prepared and signed."[46] Notwithstanding, Cube concedes that its decision not to renew the extension of the Letter Subcontract Agreement to EG & G was based solely on the parties' failure to reach an agreement as to two terms of the definitized subcontract-a cap on EG & G's G & A rate and a termination for convenience clause.[47]

DISCUSSION

The issue presented is whether the Teaming Agreement, the Initial and Final Proposals, and the Letter Subcontracts entered into by EG & G and Cube contain essential terms sufficient to govern the parties' performance on the WICC, and whether the parties had the requisite intent to be bound by such terms, so as to constitute an enforceable subcontract?

Teaming agreements are special arrangements among different companies that are commonly used in connection with federal procurements of numerous and various types of services.[48] Prime contractors often enter into such agreements with other companies known to have specialized experience in providing discrete types of services in anticipation of submitting a bid in response to a government agency's Request for

---

[42]Based upon the RFP, EG & G contends that it is the Government's expectation that Cube and its team members on the WICC will seek business opportunities to commercialize portions of the functions being performed under that contract in order to reduce costs to the Government, opportunities that EG & G will lose if Cube is permitted to terminate the contract. Additionally, EG & G points out that Cube's termination of EG & G may result in unwarranted negative inferences by future government contracting officers when examining its past performance on the WICC.

[43]*Defendant's Proposed Findings of Fact and Conclusions of Law*, ¶ 72. Cube argues that the Teaming Agreement only provides that if the parties are successful in having the WICC awarded to Cube that they would then agree to enter into "a prime/subcontract agreement for the sole purpose of performing the contract [the WICC] requirements" and that "The Cube will enter into a formal subcontract agreement upon award."

[44]"Agreements" here refer to both the Teaming Agreement and the Letter Subcontract entered into by the parties and extended eight times over the course of ten months. Cube argues that EG & G and Cube entered into the Letter Subcontract with the intent that such would govern performance under the WICC on an interim basis only until they negotiated and reached a final definitized subcontract.

[45]This refers to the Definitized Subcontract under negotiation.

[46]*Defendant's Proposed Finding of Fact and Conclusion of Law*, ¶ 73.

[47]See both trial and deposition testimony of John Schultheis, presented September 16, 2002.

[48]*See Northrop Corp. v. McDonnell Douglas Corp.*, 705 F.2d 1030 (9th Cir.1983); *Experimental Eng'g v. United Tech Corp.*, 614 F.2d 1244 (9th Cir.1980); *Air Tech v. General Elec. Co.*, 347 Mass. 613, 199 N.E.2d 538 (Mass.1964); *see also Colsa Corp. v. Martin Marietta Servs., Inc.*, 133 F.3d 853 (11th Cir.1998).

Proposal. Thus, pursuant to such an agreement, subcontractors generally provide technical expertise, financial support, and other general assistance in preparing the prime contractor's bid submission, in exchange for the prime contractor's promise to award a subcontract.[49]

The federal government acknowledges the validity and desirability of teaming agreements and recognizes that such agreements permit the government contracting industry to "offer the government the best combination of performance, cost, and delivery."[50] Moreover, government agencies routinely consider proposed subcontractors when evaluating proposals.[51]

The validity and desirability of such agreements notwithstanding, for any contract to be enforceable there must be mutual assent of the contracting parties to terms reasonably certain under the circumstances. See *Allen v. Aetna Casualty & Surety*, 222 Va. 361, 281 S.E.2d 818 (1981). That is, a contract cannot exist if the parties never mutually assented to terms proposed by either as essential to an accord. *Progressive Construction v. Thumm*, 209 Va. 24, 30-31, 161 S.E.2d 687, 691 (1968). Thus, where the evidence is that the parties merely *agreed to make an agreement* in the future, and where a determination of the terms and conditions under which the obligation would be assumed are vague and uncertain, Virginia law treats such agreements as unenforceable "agreements to agree." *Allen v. Aetna Casualty & Surety*, 222 Va. 361, 281 S.E.2d 818 (1981).

*7 In considering whether an agreement is an enforceable contract or merely an agreement to agree, courts consider not only whether the document at issue includes the requisite essential terms, but also whether the conduct of the parties and the surrounding circumstances evince the parties' intent to enter into a contract.[52] A Teaming Agreement is an enforceable contract if it is clear that the parties intended to enter into a binding contractual relationship and the agreement contains sufficient objective criteria to enforce.[53]

Agreement, or agreement to agree?

Cube argues that the Teaming Agreement between it and EG & G was nothing more than an agreement to agree. According to Cube, the parties regarded the Teaming Agreement as simply a "formal vehicle with a single purpose: to establish an exclusive relationship to prepare and submit a winning proposal for the WICC."[54] In other words, Cube argues that neither it nor EG & G intended the Teaming Agreement to state the terms of

---

[49]*See Atacs Corp. v. Trans World Communications, Inc,* 155 F.3d 659, 666 (3d Cir.1998).

[50]See FAR 9.602(a)(2); see generally FAR 9.601 et seq.

[51]See FAR 9.103(c), FAR 9.104-4; *see also John Carlo, Inc. v. Corps of Engineers of the United States Army,* 539 F.Supp. 1075, 1077 (N.D.Tex.1982).

[52]*See High Knob v. Allen,* 205 Va. 503, 138 S.E.2d 49 (1964).

[53]*Atacs Corporation,* 155 F.3d. at 666; *see generally,* E. Allan Farnsworth, *Precontractual Liability and Preliminary Agreements: Fair Dealing and Failed Negotiations,* 87 Colum. L.Rev. 217 (1987); Brent E. Newton, *Note, The Legal Effect of Government Contracting Teaming Agreements: A Proposal for Determining Liability and Assessing Damage in Event of Breach,* 91 Colum. L.Rev.1990 (1991).

[54]*Defendant's Proposed Finding of Fact and Conclusions of Law,* ¶¶ 63, 64.

a subcontract between Cube and EG & G for performance of the WICC.[55] Rather, Cube contends that the intention of the parties was that a subcontract would be entered into as a result of good faith negotiations that would occur if Cube were awarded the WICC.[56]

In support of its contentions, Cube relies on the cases of *W.J. Shafer Associates, Inc. v. Cordant Inc.*, 254 Va. 514, 493 S.E.2d 512 (1997) and *Dual, Incorporated. v. Symvionics, Incorporated,* No. 97-1228 1997 U.S.App. LEXIS 23959 (4th Cir.1997) (unpublished).

In *Shafer*, the Virginia Supreme Court addressed the issue of whether a so-called "teaming agreement" constituted an enforceable contract for the sale of digitizers.[57] The Court found the teaming agreement to be merely an agreement to agree in the future in the event that Cordant became the prime contractor on the project.[58] In finding the contract unenforceable, the Court noted that there was no mutual commitment by the parties, no obligation on the part of one of the defendants to sell the digitizers or on the part of the plaintiff to purchase them, no agreed purchase price for the product, and no assurance that the product would be available when needed.[59]

In *Dual, Incorporated v. Symvionics, Incorporated*, 1997 U.S.App. LEXIS 23959 (4th Cir.1997) (unpublished), the United States Court of Appeals for the Fourth Circuit held that a teaming agreement between a prime contractor and subcontractor was not enforceable.[60] The Court of Appeals reasoned that the teaming agreement between Symvionics, the prime contractor, and Dual, the subcontractor, did not require Symvionics ultimately to enter into the subcontract with Dual, but only to negotiate in good faith to arrive at such a contract.[61]

Neither of these cases is dispositive of the issue presented here. First, unlike the facts set forth in *Shafer*, the facts in the present case do sup-

---

[55]*Id.* at ¶ 65.

[56]*Id.*

[57]*Shafer*, 254 Va. at 516, 493 S.E.2d at 513.

[58]254 Va. at 520, 493 S.E.2d at 515.

[59]Id.

[60]In *Dual*, Symvionics, the prime contractor, and Dual, a subcontractor, entered into an agreement by which the contractor used the subcontractor's bid in its proposal to the United States Air Force (USAF) to build a flight simulator. After the proposal was submitted, Dual's anticipated costs increased substantially. USAF informed Symvionics that Dual's proposed costs were excessive. In response to USAF's concern about its costs, Dual agreed to reduce it costs to a "firm fixed price." Based in part on Dual's agreement to reduce its costs, USAF awarded the prime contract to Symvionics based on the latter's bid which included Dual as the subcontractor.

Subsequent to being awarded the bid, Dual and Symvionics signed a Letter Subcontract allowing Dual to begin work on the project. Meanwhile, Symvionics and Dual began negotiating the subcontract. Nine months into the project, however, Dual informed Symvionics that its costs had increased significantly. Concerned over these cost increases and that Symvionics might lose the simulator contract because of difficulties in completing the subcontract in time for USAF's Preliminary Design Review, and possessed of additional information that Dual had acted in bad faith, Symvionics terminated its negotiations with Dual.

[61]The Court in *Dual* acknowledged that under California law (which governed that case) the parties may contract to create the obligation to negotiate in good faith with one another as long as they did not require formation of the subsequent contract. *Dual,*

port a finding of mutual commitment between the parties with respect to the level of EG & G's involvement and type of work that EG & G would perform if Cube were awarded the WICC contract.[62] Moreover, contrary to the Court's finding in *Shafer*, this Court does find an affirmative obligation on the part of the Cube to subcontract those portions of the WICC it promised to EG & G. Indeed, EG & G's work on both the Initial and Final Proposals was performed in, and served as, consideration for Cube's promise.

*8 The facts set forth in *Dual* are also distinguishable from the facts of the present case. In *Dual*, it was the substantial increase of the *subcontractor's* anticipated costs over and above those costs previously agreed to by the parties (not an increase of the prime contractor's costs),[63] *combined with evidence of bad faith on the part of the subcontractor,* which factored into the prime contractor's decision to terminate negotiations with the subcontractor. Here, the facts do not suggest a scintilla of bad faith on the part of EG & G, nor has Cube presented any evidence that EG & G is in breach of any prior agreement with respect to the amount of G & A that EG & G can charge. The facts are not at all similar. Everything was agreed to here except minor functional details. And the testimony at trial made clear that those details were resolved by the parties and never an issue at all.

Intention of parties

Consideration must be given to the intention of the parties, and such intention should be given effect. *High Knob, Inc. v. Allen et al*, 205 Va. 503, 508, 138 S.E.2d 49, 53 (1964). To arrive at this intention, regard is to be had to the situation of the parties, the subject matter of the agreement, and the object which the parties intended. *Id.* Here, it is plain that the parties intended to act, in effect, as partners in performing the WICC contract. EG & G had the lion's share of the SOWs, EG & G was the key subcontractor, and EG & G was essential to Cube's receiving the award of the WICC contract.

Settled law makes clear that if the parties do not intend to be bound until a formal contract is prepared, there is no contract. *Boisseau, Trustee, and Others v. Fuller and Others*, 96 Va. 45, 30 S.E. 457 (1898). And circumstances which show that the parties do intend a formal contract to be drawn up is strong evidence demonstrating that they did *not* intend the prior negotiations to amount to an agreement. *Id.*

Incorporated. v. Symvionics, Incorporated, No. 97-1228, 1997 U.S.App. LEXIS 23959 (4th Cir.1997) (unpublished).

[62]See generally notes 9, 16, 18-21, and 27, *supra*. Additionally, the facts in *Shafer* are quite different than those here. In *Shafer*, Cordant-the successful general contractor as is Cube here-was suing its subcontractor-there Shafer as is EG & G here-under the teaming agreement. Cordant asserted that Shafer had agreed to furnish digitizers if Cordant were selected as prime contractor. No terms of sale were agreed to whatsoever. There was no price for the product, or even an assurance of its availability. Here, all of the relevant terms were agreed to by Cube and EG & G. Furthermore, there is no product here, only services, all of which were fully set out and all of which have been satisfactorily performed to date, and all of which have been paid for by Cube.

[63]At trial, Mr. Jay Huston, Cube' Project Manager on the WICC, testified that Cube-not EG & G-experienced cost increases over the course of the WICC project. Testimony of Jay Huston, September 12, 2002.

Conversely, where there is a proposal or agreement made in writing where it is not expressly stated to be subject to a formal contract, it becomes a question of construction whether the parties intended that the terms agreed on should merely be put into form, or whether they should be subject to a new agreement, the terms of which are not expressed in detail. *Boisseau, Trustee, and Others v. Fuller and Others*, 96 Va. 45, 30 S.E. 457 (1898). If the parties are fully agreed, however, there is a binding contract, notwithstanding the fact that a formal contract is to be prepared and signed. *Boisseau, Trustee, and Others v. Fuller and Others*, 96 Va. 45, 30 S.E. 457 (1898).

Cube argues that the agreements the parties did make,[64] and the parties' conduct, constitute strong evidence that Cube and EG & G intended to be bound under a subcontract *only if* a formal subcontract were prepared and signed. The evidence does not support such a conclusion.

First, unlike the circumstances set forth in either *Shafer* or *Dual*, the Teaming Agreement and subsequent proposals required Cube to do more than just "negotiate in good faith" to arrive at a final subcontract. Cube itself admits that the Teaming Agreement required EG & G to work with Cube in an "exclusive" relationship to prepare a response to the RFP for the WICC.[65] In exchange for EG & G's efforts on the proposal, the Teaming Agreement expressly stated that if Cube were awarded the WICC as prime, EG & G *would* be a subcontractor on the WICC and perform a substantial amount of the work—up to 49%—under the government contract.[66]

*9 Second, in the context of Teaming Agreements, the court may examine the parties' conduct, including any proposals submitted in response to a government RFP, to ascertain whether they intended that the proposed subcontractor receive a subcontract upon award to the prime. See *Experimental Engineering, Inc. v. United Technologies Corp.*, 614 F.2d 1244, 1246-47, n. 2 (9th Cir.1980).[67] The language of both the Teaming Agreement and the subsequent proposals submitted to NASA makes clear that it was the plain intent of both EG & G and Cube that EG & G would be awarded a subcontract upon Cube's award of the WICC project. This understanding that the parties would work together as prime and subcontractor on the WICC from the time of award until June 2002 is further confirmed by the parties' performance.

Third, EG & G was more than just a name arbitrarily included in Cube's Initial and Final Proposals. EG & G's abilities and experience were touted throughout Cube's proposals submitted to NASA. Moreover, EG & G was

---

[64]Again, "agreements" as used here refers to the Teaming Agreement, the Initial and Final Proposal, and the subsequent Letter Subcontracts.

[65]See *Defendant's Proposed Findings of Fact and Conclusions of Law*, ¶ 10.

[66]*Id.* at ¶ 11.

[67]In *Experimental Engineering*, the Ninth Circuit held that summary judgment in favor of the prime contractor was inappropriate where a proposed subcontractor alleged that the temporary Authorization Agreement between it and the prime contractor was not the *only* subcontract that the parties envisioned, and when the subcontractor provided support for the prime's proposal to the government, which itself described the prime and the subcontractor as a "team." *See also Air Technology Corp. v. General Electric Co.*, 199 N.E.2d 538, 546 (Mass.1964) (looking to parties' conduct to infer intent that proposed subcontractor and "team member" would receive a subcontract upon award of the prime contract.)

described as Cube's "principal subcontractor," and a large part of the "Cube Team", and was named as the company that would be responsible for several of the SOWs. EG & G spent more than $70,000 in direct bid and proposal costs for preparing the WICC proposal. In addition, EG & G spent significant time and effort on the WICC proposal that is not accounted for in the bid and proposal numbers.

Most importantly, the agreement was not that EG & G "might" be a subcontractor "if" an agreement were worked out, but "would" be a subcontractor pursuant to previously agreed upon terms as to job responsibilities, compensation, and duration.

In sum, the Court finds both the requisite intent and sufficient criteria to enforce the Teaming Agreement. The clear intent of the parties was to establish a close working relationship and to work together, post-award, for the entire duration of the WICC. This intent is evidenced by the terms of the Teaming Agreement, the parties' conduct, and the circumstances surrounding the parties' proposals for the WICC contract, the Letter Subcontracts, and the subsequent performance on the WICC.

Parties' performance

Additionally, the parties' subsequent performance and dealings with each other over the last year are informative in determining the meaning of particular contract terms at issue in this case.

"The dealings of the parties to a contract in relation to its terms are often conclusive upon questions arising as to the effect or meaning. This may be because the parties have deliberately and mutually disregarded its plain terms, or because they have so dealt with each other as to definitely fix the meaning of the terms, which would otherwise be of doubtful import. In the former case, their plain rights have been waived. In the latter case the doubtful rights of the parties have been fixed by their practical dealings with each other."

First National Bank v. Roanoke Oil Co., 169 Va. 99, 115-16, 192 S.E.2d 764, 771 (1937) (citations omitted). The parties have operated under the agreements without any confusion as to the terms, the responsibilities, the work to be performed, and, very importantly, the method of determining the amount of compensation.

Essential terms

*10 Finally, Cube argues that the promise in the Teaming Agreement relied upon here by EG & G-that Cube committed to entering into a subcontract-is similarly not enforceable where certain material subcontract terms were not mutually agreed to in the Teaming Agreement. Specifically, Cube argues that the parties did not come to an agreement with respect to the G & A rate that EG & G could charge under an agreed upon subcontract and the parties' rights concerning the termination of the subcontract.[68]

---

[68]*Defendant's Proposed Findings of Fact and Conclusions of Law* ¶ 74. The Court notes that on the one hand Cube states that "material" terms regarding G & A and termination were never agreed to by the parties, thus rendering the contract unenforceable. But on the other hand, Cube, in defending allegations of bad faith with respect to its attempt to

This apparent contradiction notwithstanding, the Court does not find Cube's arguments persuasive. At trial, the testimony of several witnesses confirmed that the Cube, in an email to EG & G dated April 9, 2002, see Compl. Ex. 21, intentionally flagged the issue of a cap on G & A, *as well as the termination for convenience clause.* The Court finds such behavior on the part of Cube inconsistent with the notion that such a provision was already contemplated and agreed to by the parties. Rather, the Court finds such an act to be more consistent with that of one attempting to *add new terms* to already existing understandings, and in the context of all the other circumstances, an act of bad faith on the part of Cube.

In Virginia, the essential terms of a contract for services are 1) the nature and scope of the work to be performed, 2) the compensation to be paid for that work, 3) the place of performance, and d) the duration of the contract.[69] Although the G & A rate and termination rights are material terms in that they involve both price and duration, the Court finds that the parties' seeming failure to agree to such terms is irrelevant where the intent of the parties as to these terms is otherwise clear.[70]

First, as EG & G points out, at the time the parties executed the Teaming Agreement, the parties were not yet in a position to specify certain terms of EG & G's anticipated contract with Cube, as NASA and the Navy had not yet issued the RFP for the WICC. As for those areas the Teaming Agreement did address, Article 2.2 of the Teaming Agreement describes the work that EG & G will perform-"certain functional areas as a subcontractor to The Cube... with the functions to be determined, once the RFP is released."[71] Yet these were not contractual matters; they were descriptions and details as to specific items of work to be performed. There was never any disagreement-and neither party so asserted-about whether EG & G would perform these "functional areas" of work.

Second, the subsequent proposals submitted to NASA clearly stated the scope and nature of the work that EG & G was to perform as subcontractor on the WICC. Such was further clarified and confirmed in the Letter Subcontracts and, also importantly, by EG & G's performance. It is clearly apparent from the evidence that the parties agreed that EG & G would perform certain and definite functional areas under the WICC. EG & G has been performing both the baseline work under those functions as well as the IDIQ work that has arisen in those areas for the last year, and is thus plainly able to perform these functions. Even Cube has not suggested that any of these items presented any areas of disagreement.

Third, the parties agreed how EG & G was to be compensated for its work. Exhibit 1 to the Teaming Agreement states that Cube "will agree with EG & G Logistics at the time of proposal submission on a fully loaded

---

add a termination for convenience provision in the subcontract, states that such a provision was already a term of the contract between the parties.

[69]*See Mullins v. Mingo Lime & Lumber Co.*, 176 Va. 44, 50, 10 S.E.2d 492, 494 (1940).

[70]*High Knob* at 508-509. In *High Knob*, court held that although agreement did not specify the amount of water to be provided or the length of time the developer would be required to provide it, there was partial performance of the agreement and the intent of the parties, while not expressed in the agreement, was ascertainable from their conduct and circumstances.

[71]Def. Ex. 1.

fee structure, to be used by both The Cube and EG & G Logistics."[72] Specifically, the parties agreed that EG & G was to receive payment from the government of its costs. At the time the proposals were submitted, EG & G offered, and Cube accepted, EG & G's summary cost data representing its anticipated fully loaded costs (including labor, other direct costs, G & A, and overhead) projected over the entire ten-year term of the WICC.[73] Although some of EG & G's actual costs may have changed during the parties' performance of the WICC,[74] EG & G has submitted invoices representing the actual costs incurred, using the same summary format structure as when EG & G's costs were initially proposed. Cube has paid these invoices without question or complaint.

*11 Fourth, the parties agreed that EG & G is entitled to share in the fee pool that Cube proposed to the government and that was incorporated into the WICC.[75] Both parties assumed that EG & G's share of the fee would correspond to its proportion of work (based on costs incurred) to total costs incurred for the entire contract.[76] These terms, too, are not in dispute.

Finally, the parties' failure to agree upon a cap on EG & G's G & A rate and a termination for convenience clause is entirely attributable to Cube's failure to bargain in good faith. That is, the Court finds that the disagreements that Cube testified to as preventing it from complying with its obligation to enter into a Definitized Subcontract with EG & G[77] were problems that Cube created in an attempt to renegotiate-or in the case of the termination for convenience clause, newly negotiate-essential terms of the parties' already established agreement.

More specifically, Cube's demand that EG & G cap its G & A rate at 3.9% is contrary to the parties' clearly established agreement on how EG & G is to be compensated. Similarly, Cube's insistence upon a termination for convenience clause that would permit it to terminate EG & G either "for cause" based upon the failure of the entire "Cube Team" to meet performance and budget targets-as opposed to just EG & G's failure-or for any reason whatsoever, is contrary to the parties' intent in the Teaming Agreement and subsequent proposals that EG & G would be a subcontractor for the entire duration of the WICC project.[78]

Although the parties agreed upon execution of the Teaming Agreement

---

[72]Def. Ex. 1

[73]The Court notes that at no time during its negotiations with EG & G did Cube request a detailed break down of the fully-loaded labor rates submitted by EG & G. Rather, EG & G submitted a detailed break out of its costs directly to NASA. Testimony of Thomas Walter, September 11, 2002.

[74]Under its terms, a fluctuation in costs does not upset the agreement as to the compensation provisions.

[75]See note 16, *supra.*

[76]Testimony of Thomas Walter, September 11, 2002. Also, according to the figures presented in Cube's FPR, EG & G's estimated share of the annual fee is roughly 41% in Year 1 of the WICC, and approximately 43% thereafter; however, actual performance will dictate the precise sharing of the fee award, just as the parties' performance under the WICC will determine the overall size of the fee that is earned and shared between them.

[77]See note 37, *supra.*

[78]Mr. Thomas Walter testified that a termination for convenience clause did not reflect the intent of parties. EG & G was akin to Cube's *partner* on the WICC and subject only to a

and subsequent Letter Subcontracts to agree to the details of a final definitized subcontract, at no time did EG & G agree to *re-negotiate* essential terms already agreed upon and adhered to over a year of performance on the WICC. The Court finds that Cube's attempt to alter the terms, under which the parties have been successfully working,[79] was made in bad faith in order to be able to terminate EG & G in order to reduce Cube's costs, while at the same time increase the amount of fee that Cube could collect under the WICC.[80]

Cube admitted through its Director of Contracts, John Schultheis, that the only two impediments to the definitized subcontract agreement were the cap on G & A and the termination for convenience clause. Yet after two years of working together on the Teaming Agreement, the Initial and Final Proposals, the letter subcontracts, and the negotiations on the definitized subcontract, *only* when the draft of that agreement was reformatted and sent by Cube to EG & G were those two items flagged. Compl. Ex. 21 at page EG 03541. And this was in April 2002. EG & G's surprise was understandable.

And what was Cube's response to EG & G's surprise reaction to these two new terms? Not an assertion that EG & G has already agreed to them- Cube knew full well that EG & G had not. Instead, notwithstanding Cube's new demands, EG & G, in uncontroverted good faith, negotiated over these two newly injected terms to an impasse. (During the negotiations Cube even suggested buying out EG & G's interest. Cube's wishes to be rid of

---

"flow down" termination clause whereby EG & G would be terminated in the event of Cube's termination from the WICC. Testimony of Thomas Walter, September 11, 2002.

Moreover, Mr. Robert Coffman, Cube's Contract Manager on the WICC, testified at trial that there was no provision in its prime contract with NASA requiring the inclusion of a termination for convenience in any of Cube's subcontracts. Additionally, Mr. Coffman testified that the termination for convenience issue was not raised with EG & G until sometime between March and May 2002, some 7 months *after* EG & G's performance on the WICC officially began under the initial Letter Subcontract of August 29, 2001.

[79]Although Robert Coffman testified at trial that Cube had discussed internally the termination of EG & G from the WICC some 3 or 4 months prior to the date when EG & G was officially terminated, Mr. Coffman admitted that no one from Cube ever told EG & G that it might be replaced on the WICC project. Testimony of Robert Coffman, September 12, 2002.

Furthermore, EG & G offered testimony at trial that Cube at no time reported any problems with EG & G's performance on the WICC, either before and after the 90-day temporary injunction issued by the Court on June 27, 2002. Testimony of Clayton Wetsell, September 12, 2002. Moreover, at no time did Cube withhold any payments to EG & G as a result of performance, or lack thereof. Testimony of Jay Huston, September 12, 2002.

[80]Furthermore, insofar as bad faith is concerned, that Court notes that Cube's transmittal of the letter subcontracts subsequent to the initial one was at best disingenuous, and at worst fraudulent. Terms were not included that appeared in the terms of the initial letter subcontract. Yet these changes or additions were not flagged for EG & G's attention. Compare Compl. Ex. 13 at page EG 03150 with Compl. Ex. 14 at page EG 03166. Cube admitted that this was done so "partially intentionally". Testimony of Robert Coffman, September 12, 2002. Terms that were changed on the transmittals from Cube to EG & G for purportedly routine signature were not flagged for EG & G. See Compl. Ex. 14 at page EG 03196. By Mr. Coffman's own admission at trial, he did not like the Teaming Agreement and set about to "fix" some of its terms, changes that he admittedly did not discuss with Thomas Walter of EG & G. Testimony of Robert Coffman, September 12, 2002. Such conduct plainly smacks of bad faith.

EG & G-for purely monetary reasons-could not have been made more plain.)

*12 In sum, the Court finds that the Teaming Agreement, combined with the terms of and subsequent performance under the proposals submitted to NASA and the Navy, constitute a binding and enforceable contract. Even though the Teaming Agreement itself does not set forth the *minor functional details* of the subcontract that EG & G was promised, the *essential contractual terms* were plainly stated in by the Teaming Agreement and were in fact agreed upon by the parties during the preparation of their proposals to NASA and the Navy.

Most importantly, Cube could not point to a single term in the drafts and negotiations of the definitized subcontract that were of any concern. (Indeed, they were substantially all agreed upon.) The only stumbling blocks were the two *new* terms—a cap on the G & A rate, and a termination for convenience clause—that were never a part of the parties' prior agreement. To the contrary, the parties had agreed on G & A without a cap, and had never contemplated a termination for convenience provision. Such a clause in and of itself is antithetical to the concept of partnering or teaming as envisioned and agreed to by EG & G and Cube.

Remedy

With respect to the remedy that EG & G seeks, the Court finds specific performance not only appropriate, but necessary.

Whether specific performance is an appropriate remedy is a matter of the Court's discretion. *First National Bank v. Roanoke Oil Co.*, 169 Va. 99, 117, 192 S.E.2d 764, 771 (1937). The availability of this equitable remedy depends on whether the party seeking such has an adequate remedy at law and whether the party against whom relief is sought would be subject to undue hardship if the relief is granted. *Id.* Thus, under Virginia law, a party seeking specific performance must demonstrate that there is no adequate remedy at law and that the terms of the contract sought to be enforced are sufficiently definite. *Manassas v. Board of County Supervisors of Prince William County*, 250 Va. 126, 132-34, 458 S.E.2d 568, 571-72 (1995).

The adequacy of a legal remedy "is to some extent relative, and the modern approach is to compare remedies... [but] doubts should be resolved in favor of the granting of specific performance or injunction." *Restatement (Second) of Contracts*, § 359 (1981). See also, 197 Va. 208, 212-13, 89, 973 F.2d 501, 511 (6th Cir.1992) ("injury is not fully compensable by money damages if the nature of the Plaintiff's loss would make damages difficult to calculate.")

In the present case, Cube contends that specific performance is not available as a remedy, as no subcontract has been proved and certain of the terms discussed by the parties are not only *not* definite, but categorically not agreed to.[81] But as previously stated, even if some of the terms of a contract are uncertain, if its meaning may be determined in light of the

---

[81]*Defendant's Proposed Findings of Fact and Conclusions of Law,* ¶ 79. See City of Manassas v. Board of Supervisors, 250 Va. 126, 133, 458 S.E.2d 568, 571-72 (1995).

surrounding circumstances, the contract will be enforced.[82] And, simply put, there are no uncertain terms here.

*13 Moreover, the Court recognizes that a legal remedy is especially difficult to fashion where damages are too speculative to calculate, such as where the contract at issue may be extended or renewed based on performance which has not yet occurred, and where extra-contractual opportunities are also lost or jeopardized.[83]

In this case, due to the award term feature of the WICC, it is uncertain whether the contract will last for only four years, or up to ten years. If terminated by Cube, EG & G will have a difficult if not impossible task calculating and quantifying the earnings it might have received under the WICC. Moreover, EG & G's involvement is a factor that arguably affects the success of that contract and whether it is extended to its full ten-year potential.

A second characteristic of the WICC that makes it difficult to calculate damages is that the incentive and award fees that can be earned each year will vary based on performance. Again, if EG & G is terminated from the contract, it will be unable to help Cube maximize the annual fee pool. In either event, the anticipated profits by virtue of the fee sharing are impossible to forecast.

The Court concludes that the loss of EG & G's participation in the WICC-a major government contract-constitutes a substantial irreparable injury to EG & G that cannot be adequately remedied at law.[1] As for Cube, the Court does not believe, based on the evidence, that it will suffer similar substantial harm by the Court granting EG & G's requested relief and by requiring Cube to live up to the bargain it made with EG & G.

CONCLUSION

Upon consideration of the object which the parties here intended to accomplish under the Teaming Agreement, the circumstances under which the Teaming Agreement was made, the parties' negotiated terms in the Teaming Agreement, the Initial Proposal, the RFP, and the Letter Subcontracts, combined with the parties' performance on the WICC over a year, the Court finds that it was the clear and plain intention of the parties that EG & G would, in its capacity as subcontractor, perform on the WICC.

In addition, the Court finds that the essential terms of the subcontract that Cube promised to give EG & G are more than sufficiently clear and

---

[82]See note 64, *supra.*

[83]*See e.g., Purdue Pharma L.P. v. Boehringer Ingelhein GMBH,* 98 F.Supp.2d 362 (2000) (injunction granted where future market circumstances made calculation of damages difficult and where, without an injunction, plaintiff would lose future opportunities in the relevant marketplace); *Aero Corp. v. Dep't. of the Navy,* 540 F. Supp 180, 214 (D.D.C.1982) (lost opportunities constitute irreparable injury "which no legal remedy could either value or redress.")

[1]*See Dairy Maid Dairy, Inc. v. United States,* 837 F.Supp. 1370, 1381 (E.D.Va 1993); *United Power Corp. v. United States Defense Mapping Agency,* 736 F.Supp. 354, 357 (D.D.C.1990); *Quality Transport Services, Inc. v. United States,* 12 Cl.Ct. 276, 282 (Cl.Ct.1987) (because loss of anticipated profits cannot be recovered on a government contract, loss of contract constitutes irreparable harm.)

definite so as to permit the Court to order the specific performance that EG & G seeks. The parties established all of the essential terms of the promised subcontract through the mechanisms provided for in the Teaming Agreement, and those terms are supported by substantial evidence, including the parties' Initial Proposal and FPR, the Letter subcontracts, and the parties' performance under the WICC since September 1, 2001. As to the two disputed terms-capping of the G & A rate and termination for convenience-the parties never had as part of their agreement that EG & G would have to cap its G & A rate or that EG & G could be terminated for convenience. Those terms were not a part of the parties' agreement, and, more specifically, were not left open for the parties' negotiations.

Index